FUNERAL CULTURE

AIDS, Work, and Cultural Change in an African Kingdom

Casey Golomski

.

Indiana University Press

This book is a publication of

Indiana University Press
Office of Scholarly Publishing
Herman B Wells Library 350
1320 East 10th Street
Bloomington, Indiana 47405 USA

iupress.indiana.edu

The paper used in this publication meets the minimum requirements of
the American National Standard for Information Sciences—Permanence
of Paper for Printed Library Materials, ANSI Z39.48-1992.

Manufactured in the United States of America

Cataloging information is available from the Library of Congress.

ISBN 978-0-253-03644-5 (cloth)
ISBN 978-0-253-03645-2 (paperback)
ISBN 978-0-253-03646-9 (ebook)

1 2 3 4 5   23 22 21 20 19 18

FUNERAL CULTURE

Contents

Acknowledgments

Cᴏᴏᴘᴇʀᴀᴛɪᴏɴ, ᴄᴏʟʟᴇɢɪᴀʟɪᴛʏ, ꜰʀɪᴇɴᴅsʜɪᴘ, and love are qualities that I value in mutual relationships and are what I received from many people as I developed robust interests in culture and humanitarian concern into ethnographic research for this book. I have been waiting to graciously thank many of them here. *Siyabonga tsine.*

Doing sociocultural anthropology as a richly descriptive comparative study of human being means learning about, listening to, and empathizing with others around us. I learned these skills first from my family: my dad, Kenneth Edwin Golomski, or "G," a social studies educator and coach, and my mom, Monica Kathleen Brady Berg Golomski, a business educator and heartening citizen. Our own rituals together of dinners, holidays, and Friday-night football games gave me grounds to think creatively about the cultural and ritual life of our own communities and others. I have to begin with them, because they gave me life and let me become who I am.

In Swaziland, people who gave me a hand, a chance, and a tip or two were: Darrin Adams, Doug and Jen Armitage, Ivy Bennett, Nelly Bennett, Teresa Bennett, the late Phil Bonner, George Choongwa, Bongani Dlamini, Lindiwe Dlamini, Mlungisi Dlamini, Velabo Dlamini, Rebecca Fielding-Miller, Simphiwe Groening, Barb Houle, Shorty Khumalo, Hlanhla Lukhele, Mzwandile Lukhele, S. T. Lukhele, Zodwa Mabuza, Nkosingiphile Makama, Veli Matsebula, Themba Mavuso, Vusi Mbatha, Nokuthula Mbatha, Vukile Mbatha, Vusi Mbatha, Almon Bingo, S'thembile Mbingo, Esther Mbuli, Bill and Erin McCoy, Bakhetsile Mdluli, Buhle Mdluli, Busi Mdluli, Sizwe Mdluli, S'busie Mpungose, Cebsile Ndzinisa, Thabile Ngubane, Fire Ngwenya, Comfort Ngwenya, Lindiwe Ngwenya, Phindile Nsibande, Buhle Shongwe, Khole Shongwe, Martha Shongwe, Mbabane Shongwe, Phumlani Shongwe, Sebenele Shongwe, Xolani Shongwe, and Martha Vankampen Hertslet.

Thank you to the staffs at the United States Embassy and the National Archives, and to Rosemary Andrade and Donald Nkonyane at the National Museum for access to the collections and coordinating illustration permissions with Aleta Armstrong. Nicodemus Fru Awasom, Nhlanhla C. Dlamini, Hebron L. Ndlovu, and Sonene Nyawo at the University of Swaziland's Department of History and the Department of Theology and Religious Studies were all innovative interlocutors, pushing me to rethink my understanding of culture and Swaziland.

Colleagues I met on a postdoctoral fellowship in South Africa at the University of the Witwatersrand from 2014 on enlightened me and continue to inspire me. The university is a cosmopolitan place drawing in itinerant citizens who are also well imbricated in the lifeworld I describe in this book. On cold Johannesburg evenings over dinner and glasses of red wine, in the office, and in seminars, the times I spent together with the following people encouraged me to forward my work as part of a shared humanist and social scientific endeavor: Max Bolt, Cath Burns, Sharad Chari, David Coplan, Gabby Dlamini, Claudia Gastrow, Kelly Gillespie, Pamila Gupta, Julia Hornberger, Deborah James, Lenore Manderson, Achille Mbembe, Fraser McNeill, Dilip Menon, Nolwazi Mkhwanazi, Polo Moji, Danai Mupotsa, Kirk Sides, Robert Thornton, Daria Trentini, Joshua Z. Walker, Hylton White, Tim Wright, and Eric Worby; the staff of the Department of Social Anthropology, Wits Institute for Social and Economic Research and its Humanities Graduate Centre; and colleagues at several writing retreats and workshops, including the 14th and 15th Johannesburg Workshops in Theory and Criticism.

I learned siSwati by way of isiZulu. Many of my first words in these tongues I spoke with Zoliswa Mali and Beth Restrick at the Boston University African Studies Center, where I also thankfully met Parker Shipton. A Fulbright-Hays grant and the United States Department of Education sponsored my isiZulu language training at the University of KwaZulu-Natal Pietermaritzburg with Audrey Nonhlanhla Mbeje and Thabile Mbatha Ngubane. From there, T. J. Tallie, Joseph D. Napolitano, and April Sizemore-Barber became ongoing language and writing partners. Martha Shongwe and Cebsile Ndzinisa were also special teachers of siSwati.

My early academic mentors, the late Anthony Galt, Sabine Hyland, and Victoria B. Tashjian, and at Brandeis University Mark Auslander, Elizabeth Ferry, Charles Golden, David Jacobson, Nina Kammerer, Sarah Lamb, Janet McIntosh, Rick Parmentier, and Ellen Schattschneider helped cultivate my interests and analyses. My Brandeis peers and I prided ourselves on celebrating an inclusive, supportive, and rigorous environment, and I am very proud to see where it has gotten us all in life. I also thank my colleagues at the Departments of Anthropology at the University of Massachusetts, Boston, and the University of New Hampshire for being encouraging and for inspiring me to write beyond borders. At Harvard Divinity School, the theory, thoughtfulness, and kind words of Michael D. Jackson lit my path forward.

Delivering paper presentations based on this work to best reshape it for a wider audience was helpful. I was able to do so for meetings of the International Research Network on Religion and AIDS in Africa, the African Studies Association, the Society for Cultural Anthropology, the American Ethnological Society, the South African Visual Arts Historians and Comité International d'Histoire de l'Art, and the American Anthropological Association. I received exceptional feedback from audiences at invited talks based on this research. I presented these talks for Nhlanhla C. Dlamini and the University of Swaziland History Staff Seminar Series, Alan Whiteside and the University of KwaZulu-Natal Westville's Health Economics and HIV/AIDS Research Division (HEARD), Boston University's African Studies Center Walter Rodney Seminar Series, and the University of the Witwatersrand's Department of Anthropology and Centre for Indian Studies in Africa.

Dee Mortensen thankfully saw my ethnographic vision. At Indiana University Press, she, Paige Rasmussen, Rachel Rosolina, Stephen Williams, and Julie Davis helpfully guided me. Jessica Vineyard and the staff at Ninestars were exceptional copyeditors, and Cyndy Brown was a stellar indexer. Several colleagues and friends from different seasons of my life read specific parts of the manuscript, wrote comments, and helped revise it overall, securing its growth from early ideas and chapters to book proposal, revisions, and completion: James Amanze, Joel Cabrita, Shelby Carpenter, Arianna Huhn, Anna Jaysane-Darr, Casey J. Miller, Smita Lahiri, Vito Laterza, Mrinalini Tankha, Allison B. Taylor, Daria Trentini, Laura Ann Twagira, Ilana van Wyk, Hylton White, and Eric Worby. Melissa Clark helpfully produced the map. Others, such as Eric Kuzma and Teri Del Rosso made the intersection of personal life and writing extraordinary. For their final editorial efforts, wisdom, and well wishes at the very end of it all, I am indebted to Rebecca Fielding-Miller, Jessica A. Hardin, Ieva Jusionyte, George Paul Meiu, Robin Root, and April Sizemore-Barber. I am forever grateful for your gifts.

Note on Transliteration

Transliteration—notes on pronouncing siSwati words, including places and people's names:

c   The written consonant "c," as in *umcwasho* (national chastity rites), is pronounced as a dental click by clicking the tip of the tongue on the back of the front teeth.

hl   The written consonant pair "hl" is a fricative. It is pronounced like a lisp, by flattening the tip of the tongue on the roof of the mouth, then exhaling and articulating the "l," and is followed by a vowel, as in *sihlahla* ("tree").

ph   The written consonant pair "ph" is pronounced as a normal "p," exhaling to emphasize the "h."

th   Like "ph," "th" is pronounced as a normal "t," exhaling to emphasize the "h."

FUNERAL CULTURE

Introduction: Funeral Culture: Dignity, Work, and Cultural Change

INSIDE AN INKY copy of the *Swazi Observer*, one of the two newspapers in the Kingdom of Swaziland, the op-eds are just before the obituaries. Some op-eds are inspirational and others cheeky, as in one series called "Societal Scales" by Mr. Dumisa Dlamini, about the ways women and men don't get along. "Does a Man Love His Car More Than His First Lady?" (2007) and "The Forgotten, Deserted, Infected but Loyal Bride" (2015) are some colorful titles in his series. One article I read online in 2006 called "Those Tears, Roses and Messages at Men's Funerals" (November 18) stood out because of its take on "culture":

> Life is just a precious gift to mankind whose value can never be quantified. Whosoever is alive is treasured by lots and lots of people even if they were not to come out openly whilst (s)he is alive to tell him.... A man has this manner of bringing a balance within the relationships he has established with these people close to his heart.... Whilst he breathes he has made his person, love and third leg [penis] very useful somewhere beyond the parameters of his marriage.... Societal Scales has always had it that men are never neat in their intimate dealings and much of this untidiness is exposed just when the fella has breathed his last. Here is this *new culture of funerals* being extended beyond the family and publicised so that friends, acquaintances and relatives could be informed of the demise of the man. Hardly in the body the family is prepared for the shock that comes with funerals. Whilst all would be grieved and sore at heart, at times you would be shocked at the flood of tears, the bunch of roses and heap of messages from the mourners. (emphasis added)

Dlamini goes on to write about women getting angry or embarrassed at their husbands' funerals when it comes out that the men had extramarital lovers. The lovers' identities are supposedly revealed when they show up with gifts such as flowers and personal condolences printed on small cards. "Here is the biggest bunch from Mandy with love and narrating all the good times she has spent with the deceased and their beautiful daughter," he writes, describing how the man's widow would start, "wailing in shock that her husband of many years has sired bastards outside the holy matrimony. Had it not been for the flowers, nobody would have heard of the clandestine affair." In this account, flowers, cards, and ambiguities surrounding the event lay the groundwork for what, in passing,

Fig. 0.1 Artificial flowers and condolence cards at a cemetery in Manzini, 2010.
Photograph by author.

Dlamini cites as a "new culture of funerals." "Society being what it is would get a chance to gossip about the scandalous funeral where the hidden came to exposure," he concludes, "and at the wrong place—the graveside.... Whatever the situation is, be wary of the ROSES, TEARS, FLOWERS AND MESSAGES BROUGHT at a man's funeral."[1]

What at first sounded to me like a soap opera scene in many ways turned out not to be so incredible in this small country in southeastern Africa. Stories in "Societal Scales" represent a form of local social commentary. They depict a wider sense that funerals today are different from what they were in the past and dealing with death and dying is more uncertain. When I asked people about funerals during my fieldwork there, they most often told me funerals were differently organized, more frequent, and less "traditional". Most of my friends, consultants, and others I met pointed back to material cultural items such as flowers or cards (see fig. 0.1), and HIV/AIDS to explain how things have changed.

Contemporary forms of living and dying in Swaziland cannot be understood separate from the global HIV/AIDS epidemic, for which southern Africa and the kingdom itself became ground zero at the turn of the millennium.[2] In

1999, the king of Swaziland, King Mswati III, declared HIV a national disaster, following up on lobbying efforts by medical professionals, researchers, and politicians to engage with what was by then an obvious public health crisis. This led to the watershed parliamentary establishment of the National Emergency Research Council for HIV/AIDS (NERCHA) in 2001, which organizes local and international collaborations for HIV prevention and treatment countrywide.

By the mid-2000s, the effects and politics of the epidemic in southern Africa were generating numerous critical responses, ranging from local grassroots activist programs such as the South African Treatment Action Campaign to global initiatives such as the United States' Presidential Emergency Plan for AIDS Relief (PEPFAR). These entities hotly debated what would work best as treatment and prevention modalities.[3] Outside of the policy domain though, in neighborhoods, townships, and the countryside, ordinary people faced the consequences of political stagnation and curtailed financial, pharmaceutical, and health care resources.[4] They were already at work caring for the sick and burying the dead.

Because antiretroviral medications (ARVs) became available only very slowly, mass death from AIDS became a macabre reality. Citing crisis-level mortality rates of the time, health economist Alan Whiteside and colleagues (2007) called the situation in Swaziland a humanitarian emergency. Urban and rural community cemeteries were quickly reaching maximum capacity, and new ones were being opened. Since 2007, Swaziland has had the world's highest HIV prevalence for a country, and as of 2017, the world's highest HIV incidence rate. The latest figures indicate that out of a hypothetical one thousand people, twenty-four could contract HIV over the course of a single year. Nationally, more than one in three people ages eighteen to forty-nine are HIV positive, and younger women are at greater risk (Justman et al. 2016; van Schalkwyk et al. 2013; Sibbald 2012).

Today, the epidemic has stabilized. ARVs are now almost always available at most clinics to all people living with HIV, and a significant proportion of the government budget is allotted to HIV treatment with support from international and private donors. Diverse prevention initiatives are nationally operational, including neonatal and adult medical male circumcision (MMC) and educational programming in schools and public and private workplaces. Comparatively, the kingdom is a glowing example of how local states and global public health entities' collaborations can dam a cascade of death and new infections.[5] Despite these achievements, the knell of AIDS deaths echoes in popular consciousness, and stigma is problematically common.

Almost ten years ago, I began ethnographic research to document what life and death could mean culturally in Swaziland amid a disease epidemic of these proportions. What could people do about it? At the beginning of my fieldwork in 2008, I collected more than two hundred stories like Dumisa Dlamini's from the *Swazi Observer* and other local media about funeral-related conflicts: corpse custody and burial location disputes; exhumations, courts cases, and police interventions; stolen mourning gowns and funerary goods; and scandals at hospital and funeral parlor morgues of abandoned, missing, or rerouted bodies. Many writers cited the graven "unSwazi" nature of these disruptions and questioned what had become of "Swazi Culture" itself. Regarding Dlamini's 2006 op-ed, what was it about contemporary funerals that made them so centrally about a "new culture," as he and others saw it? What did stuff like roses and cards have to do with this new culture?[6]

Funeral Culture answers these questions by describing cultural transformations of dying, death, and funerals in this patriotic and traditionalist-governed nation-state. By focusing on new funerary forms and practices that emerged alongside the epidemic, this book shows how these transformations resonate with people as an instance of cultural change. Similarly, writing about conditions of life with AIDS in South Africa under neoliberal economic policies, anthropologist Jean Comaroff (2007, 203) makes a brief note that funerary wreaths, coffins, and other "banal accoutrements of death" are now conspicuous on the landscape, dotting small-town shops and roadsides. What value do these objects have? And why do they matter?

In this book, I describe such "accoutrements" of this new funeral culture in Swaziland. These include: an expanded market of life insurance with its offices and brokers, more consumer options for tombstones and caskets, funeral feasts and catering, morgues and funeral parlors, the country's first crematorium, new Christian religious practices of healing and resurrection, and pharmaceutical and social resources of global health and humanitarian aid entities. *Funeral Culture* interrogates these examples and the social relations among which they obtain value to show how they are anything but banal. The stuff of funerals is part of people's everyday socioeconomic livelihoods and takes on political implications by pushing back against state policies and practices of cultural authentication.

These claims require a bit more unpacking. In the remainder of the introduction, I first ask: What do contemporary funerals mean for people? How do they plan for and produce them? This is where the word "work" in the book's title also comes into play, as there is a lot to do for a funeral and many new and different ways to pull it off. These dynamics of cultural production have implications not only for understanding what happens in the kingdom at large but also for what culture might mean in postcolonial societies globally and under specific epidemic disease stressors. This approach is critical, I think, given the ways culture continues to animate politics and health care globally.

Hard Work as the Burden of Dignity

Funerals in Swaziland allow the living to come together to remember and bid farewell to a deceased person by putting on a complex ritual event. According to many people in the kingdom, funerals demonstrate some of the most important aspects of culture, even if today what kind of culture funerals make up comes sharply into question amid HIV/AIDS. Many people told me that for a funeral to be particularly good or memorable, it should above all be *dignified*.

Dignity as a socially animated value is interesting because of its philosophical breadth, variation, and findings about it from recent cross-cultural research by anthropologists. In neighboring South Africa, Antina von Schnitzler (2014) shows that dignity is legally and politically produced in different forms by and for impoverished citizens in their quest for basic amenities such as electricity and toilets. In his discussion of German consumers and Mayan farmers, Edward Fischer (2014, 7) twins dignity to fairness to mean the "positive value of respect, a sense of being treated fairly." Throughout Swaziland and in siSwati, the predominant language besides English, the word for dignity is *sitfunti*, which refers to perceptually related notions of shadow, prestige, influence, soul or personality, and respectability, *sitfunti sekuhlonipeka*.[7] Dignity in Swaziland colors ethical concerns similar to those in Germany, Guatemala, and South Africa. In the wake of HIV/AIDS and preoccupying concerns surrounding mass death, people now aspire to dignity as a quality of funerals, a quality that is interrelatedly social, existential, and material.[8]

A good summary of what a dignified funeral means came from the owner of a funeral parlor I met in a Manzini neighborhood. With about 100,000 people, Manzini is the oldest and largest city in Swaziland and a central hub for the country. In 2014, when I was passing through for a short visit, I visited a small new parlor near a friend's workplace. There I met a short, bespectacled woman who had worked at a loan-servicing center and had opened the shop with her husband after their retirement. We greeted each other and talked about her business, swatting away paper wasps that had already started building a nest in the shop's roof. After showing me flyers for South African–imported caskets, some decorated in cattle-skin prints, she described what a "dignified funeral" meant:

> A person should not be buried like an animal, like at a pauper's funeral, which is not a dignified funeral, one where the police or government must bury you simply when there is no one else to bury them. We wish to have respect for the dead, so when we organize a decent funeral, it makes both the living and the dead happy. The dead person most likely had wishes about how they would like to be buried, having this sort of casket or that one, and how the funeral should take place. They might have wished for the funeral to be one way, but you might find that the children of the dead person are hesitant to do it as

such. The children may want to buy what they think they can afford, but it is important to respect the dead person's wishes about what they wanted.

Her words nicely show how a dignified death emerges from one's own and others' wishes for what a funeral *could* look like. They also echo the commercial branding of the country's oldest and largest funeral parlor, Dups, which expanded its operations in the wake of the epidemic. It promotes dignity through consumption to fulfill social obligations, as one of its 2010 newspaper advertisements reads: "We appreciate that in our culture we do not only look after ourselves but also have the responsibility of our parents and family. The ability to provide a loved one with a dignified funeral is something we all want to do, but cannot always afford." Dignity was also what most people generally talked about with respect to their own preparations for death. Dignity was clearly an important value of funerals, interrelatedly social, existential, and material, and it had its own history.

The term *social* refers to a dignified funeral that is well attended, *kubakhona bonke* in siSwati. Most people would say with some ambivalence that funerals are bigger in size today than they were in the past, yet it is common knowledge that anyone can go to a funeral, including strangers. I learned this while conducting randomized interviews in the industrial town of Matsapha in 2011. When I asked one man how many funerals he had attended in the past month, he said four in total. He told me about one he had gone to after randomly passing by it during an evening walk. He was initially drawn in by the riveting words of the person preaching. He stayed through the night, and along with the other attendees, received a portion of food in the morning. Strangers at funerals are not usually deemed suspicious because hosts assume that they came with someone who knew the deceased or that they are otherwise there to get a free meal. Their presence increases the number of attendees overall, and this represents to the organizers and participants that they did a good job creating a hospitable event where even strangers felt welcome. Still, funerals entirely made up of strangers, as in the case of pauper burials by the state, are void of dignity because one's most intimate social relations have abandoned the dead completely.

Most people at a funeral have deep personal ties to the deceased and his or her family. They include the families of blood relatives and in-laws, often many times removed, as well as former coworkers, classmates, friends, neighbors, and members of churches or burial cooperatives the deceased or the family belonged to. A funeral with many people represents how valuable the deceased was as a part of others' lives and that he or she is being remembered. Family members feel obligated to do the work of hosting the event and its many attendees, but they also get a lot of help, including from contracted "strangers" such as funeral parlor employees and insurance brokers. Getting along with others at such a highly charged event is one of the major challenges of contemporary funerals. People have competing convictions about how the event should unfold, who should be there—like whether to include or exclude extramarital lovers—and how one should comport oneself.

These challenges speak to another aspect of funerary dignity: that this dignity is existential. Here, the term *existential* refers to the idea that funerals are understood to be dignified if they can engender well-being, *kukhona kahle* in siSwati. Well-being bridges people's social obligations and subjectivities, which means that attendees are encouraged to get along with each other despite what are sometimes serious affronts to what they personally feel ought to be happening at the funeral.[9] As public events, funerals compel people to reconcile their subjective opinions about the deceased or the funeral's constitutive elements with the sensibility that the event should remain coherent for the sake of respecting the dead person and the family, given the immediacy of the loss.

Funeral attendees understand that they must do work indicating particular social roles so that the event goes smoothly and dignifies the dead. In this sense, people acknowledge that when they participate in a funeral, they must often do so according to ways that others think they ought to. Affinal women—for example, those who are related to the deceased as in-laws—are obliged to deferentially approach and serve their in-laws; move grass mats, blankets, and items during the burial; sing or cry; and cook food for the postburial morning feast, at which hundreds of people are fed. When younger people who speak English and live primarily in towns attend rural funerals, they must adopt deferential forms of speech when addressing elders and exercise restraint when speaking to friends of the same age. This decorum is difficult to maintain, given the often-unbridled outbursts of grief at funerals, which are emotionally draining for both the bereaved and those who comfort them. Some attendees, especially emcees who direct the series of speakers and songs, may try to envelope these outbursts into the event's overall flow, shoring up a common sense that life and the funeral itself must respectably and harmoniously go on.[10]

Finally, dignified funerals are those that are well organized and well prepared, *kulunga kahle*. This aspect speaks more directly to a focus on materiality in that there is a lot of stuff that goes into making the funeral itself. People, including the deceased, have to be transported to and from the event, often from far beyond where it takes place. Tents and gas-powered generators for extra electricity need to be rented, set up, and taken down. Phone calls need to be made, some requiring extra cash for mobile phone airtime. A grave needs to be dug. Food and beverages need to be bought, prepared, cooked, and served. An emcee and perhaps a choir and musicians need to be invited and get their act together. Programs and obituaries have to be written up, typed, printed, and copied. All of this requires money and work. Incorporating other aspects of dignity and getting the material elements of a funeral well organized rides on whether or not people can reconcile their subjective sense of contribution with the obligation to complete the tasks that are socially expected of them. Taking these altogether, producing dignified funerals is hard work.

Contemporary funerary dignity has a history too. The term itself invokes seemingly universal ethical notions of quality and human value, yet it is born out of colonial histories of Christian religious missions and the introduction of capitalist consumerism. Historians Rebekah Lee and Megan Vaughan (2008) note that across Africa, "dignified" funerals grew out of particular moral and commercial economies in urbanizing spaces such as towns and mining settlements. These economies became grounds for historically situated notions of respectability and status through which dignity materialized. Terence Ranger (2004) showed this for colonial Zimbabwe in describing how the forms that made up a funeral of such quality changed as Ndebele peoples migrated between township municipalities and rural areas for work.[11] While promoting a collective black African community in townships, funerals also revealed cultural and economic inequalities. In this case, work in the form of migrant labor became central for the emergence of popular cultural values surrounding death.

That this material formation of dignity persists today is a testament to the systemic configurations of capitalism that have long shaped the lives and deaths of peoples across postcolonial Africa and its diasporas. Indeed, calling funerals hard work and acknowledging the production, consumption, and exchanges they entail draws our attention to the ways culture animates economies historically. It is to ask why people value what they do and make, among others, and under conditions of power. During modern European colonialism, work itself as a general form of productive action was revalued and enforced as the compulsory pursuit of wages in the form of capitalist labor. The ways people spoke, thought about, and acted on the world in relation to others, including the dead, were reconfigured as daily preoccupations became more bound up with monetized, stratified ways of being in the social world. Anthropological research attuned to history has demonstrated this.[12]

In this case of HIV/AIDS too, our attention is drawn to the ways disease epidemiology shapes and is shaped by these dynamics. One's ability to get by and live life as one would want to live is historically influenced and remade under diverse circumstances, including an epidemic. Ways of living, healing oneself and others, and dying reflect what goes on over time and what one can culturally make of those happenings with what is available to them. Under particular economic conditions, for example, Anne-Maria Makhulu, Beth Buggenhagen, and Stephen Jackson (2010, 4ff.) describe how "hard work" configures many contemporary people's subjectivities in Africa. In their words, hard work is made up of a "variety of tactical modes of being-in-the-world people adopt within the context of 'hard times,'" the kinds of daily and productive "social, physical, economic, spiritual, and imaginative labor" that "always involve political stakes."

Their description is not limited to work as labor, as a moneymaking pursuit within an inherently unequal and global system of capitalism, although it is this, too. "Hard work" is something broader, what I think Michael Jackson (1989) aimed for in describing initiation rites of Kuranko people in Sierra Leone. Jackson writes that construing coming-of-age ceremonies as "ritual" might only overshadow the ways it is not so practically distinct from "work" for people themselves. This is a difference that Western thinking might initially presume. Farming, raising children, lighting a fire, and burying the dead are inclusively human cultural experiences and manifest a will to do the best one can with what is at hand at the time.

Importantly then, calling funerals hard work also reflects the ways they are talked about by most people I know in Swaziland. In siSwati, the word for "funeral" is *umsebenti*, which is the same word for "work" or "wage labor." One can be working in an office *or* taking part in a funeral, *uyasebenta*, or be at a workplace *or* a funeral itself, *usemsebentini*. Of course, its use is context dependent, and there are more precise words for different elements of a funeral. For instance, burial as a funerary rite is *umngcwabo*. The night vigil preceding the morning burial is *umlindzelo*, a noun derivation of the verb to wait for, keep watch, or guard, *kulindzela*.

Yet *umsebenti* is the widely used term to refer both to funerals and other life-cycle events such as marriage, coming-of-age rites for children and young adults, and postburial mortuary rites. These last rites include "cleansing" or "purifying" the bereaved one to three years after the death to bring them out of mourning. Newer rites described in this book involve tombstones purchased on credit and their ceremonious unveilings at the gravesite. Many people in Swaziland might translate *umsebenti* as a "function" or an event generally, but most people I met understood its use to refer to a funeral. As an endogenous concept, *umsebenti* ingeniously describes how funerals are work-like and the complex of social, existential, and material forms needed to produce one with dignity.

As for local embodied experiences of this work, the feelings surrounding funerals are talked about as being heavy or difficult, *kulukhuni*. Funerals in Swaziland are not lauded, boisterous, festival-like occasions seen elsewhere cross-culturally.[13] To deal with death is an existential burden (*umtfwalo*) often seen as placed on people by God or other forces of the world and to be carried. It is "something that has befallen us that we have already faced," *akwehlanga lungehlang'*. Death is an eternal problem, even if, for the majority of Swazis who are variably Christian, God may provide eternal life. People are averse to funerals and find them hard because of their experiential qualities. For some people I met, death imbues a negative shadowed force called *sintima* or *sinyama*, connoting blackness, badness, and depressive qualities.[14] Likewise, newer Christian religious practices discussed in this book have darkly revalued perceptions about bodies, memories, and death itself and lead some people to perceive elements of funerals to be demonic.[15] The macabre essence of funerals coheres feelings associated with emotional, physical, social, and financial burdens and complicates establishing already fragile forms of dignity.

Contemporary funerals themselves do important work for people's historical consciousness in Swaziland, as funerals' changing forms incite conversations about the meaning and value of culture. Things that go into preparing for death and dying, and the things that happen at, go into, and come out of funerals, materialize something that goes beyond tenets about what Swazi Culture is.[16] Before getting this far out in scale though, it will be helpful to see concretely how a funeral turns out to be hard work for a few people in Swaziland I know well, and what culture has to do with it. Swazi literary scholar Sarah Mkhonza once explained to me that "*umsebenti* is that work I must do when I go home for an event, and today, we must go home all the time to do work for funerals." Via ethnography, a story of people's lives, home is where we go back to now.

LaGija's *Skon'*

Commuters and frequent visitors to Swaziland know the notoriety of the Malagwane Hill. The well-developed, steeply winding urban corridor highway descending from the country's administrative capital, Mbabane, and into the royalist capital, Lobamba, in the Ezulwini Valley, is a risky spot. It has been the site of several horrific truck and car crashes. It is a memorable site of past dangers and potential new ones with its own cultural history (L. Simelane 2014). In 2009, a week before Christmas, on this same stretch of road, one crash claimed the lives of three government employees, including Roxanne, my friend and main consultant LaGija's *skon'* (sister-in-law).[17]

Roxanne spent a week in a coma at the government hospital in Mbabane. LaGija's office was nearby, and she went to see her dying sister-in-law three times that week to bring food for Roxanne's mothers, who kept a longer watch. The day I arrived at LaGija's home near Manzini was the day Roxanne passed away. "Here come the condolences," LaGija said, scrolling through text messages she received while we were in the car. She patted her mobile phone as it buzzed throughout the day. LaGija's mother also called to make note of the death and to quickly say hello. Because Roxanne was an unmarried adult woman, her family arranged for her burial at her parental home per Swazi Culture. If married, she would have been buried at a home of her husband's people.

Fig. 0.2 Women sitting by a church before a night vigil near Madlangempisi, 2009. Photograph by the author.

LaGija and her sisters were genuinely saddened by the loss and spoke with trepidation about their obligations and some of the potentially difficult people they would face at the funeral. With the gospel band Joyous Celebration playing on DVD in the background, LaGija's sister Buyiswa explained that they would have to go there as "outsiders." "'Oh, *makoti* (daughter-in-law), you are bringing me bread and jam? I don't want bread, I want scones!'" she said, imitating a creaky-voiced old woman. "Listen," she went on, "when someone dies, the older women will come and gather at the house for one or two weeks. They're mourning there. The women say their respects, but they expect to be waited on and served by all the *makotis*. The things you must do for a funeral!" (see fig. 0.2.)

Buyiswa railed against the ways younger women should be deferential to older women at the event, even when the older women ask for unnecessary delicacies such as scones. "Shouldn't brown bread slices be good enough for a small meal?" she asked. Her sister agreed. LaGija is an educator, a Pentecostal-style preacher with a master of arts degree whom I had met about a year prior to my first stay at her home. The day of the funeral was the first time I saw her wear *liduku*, a customary but not uncommon headscarf, and *sidwashi*, a blue or brown calico print dress, both garments that can point to a woman's married status and domestic role. Soon after I arrived, I also learned that LaGija and her husband had been estranged for several years and did not regularly talk to each other. The social and physical distance between who she identified herself as and who she was in the eyes of her in-laws were now collapsing as she prepared to go.

On the Saturday evening of the funeral, four of LaGija's sisters, a brother, a sister-in-law to one of her sisters, LaGija's own mother, and another wife and son of LaGija's father convoyed two hours to Roxanne's family's countryside home. Incidentally, we took the MR3 highway back up the Malagwane Hill and past the scene of the accident. We passed the spot without anyone in the car remarking on it. When we pulled off the tarred road onto a dirt one to head toward the homestead, one of LaGija's husband's cousins was tacking to a sign pole an A4-size piece of paper with the word "funeral" and a drawn arrow pointing to a nearby churchyard. We went to the small church near the home, where several older women sat on the floor on mattresses overlaid with grass mats. They were Roxanne's mother and three paternal aunts, some of whom had watched over her at the hospital. After a muted exchange of greetings and a short song, LaGija went off to prepare a tray of drinks and scones for the women at their request, as Buyiswa and LaGija had predicted.

Over the course of the night, I didn't see LaGija much, as she sequestered to the backyard of the house, where potatoes, beetroot, and other foods roiled in the waters of four large black cauldrons. Several women stood there at makeshift tables with large knives, slicing vegetables and sawing up bite-size portions of meat. Earlier, we had come upon the women and greeted them, and they had given us a short acknowledgment. LaGija's sisters moved between the church and the kitchen space to help her out. In doing so, they also tried to prevent themselves from falling asleep, although LaGija's youngest sister eventually went to lie down in the back seat of her car. Also, to do something else besides listen to the night-vigil preachers' sermons, the sisters helped me trace who was related to whom in both LaGija's and her husband's extended families. Roxanne's immediate family members were easy to point out because all her sisters and brothers took turns giving speeches throughout the six-hour event. They called us to acknowledge God's plans despite worldly suffering and to count good social relations as instrumental to salvation—these themes, I would later learn, are part of the standard genre. All of Roxanne's siblings were present except one, an older brother who could not get time off from work. He was one of several drivers for one of the kingdom's queens.

LaGija returned to the church around 4 a.m., bearing a tray of scones and brown bread slices to serve with the tea. The early morning tea service is common at contemporary funerals and is coordinated by younger or socially junior women, such as daughters-in-law, in a family. People often cluck their tongues in a way to critique the tea, which they will say is exorbitant because it is costly. Yet when tea is actually served, it does not often get turned away. Hot tea feels good to hold and drink when one has been sitting inside an unheated vinyl tent all night. A crusty scone to go along with the drink is a good way to tide one over until the chance to eat again, which will still not be for another several hours. Teatime marks a relative break in a night vigil's proceedings, and that night we all sat still afterward, snoozing until dawn.

Around 6 a.m. we started waking up, covering ourselves in our blankets to stay warm and arranging ourselves for the burial service. This service involves more speeches by family and church members and local authorities, a procession to the grave, and interment. Roxanne's nephew distributed programs provided by a funeral parlor that outlined the proceedings and gave a short obituary detailing Roxanne's education and where she had worked. With directions from the pastor, both Roxanne's father's and mother's families then had someone speak on their respective group's behalf, giving condolences and thanks for those who helped make the funeral possible. The funeral parlor employees, along with some older men, helped load Roxanne's body and a few of her bereaved mothers and aunts into the hearse for the short ride to the gravesite while the rest of us followed on foot.

Roxanne was buried about a kilometer outside of her parent's yard. Amid the immense numbers of AIDS deaths, those by injury from events such as a car accident, like Roxanne's, are sometimes considered bad. Customarily, there is something more ominous surrounding the circumstances of these deaths that compels families to place their loved ones' bodies outside of the confines of their homestead. Death by accident evacuates the potential for others to socially mitigate a person's dying. It is instantaneous, unlike a wasting death from AIDS or other illnesses, and others are not able to care for the person over a long-term decline and in the final days of life.

At the gravesite, a small woodland grove overlooking a ravine, the funeral parlor set up a small tent with chairs for the principal mourners. On each chair were a rose, a bottle of sparkling water, and a packet of tissues, accoutrements evidencing the family's consumer commitment to supply such dignifying goods for the bereaved. Runners of artificial grass were draped over the side of the muddy grave and framed a brassy contraption eventually used to lower the casket. Standing around the grave, we bowed our heads in silence and listened as the pastor reminded us to stay mindful of who we were and who we lived among as God's children: we are all heading on the same path toward "home" and will eventually make it there when God calls on us. With a nod and shout of the first few lines of a hymn, the burial began.

A few young children took the roses from the seats and tossed them into the grave while men began tossing in shovelsful of earth. Chairs in the small tent toppled as Roxanne's mother and another woman rolled onto the ground, crying.

A grass mat belonging to Roxanne was held out above the grave and sliced with a machete. It was laid inside with logs, the printed programs, more earth, and a piece of sheet metal layered on top to finish the task. Lastly, we were directed to turn away from the grave and sit. Gazing over the ravine, a large man, a representative of the area's chiefly council (*libandlancane*), arose and made a final statement to effectively close the proceedings. The burial was done.

"Some things in Swazi Culture are bogus," said Buyiswa laughingly after the burial. We sat together eating stews, salads, and meat from Styrofoam takeaway boxes, food that LaGija and the other women had prepared throughout the night. Buyiswa was speaking for herself and her sisters as self-professed Christians who were "too scared" of what some saw as traditional elements of the funeral, such as burying Roxanne outside of the homestead. Most of the attendees were finishing their food and grabbing more for the journey ahead. LaGija, her sisters, and I were ourselves heading to a worship service at their family's new Pentecostal-inspired church about an hour's drive away. Suddenly, LaGija was beckoned to speak to her estranged husband, who aggressively demanded cash from her for his bus ride home. She said she never knew her husband drank until she saw him at this funeral. This had also been obvious to her sisters when he stood up and testified incoherently at the vigil.

After that, LaGija drew me aside so I could bid farewell to her mother-in-law, who ate with the other principal mourners in the main house. The day before, I had purchased a blank greeting card at a supermarket. I had penned a few words of condolence but made the apparent mistake of writing "Thank you for letting me grieve with you" inside. "Why would you thank someone for letting you come here?" asked LaGija. "Anyone can go to a funeral!" I fumbled a few words of confused remorse to her mother-in-law while handing her the card. Aside from those smaller cards with messages attached to the flowers laid at the casket, mine was anomalous as a gift. In the car ride to their church, while eating the last food bits in the takeaway box, the sisters reiterated how "bogus" the husband and aspects of the funeral really were.

The story of LaGija's *skon'* illuminates how funeral culture emerges practically. It speaks to bigger questions that should not be unfamiliar to many: wellness; religion; gender and sexism; family; and the right, ability, and will to do work as something that matters. It shows what has to be done at a funeral, who has to do it according to age, gender, and status, for example, and how people there will or will not get along. Importantly, a bit more background on the funeral shows how pride and the state's authentication of Swazi Culture has unsettled contemporary dying amid HIV/AIDS.

Roxanne's brother, for example, as a driver for one of the queens, was a member of the Umbutfo Swaziland Defense Force, the state military. Earlier that same year, a directive had been given to some senior members of Umbutfo, along with those of the Royal Swaziland Police and His Majesty's Correctional Services (of state prison wardens), that they were prohibited from attending their families' funerals, in part in response to high rates of people missing work due to HIV/AIDS-related deaths. In a news article titled "No More Funerals!" Sibongile Sukati (2009) describes:

> In Swazi culture, it is prohibited for a person to attend or be around the royal family if they have attended a funeral or have had a death in the family usually for a period of seven days after burial. "We were told that the only funerals we could attend were those of our biological mothers and biological children and none else," said one senior member of the armed forces, who wished to remain anonymous.... "We are not even allowed to attend a sibling's funeral and sometimes it is just stressful because some of our family members do not understand why one cannot be allowed to bury their relative."

In response to the media and affected officers, then-army commander Lieutenant General Sobantu Dlamini noted that they could apply for permission to attend funerals if they felt compelled to; they were told to otherwise just send money. "Dlamini said that there was nothing out of the ordinary as the officers chose this line of duty, which of course came with certain obligations if not sacrifices" (S. Sukati 2009). Over dinner one night at my friends' home, the wife, Nobunye, explained: "If you are otherwise working for royalty, you can't go near the body. It is difficult, but they could make arrangements to be away from work for the funeral by getting someone to work for them. You can't be around royalty then for seven days to a month." The husband, Alfred, disagreed over the duration, but the two laughed. "It is like mourning," they said. "You have to take a break from work!"

Part of the explanation for the prohibition has to do again with *sinyama* as a shadowed contagion that could pollute mournful commoners and afflict royal employers. Close family members of the dead—more often older and married women as widows—embody *sinyama* and are more likely to emit it to others. The bereaved have to be kept away, or here, be preoccupied at work. For example, widows feel they must sit at the back of public transport and in church or else get comments from people around them, and noticeable space is given between widows and others in queues and public spaces such as banks and supermarket checkout lines. In the past, widows have been barred from attending royalists' national ceremonies yet have also been told to take off their mourning gowns en masse to celebrate momentous events such as the king's birthday and Independence anniversaries.[18] In this case of the military's injunction, Roxanne's brother's *sinyama* would harm royal employers in a way that would undo both their power and relationship to their citizens. The fact that some can be forced to stay at work instead of going home to a funeral is telling, given that HIV/AIDS- and funeral-related absenteeism has been a problem for the formal employment sector.[19]

For some Dlamini royalists, the production of funerals for members of their own families are also outsourced to a special group of people, *bantfu bentsaba*, "people of the mountain," who host the event or undertake rites to absorb, separate, and deflect the effects of death from people closest to kingship. Some senior royalty are buried at night in sacred mountains, which are guarded by the military.[20] LaGija's sister-in-law, like the majority of Swazi, do not have such mystical ritual service providers. If they had someone help them out, it would likely be their own family, a church, or today, insurance companies and funeral parlors, all of whom could help transport and inter the body. The majority of Swazi bury their dead at rural homesteads and increasingly in urban municipal cemeteries. LaGija had earlier offered to take me to visit one of the homesteads where this almost tributary form of funeral labor for royalists took place. One of her office's secretaries belonged to one of the families who hosted royal funerals, but the secretary herself died a few months later.

Other concerns haunted families, brethren, and coworkers of ordinary people such as LaGija. Why would we need to bury someone outside of the homestead, fearing the specter of *sinyama* or polluting royal employers, if we live in a world where God already has power over such dark forces? For them, such darkness is indeed there, but are we not protected from them by living a godly life? Does our persistent concern for them in funerals suggest otherwise? If Roxanne's brother had taken off from work for the state to come to the funeral, would this mean they were unpatriotic or not following Swazi Culture? As the sisters said the week before, cooking all night could be an affront to being an independent woman, yet the work also showed they cared for their in-laws. Costliness was part of our conversation, too. Do we need those roses and programs? They just end up buried in the grave anyway. These questions require us to ask directly how social reproduction occurs in a context like this and what we might learn more broadly about culture, illness, and politics.

Cultural Production, AIDS, and Politics in Postcolonial Africa

What is "funeral culture"? And how is it related to what I capitalize and call Swazi Culture? Culture has been a tricky thing to make sense of, and especially so in often desperate situations of epidemic disease. Anthropologists have approached the relationship between HIV/AIDS and culture in Africa from different angles. Some take culture to be more about beliefs and practices, others about contexts, and still others somewhere in between. Some are more applied, some more theoretical, but most try to illuminate culture's lived and human dimensions. AIDS is generative as much as it is destructive. It viscerally forces people into matters of life, illness, and death. These are basic concerns of human beings, and dealing with them manifests culture as an "existential imperative," to use anthropologist Michael Jackson's (2011, xxii) term. The will to live well may be culturally universal but constrained too by political, economic, ecological, and here epidemiological circumstances in place.

Studies focused on AIDS-related global public health, activism, and clinical work show how interventions structurally "corroborate cultural processes" (Biehl 2007, 67) or "cultural logics" (Nguyen 2010, 6, 138) of biomedicine.[21] In their applied approach to HIV/AIDS prevention in sub-Saharan Africa, Edward Green and Allison Herling Ruark (2011) take culture to be a complex adaptive system and focus on understanding cultural systems in order to change health-related behaviors. They see their approach to culture as different from most others, which focus on how cultural ideas influence uptake of biomedical technologies such as condoms. Both approaches are important, I think. Culturally routine behaviors are not removed from the material worlds people inhabit and use to get by. For example, health-related information can come from non-biomedical places where people spend a lot of their time, such as a church, and access to biomedical technologies such as contraceptives cannot be taken for granted, as they are sometimes structurally unavailable or out of reach. *Funeral Culture* takes a middle ground here to depict how people practically live out their lives because of changed material and social circumstances.

Such medical and applied approaches are crucial but focus strongly on the ways people are re-oriented toward biomedical frames. Sociocultural anthropologists have taken a broader view of HIV/AIDS that constellates embodiment, relationships, representations, and socioeconomic dynamics to conceptualize the disease "as an optic … to learn about people and about society" as well as "a symbol of social crisis" that "dominates public discourse beyond its actual health impact."[22] In this approach, as Daniel Jordan Smith (2014, 17) writes about southern Nigeria, AIDS shows that the ways people "grapple with the epidemic" reveal "broader anxieties about their culture, their values," and inequality. How people actually "grapple" or get by amid HIV/AIDS is a profoundly relational and culturally "creative" process, as Paul Wenzel Geissler and Ruth Prince (2010) describe for Kenyan Luo-speaking communities. In their ethnography, cultural creativity can emanate from basic tactile engagements between people, in assessing each others' pleasures and bodily pains, as part of being together in a community. Discussing the epidemic in South Africa, Didier Fassin (2007, 23) writes that while all people "share a destiny" as part of life together in a community or world affected by the disease, the world itself is also shared unequally.[23] The task of anthropologists is to then document peoples' experiences of AIDS because they reveal memories and histories of this inequality, mobility, and violence.[24] Women's experiences are especially illustrative as burdensome in this respect.[25] It should not be so.

A final approach is one I term "cultural production" that draws on aspects of these sociocultural and medical approaches. With respect to HIV/AIDS-related biomedical intervention, indicators of "culture" often get re-produced in technical or policy papers as something unmoored from the creative flow of everyday life, insofar as culture may be construed as a problematic barrier *or* a resource to capture to encourage health-related "best practices" in a population.[26] Indeed, culture has been incredibly resourceful amid HIV/AIDS for health-related practitioners and organizations, but also, importantly, for the communities targeted by said practitioners and organizations. To various ends, and by diverse groups, particular phenomena get reified, codified, and copied in colorful symbols, images, and sounds *as* culture. As content and theme, HIV/AIDS has been culturally expressed in writing, folklore, art, music, television, and social media at local, regional, and international levels. These expressions, or cultural productions, are often in direct and political response to the epidemic in Africa.[27] Overall, I find this approach helpful to show how culture is multiply or contrastively produced, often in the same community, and under different sociopolitical circumstances in history. *Funeral Culture* shows how this occurs within the Kingdom of Swaziland.

A main claim of this book is that social and demographic shifts due to the disease compel people there to reconsider the value and use of what they know to be Swazi Culture, especially as it is reproduced by the kingship. Swazi Culture has long been associated with the politically dominant Dlamini clan, since at least the early eighteenth century. The clan moved southward from the Indian Ocean coastal inlands to the area of the present-day nation-state and interacted with other groups such as Sotho, Ngwane, and Pedi and the Zulu kingdom. These interactions—of both interdependency and domination—resulted in an inchoate polity defined by selected customary practices of several groups. Unlike many neighboring polities that were dominated during modern European colonialism, Dlamini royalists commandeered an amalgamation of other local kingdoms and clans in its dealings with Afrikaner settlers and British colonialists through the end of the nineteenth century on to independence in 1968.[28] The previous King Sobhuza II (1899–1982) who oversaw the Swazi nation before and after this transition, effectively shut out political opposition. To do so, in part, he played on enduring, popular symbols, such as a stone to grind grain, *imbokodvo*, which increasingly came to reference Swazi Culture and Dlamini kingship's authority. This process unfolded similarly across the African continent amid decolonization, leading to culture's centrality in postcolonial political life.[29]

Contemporary Swazi Culture is represented as monocultural rather than multicultural and is widely lived out and promoted by people who are called traditionalists or promonarchic. Many citizens revere the state leaders, King Mswati III and the Queen Mother, his mother, Ntfombi Tfwala, both of the Dlamini clan. There are many princes and princesses—Mswati has more than fifteen sons and daughters and more than two hundred of his own brothers and sisters by his father Sobhuza II, who had more than eighty wives. Many royalists live well, and some have major economic and political power. Other traditionalists include the governors of royal capitols, such as the late T. V. Mthethwa and Jim "Mbhokane" Gama at Ludzidzini, and state-appointed princes who govern districts of local chiefdoms in a postcolonial sovereign system called *tinkhundla*.

Various state-owned television and radio channels broadcast popular shows that boldly claim what is definitively cultural as Swazi.[30] They are also platforms for national royal decrees from the capitals to annually summon citizens to do tributary labor, such as weeding royal fields. The late state historian James S. M. Matsebula (1988 [1972], 9–11), head of the national council governing cultural and heritage sites, described how kingship holds chiefs and "commoners" together in "oneness." This was done through administrative capitals, councils, and state-sponsored ceremonies. The vernacular terms he notes for commoners, however, are telling: *tinja tenkhosi* (the king's dogs) and *tibi tendlunkhulu* (insignificants or trash of royal households).

Today the state promotes Swazi Culture in large, annual, national ceremonies that draw tens of thousands of participants and also effectively regiment the population into gendered age grades. From the harvest "first fruits" rites of kingship, *iNcwala*, undertaken by young and older men to the new national *Buganu* rites of older women celebrating the *marula* fruit harvest and brewing, these ceremonies have been central to Swazi Culture's constitution in public life and scholarship for almost a century.[31] Amid HIV/AIDS, these ceremonies have become central for more global audiences to see cultural efforts to fight the disease while also drawing in tourists, a point taken up in chapter 1.[32] These national forms are produced by royalist state and parastatal arts and tourism entities that market the country as a premier cultural destination, insofar that anthropologists John L. and Jean Comaroff call the kingdom "ritual-saturated" (2009, 113, 156n25) and note that the perception outsiders have of Swaziland as a total "culture park" is not at all far-fetched. Susan Cook and Rebecca Hardin (2013, 227) characterize Swazi royalty as a bastion of "defiant African alterity," showing how corporate entities visit the kingdom to learn how to better cash in on culture for financial benefit. These interpretations elide with more critical perspectives on Swazi Culture generally, which see it as politically reproduced to maintain elite rule.[33]

Much of this criticism is not totally off the mark in the perspective of many Swazi citizens themselves. The national ceremonies are ebullient, symbol-rich, and widely marketed across the world, yet local participation tends to be incongruent with the public valorization of the ceremonies. The majority of Swazi people I met had never been to *iNcwala*. Many women I spoke with said they had

Fig. 0.3 Girls' age grade regiments at the Reed Dance, Lobamba, 2010. Photograph by author.

participated in *Umhlanga*, the annual state ceremony for young girls, enjoyed it immensely, but had only gone once or twice in their youth (see fig. 0.3). As the majority of the country is Christian, many also feel that these traditionalist ceremonies do not align with their churches' principles, despite the argument that theologically the ceremonies evince religious tolerance (Ndlovu 2007). Others are unable to afford the traditional attire (*imvunulo*) needed to participate unless it is rented or donated by the state. Shortly after independence, the most prominent anthropologist of Swaziland and a lifelong friend of Sobhuza II, Hilda Kuper (*Mam'* Kuper as she is still locally known), forecasted the waning efficacy of Swazi Culture in these ceremonies. She wrote: "With the economic and political diversity and complexity of a modern State it is no longer possible for a single ritual to symbolize the totality" of the Swazi nation, given its increasingly heterogeneous population, nor are such ceremonies now "more important than other public holidays" (Kuper 1972a, 614).

The politics of rounding off what Swazi Culture is and is not and for whom it is important is clear. In historical moments of noticeable social change, certain phenomena have been locally decried by elites as unSwazi, including Western constitutional law as was suspended in the kingdom from 1972 to 2005; divorce; forms of women's dress; outsiders who do not treat local people as equal or human beings; and more recently, the suspended burial, abandonment, and mistreatment of the dead.[34] Usually, that which is said to be unSwazi points to an affront

Fig. 0.4 Children's street parade organized by a church. The center placard reads, "God gives us the work to bring people together," Hlatikulu, 2011. Photograph by author.

to traditionalist sensibilities, but dramas that play out surrounding contemporary funerals go beyond this purview. Practically, culture has never really added up to social consensus nor a single moral truth.[35] What people find valuable to accomplish their immediate plans and projects, especially surrounding death, does not always line up with the best ideations of culture proposed by those who claim to be its primary arbiters. The burdensome, complex efforts needed to pull off funerals today, for many people I met in Swaziland, felt patently unSwazi.

Still, the majority of people I met and know well are not interested in a radically deconstructive project of culture. They are aware that culture, writ small, is ever-changing and dynamic. Most are proudly patriotic despite local and global pro-democracy criticism of the monarchy.[36] Most love Swazi Culture in its popular forms of singing, dancing, joking, telling riddles and folklore, and wearing *imvunulo*. Some of these are also listed as part of "Swazi Traditional Religion." Still, mission-originated and newer Pentecostal churches, workplaces, and schools organize popular "culture days," where members enjoyably undertake all of these activities with Christian commitment and flair. Some of the happiest moments I have had with my friends, informants, and consultants there have been in sharing in these events, church services, weddings, and weekend afternoons.

Many everyday cultural practices unfold in more common ways: Braiding, dreading, or cutting hair to make oneself look beautiful. Wearing clean, well-pressed or -ironed, fashionable clothes to look good and for mobile phone selfies. Children's schoolyard and afterschool play (see fig. 0.4), like skipping rope and make-believe. Watching weekend soccer games at neighborhood fields or the National Stadium. Indulging in ripe indigenous fruits such as *emantulwa* and *tingcosi*. For those in town, buying commercially farmed "whiteman" chicken (*ramtutu*), for Sunday dinner and comparing it to more flavorful indigenous ones (*tinkhukhu tasekhaya*), or knowing the best roadside vendors of "chicken dust," named for succulent flame-grilled portions of chicken laced unintentionally with dust kicked up by vehicles and passing feet. Knowing which of the differently colored flags flying above a homestead means a Zionist church family lives or congregates there or whether the family sells milk, beer, or meat.

These beloved practices are best characterized in siSwati as customs (*emasiko*) and ways of life (*imihambo*). Museum and heritage specialist Bob Forrester and anthropologist Vito Laterza (2014, 26) importantly differentiate Swazi Culture from customs; the latter they define as "a flexible and shifting set of practices that change over time and adapt to changing circumstances." They note that "these logics and activities [of *emasiko*] are often simplistically associated with 'Swazi culture'" yet extend beyond any particular social group. They also note that "most Swazis continue to draw upon customary practices and idioms to pursue their own interests and aspirations outside the arena of national politics." This kind of everyday cultural production can be traced ethnographically, a documentation that supports Cook and Hardin's (2013, 229) call for "analysis of new and nuanced deployments of 'culture'" in Africa and globally.[37]

Funeral Culture expands on these important ideas in demonstrating diverse formations of culture in the wake of disease and demographic and historical changes, describing how the materiality bound up with contemporary funerals incites renewed consciousness about the value of culture in everyday life. This book is not a comparative inventory of what is "old" as part of Swazi Culture and "new" as part of funeral culture's mortuary goods, global public health resources, and the like. It is rather about how this renewed consciousness surrounding things used to get by in life and death registers as cultural change. It also shows how this dynamic plays out due to the effects of HIV/AIDS and how answers to existential questions surrounding death are renegotiated through seemingly banal accoutrements: flowers to lay at a grave, printed funeral programs, and Tupperware containers of scones served at night vigils by daughters-in-law like LaGija.

Before turning to why I chose the method and writing style I did for this book, I offer three last points on culture via insights of a few seasoned anthropologists from around the world. First, some food for thought: once, over platters of pan-fried fish at a Congolese club in Johannesburg, Lebanese anthropologist Ghassan Hage suggested to me that culture is immersion in a milieu. Citing philosopher Georges Canguilhem (2001; Marsland and Prince 2012), a milieu is an environment formed from life forces, inert elements, and ideations—including other people and preexisting notions of what dignity, a good death, and culture are. Dealing with death is not new work for people in Swaziland or elsewhere, because death and its commemoration are eternal problems—and not just for the human species.[38] What is new is the stuff populating this particular milieu by which people are able to differently deal with death. Some of these practices and material forms are novel because they are newly available commodities, ideas, and spaces. Others are preexisting but spun with new values in social marketing and global public health communications. Altogether, by funeral culture I mean people's historical consciousness of being part of this present milieu and getting by therein, and their ways of envisioning how to overcome its challenges with dignity.

Culture is not *"inherently* a conservative or dangerous concept," argues American anthropologist Sherry Ortner (2006, 114ff., original emphasis), and "there is a kind of category mistake in seeing it as such." While acknowledging the "very real dangers of 'culture' in its potential for essentializing and demonizing whole groups of people," she says—and of which people in sub-Saharan Africa, for example, have been grossly misrepresented in writing and research on their sexualities[39]—"we must recognize its critical political value as well, both for understanding power and for understanding the resources of the powerless." In this way, funeral culture is not always a critique by commoners or ordinary citizens of royalists' use or appropriation of Swazi Culture, although as the following chapters show, aspects of it may be. It is a practical, popular production of culture in a pluralistic, postcolonial setting—a place of people's own making, where relationships, often unequal, get reproduced in everyday practices of ritual, healing, remembering, saving, living longer, and dying. Funeral culture then is also a kind of practical consciousness through which claims about the value of life and death are made in everyday cultural production.

Lastly, Ugandan anthropologist Christine Obbo (2006, 165), writing about Africans' cultural self-representations and AIDS, notes that "despite the trappings of globalization in many aspects of urban life in Africa, local cultures still matter; they are the lived experiences of the majority of people." In this respect, and to do a respectful ethnography of people with whom I worked and lived, it does not make sense to throw out culture singly as a stereotype or façade for hegemony or oppression. Its use, embodiment, and reproduction are much more circumstantial and creative. To do so would be to throw out most people's sense of their fundamental humanity—for many people in the kingdom, to be Swazi is indeed to be human.[40] Thus this book is less a continuation of this critical scholarship on Swazi Culture's misappropriation or inventedness, although these processes are undeniable in any examination of human cultural production. It is more about how funeral culture emerged alongside of it due to HIV/AIDS.

Ethnography: Getting By, Getting Along, and Getting Well

The people you meet in this book are not political progressives, royalists, or socioeconomically upper class. They are wonderfully "ordinary," to use Swazi librarian Balam Nyeko's (2005) term.[41] Their everyday lives mattered to me, as they are who most Swazi are. Unlike Hilda Kuper (and like most outsider anthropologists since her), I did not live or work with royal Dlamini or traditionalist elites. My friends, host families, and consultants were ordinary people who lived productive, healthy, and mostly happy lives under various material living conditions: some with running water for drinking, washing, and toilets, some without; some with their own cars, televisions, and other nice amenities, and some without; some who bought foods at markets and grocery stores, and some who grew much of their own starches, fruits, and vegetables and raised animals.

Teaching about peoples and cultures of sub-Saharan Africa has been the way I make my colloquial bread and butter for some time now. For most people completely unfamiliar with what life in southern Africa is like—students and others newly traveling there with development, evangelical, volunteer, or biomedical treatment intentions—I frame the approach in what I think are more recognizable terms. The unit I teach on the intersection of medicine and religion I call "Getting Well," the unit on kinship and relatedness "Getting Along," and the unit on economics "Getting By." These more easily depict a common humanity and cast more equitable terms through which to relate to people cross-culturally. Ethnography as a method of long-term fieldwork in which one lives locally incorporates these in documenting how people go about their everyday lives. Appreciatively, nearly everyone I met in Swaziland was willing to go along with me (and sometimes laugh) on this journey.

Trying to do a sensitive, sensible account of life and death led me to live alongside several families in their homes to see their larger respective communities. I lived at LaGija's home with her and her sister Buyiswa and LaGija's adult daughter and sons. They all shared a small three-bedroom house in a suburb of Manzini, and all of them kept busy with schedules of work, university classes, church worship services and Bible study sessions, shopping, watching television and reading, and visiting friends. There was a lot to do in town, and if I did not have other interviews with local businesses such as insurance companies and funeral parlors, or with global health or development entities, I went along with them on their activities. In this way I met many of their coworkers, church brethren, and extended family members spread throughout the kingdom. I first met LaGija in 2008, and stayed with her and her family for six months in 2010, with shorter visits in 2009, 2011, 2014, and 2017.

Given Swaziland's small size (see map 0.1), nearly everyone in town has ties to the countryside. Life in rural communities is different from life in towns,

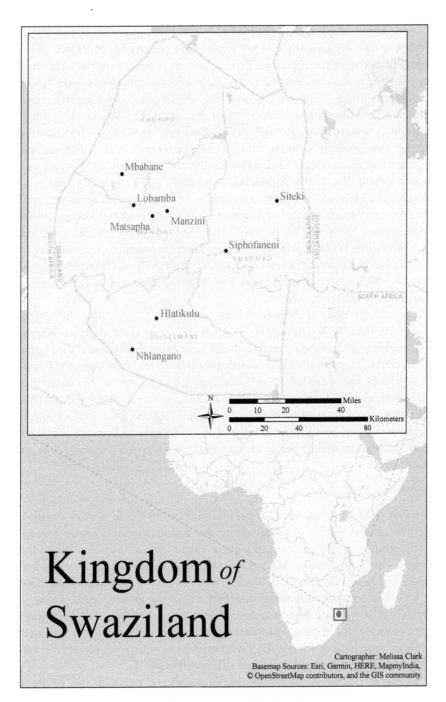

Map 0.1 Maps of Swaziland and Sub-Saharan Africa, 2017 © Melissa Clark.

as in the latter, people govern themselves in more customary ways. I spent six months in 2011 living with a young family in a countryside chiefdom I call Madulini in the southern part of the kingdom, near Nhlangano. At that time, Vuyo Matimba, his wife, Nokwenza, and their three daughters were in the home. I met them through Vuyo's oldest sister, who, like LaGija, I met through an educational fellowship. Vuyo commuted to work in town each day, and Nokwenza kept house. I stayed around Madulini and helped Nokwenza with the weeding, farming, washing, cooking, and keeping the family's cattle, chickens, and pigs well fed. Like LaGija's family, this family went to church. Their house was located next to the chief's compound (*umphakatsi*), so I attended many public council meetings, with most involving family dispute mediation and citizen reports of deaths, births, and crimes. At the community or *kagogo* center, I documented global and public health and development programming for the likes of Doctors Without Borders, the World Food Programme, the Ministry of Health, and World Vision. I went back to visit this family several times in 2014, 2015, and 2017, and by naming me as a godfather to their new daughter—their fourth—I am obliged to return.

Thankfully, none of these friends or consultants passed away while I was living with them, although several of their friends, coworkers, church brethren, and relatives did. I was welcomed to attend these funerals, given that they knew my interests. They welcomed my additional condolences, since dignified funerals should be well attended by well-intentioned people anyway. My account is built up from more than sixteen months of interviews, conversations, and participation in and observation of everyday life in Swaziland from 2009 to 2017. It was born from my best attempt to respectfully, sensitively, and sensibly represent what I learned about how people in Swaziland got well, got along, and got by, or died trying.

Charting a Path

The first three chapters describe cultural changes in the long-term physical, spiritual, and economic preparations for death and funerals. Chapter 1 traces HIV/AIDS and its related mortality at the turn of the millennium. When the royalist state was unable to singly accommodate the high disease burden, global health and humanitarian aid entities collaborated to help coordinate the rollout of ARVs and organize community- and faith-based non-governmental organizations (NGOs), to which many people flocked. While not without their own problems, these entities' material interventions of food and medication and novel sites of social organization enabled HIV-affected people to stave off forms of social and physical death and reckon a more risk-sensitive life.

Chapter 2 explains the popular rise of neo-Pentecostal Christian religious practices coterminous with the epidemic. These religious practices engendered physical, social, and spiritual well-being and preparations for a millennial resurrection in the afterlife. This chapter describes their important material dimensions and how healing-related practices involve a counterintuitive process whereby the afflicted understand that healing is not immediate but occurs only at a later time. Framing these practices through the locally popular Bible verse James 2:26—"Faith without works is dead"—people identifying as Christian saw that without doing the hard work of religious ritual, there was no chance for healing or life after death.

The last chapter in this section, chapter 3, situates the effects of neoliberal economic policy reforms and AIDS on death by focusing on Swaziland's life insurance market. This market expanded threefold in the course of a decade and diversified a preexisting field of burial cooperatives found in communities, workplaces, and churches. This chapter shows how people bought into and used new cash-heavy policies and traces the effects that policies had on family care practices and ideas about ethical and economic value. Insurance was marketed as a novel panacea to care for others by providing a future decent funeral, yet investment in policies was often a secretive process that had uncanny qualities of witchcraft.

Chapter 4 is the first chapter of the second thematic section of the book in that it describes how funerals are produced. This chapter revolves around two enigmas: Why has there been a rise in corpse custody and burial location disputes? and, With the country's first crematorium opening in 2007, why are most people averse to cremation? Focusing on the materiality of human bodies, it looks at the work people do to make sure dead bodies remain whole in their move from the site of death to the mortuary and to the funeral and the burial site. Disputes about bodies surrounded their use in future claims of gendered belonging and social and ritual obligations, which were all vital amid increasing material dispossession. In this context, cremation was seen as a theological aporia and culturally and unsettlingly disembodied because there is no body to put in the ground.

Chapter 5 examines eating food at funerals and foregrounds two contradictions of eating as it has turned into a large, feast-like rite. First, why are feasts considered excessive events amid poverty and food insecurity? Second, why is it that, as people say, visitors to the funeral brought food for the bereaved in the past, while today the bereaved must feed the visitors? Outlining the effects of regional labor migration and changing work roles for kinswomen and bereaved families reveal how cooking for feasts functions to purify and make food culturally wholesome for its consumers both at and far beyond the funeral itself. Amid food insecurity and labor migration, food gets mobilized as a satiating form of life.

The last chapter focuses on the materiality of commemoration as a form of radical mourning. I compare it to royalist practices. In an ethnographic method of following objects and their social lives, the chapter looks at two media used to remember the dead: tombstones and personal ephemera such as clothing. The public memory of the epidemic is driven particularly by an expanded market of funerary wholesalers, who encourage the erection of more permanent personalized tombstones and preoccupy the living with new funerary rites at public cemeteries. Circulating at and beyond the grave are contested forms of adornment in mourning attire and memorabilia that likewise force citizens and the state—with its more secretive commemorative rites—to face the dead.

Contemporary funerals are understood as hard work involving embodied, consumptive practices surrounding new material forms associated with the millennial rise of HIV/AIDS. In the conclusion, I expand on the political and ethical implications of these claims about cultural production and change in postcolonial Africa. Doing so lays out the intersection of illness, wellness, and power in comparative perspective to show how popular forms of cultural production emerge and resonate alongside culture's historic abstractions by states and markets in postcolonial societies. Culture still matters, less perhaps for theory and more in everyday practice for those who live and die by it.

Notes

1. This is the original emphasis.

2. The social science literature on the HIV/AIDS epidemic in sub-Saharan Africa and globally is now legion and interdisciplinary. Monographs and edited volumes on AIDS in Africa or comparatively that have informed this book include, chronologically: Green 1994; Treichler 1999; Kalipeni, Craddock, Oppong, and Ghosh 2003; Campbell 2003; Nattrass 2004; Booth 2004; Poku 2005; Barnett and Whiteside 2006 (2002); Farmer 2006 (1992); Illife 2006; Rödlach 2006; Fassin 2007; Epstein 2007; Biehl 2007; Feldman 2008; Steinberg 2008; Thornton 2008; Susser 2009; Becker and Geissler 2009; Nguyen 2010; Hunter 2010; Klaits 2010; Geissler and Prince 2010; Dilger and Luig 2010; Zigon 2010; McNeill 2011; Henderson 2011; Green and Herling Ruark 2011; Niehaus 2013; Mbali 2013; Decoteau 2013; Wilson 2013; Mojola 2014; Smith 2014; Sangaramoorthy 2014; van Dijk et al. 2014; Whyte 2014; Burchardt 2015; Benton 2015; Rhine 2016; Wyrod 2016; Parikh 2016; Hunleth 2017; and Kenworthy 2017.

3. HIV/AIDS-related politics in Southern Africa, for example, have been well documented. See: Nattrass 2004; Fassin 2007; Susser 2009; Mbali 2013; Decoteau 2013; Burchardt 2015; and Kenworthy 2017.

4. Hickel (2012) describes how HIV transmission in Swaziland has been shaped by the history of labor migration; gender inequality; and economic policies, including matters of pharmaceutical patents governed by the World Trade Organization.

5. I describe these successes more in chapter 1.

6. I like what the anthropologist Daniel Miller (2010, 1–2) has to say about the word "stuff." It is a basic, familiar word for most English-language speakers around the world that

simply refers to "material culture." To use Miller's words, "stuff as a term serves just fine" for my narrative purposes in this book.

7. These are common translations also denoted in the most recent siSwati-English dictionary (Macmillan Boleswa 2010). Werbner (2015) and Klaits (2010) describe similar percepts of *seriti* for Christian peoples in Botswana amid AIDS.

8. Dignity is a useful concept around which I organize my ethnographic description of people's everyday funeral-related actions as a form of work. Dignity was valuable to people as an embodied experience and ethical principle. It was not of course determinative of all people's experiences or ideals. Vito Laterza (2012) brilliantly considers *umoya*—a siSwati percept of breath, wind, or spirit—as a way to situate Swazi people's experience of work as an imminent worldly activation of people's lives and the forces surrounding them. See also Laterza, Forrester, and Mususa 2013.

9. Explaining Swazi funerals in this regard, I find Jackson's (2005; 2011) existential anthropology useful. Focusing on people's lived experiences within events, he shows how multiple subjective and external forces play into shaping experience. Jackson foregrounds well-being as an condition of struggle wrought between what one has and lives by and what one desires and how one could or would want to live. *In extenso*, this speaks to the concept of intersubjectivity, where people struggle to recognize and relate to each other, and yet they forge something extraordinary in the in-between space of their relationship.

10. The collective orchestration of subjective sentiments and social obligation is in some ways akin to what Rose (1992) described as the "politics of harmony" that many Swazi undertake even when engaged in more tense matters such as land tenure disputes. Rose demonstrates that ordinary people are able to strategically, indeed harmoniously, negotiate for and achieve their personal goals despite state-propagated economic inequality. To be able to get along with others who are dispossessive, uncaring, or of a different class is a paramount example of how collective well-being is produced to qualify an event such as a funeral as dignified.

11. Ndebele *umbuyiso* rites, he describes, involving forms of cattle sacrifice, beer consumption, and verbal rites to the deceased, persisted and were renegotiated. Funerals in the new townships were "modernized" by the use of coffins, mourners' "proper" adornment, and processions to urban cemeteries, all forms promoted by Christians. These modernized forms were more expensive, and their mobilization entailed participation in social networks of new churches, businesses, and community or ethnic associations.

12. Regionally in Southern Africa, for example, Jean and John L. Comaroff (1987; 1991) trace Tswana-speaking people's historical consciousness of these colonial-era transformations of productive action, which resulted in a bifurcated value system opposing work and labor, and perceptions of oneself and others: ways of being and acting *setswana*, Tswana, and ways of being and acting *sekgoa*, (British) European. For Zulu-speaking peoples in the late nineteenth century, Keletso Atkins (1993) shows how roles and organization of work, *umsebenzi* in isiZulu, involving generational and patriarchal hierarchies were revalued as labor under British colonial economic policies. At that time, young Zulu men moved away from rural chiefdoms to try success at being clothing launderers in urbanizing colonial Durban, evincing a new cultural work ethic. In post-apartheid South Africa, Hylton White (2004; 2010) shows how inabilities of contemporary Zulu-speaking peoples to find sustained wage labor may confound intergenerational relations with their long-deceased relatives—some of these would be the

descendent individuals described by Atkins. White's informants explained how the dead made spiritual calls on them to make sacrifices or build small commemorative houses in traditionalist style at rural homesteads. Without steady income, however, they sometimes failed to deliver these material goods to their (deceased) families, thus compromising their sense of dignity and location within ideations of culture itself.

13. This holds for West Africa in particular, where funerals are multiday party-like events that involve overt displays of wealth in elaborate coffins and glamorized consumables (de Witte 2001; 2003; 2011). In Madagascar (Graeber 1995) and Indonesia (Yamashita 1994), funerals are often described as exciting events where attendees boisterously engage or dance with the corpse.

14. *Sinyama* is said to powerfully affect older women relatives of the deceased, such as one's mother and other "mothers"—the sisters to one's parents—and who are the principal mourners at funerals. Widows are especially surrounded by darkness and are separated from other funeral participants in a room or small house on the homestead. They are usually confined there in mourning until they are later healed or purified from their condition. Wrongly, they are sometimes avoided or joked about for apparently emitting to others. The sensorial affront of *sinyama* is similar to experiences of other unsettling transcendental phenomena, which inflect funerals and make them hard to bear.

15. See chapter 2.

16. I capitalize the term "Swazi Culture" to signal how some customary rites and practices are nationalized, politicized, and commodified by the governing royalist regime. I discuss the state's process of postcolonial cultural production later in the introduction and throughout the book.

17. The names of individuals and their families with whom I lived and worked are changed, as are some names and details about their places of employment, schooling, or residence as matters of anonymity. The names of individual churches, businesses, and organizations are likewise changed to not single out any person or entity as extraordinary or solely representative of claims I make about cultural change in Swaziland or the value of reified forms of Swazi Culture.

18. See the United States Department of State 2011, 2013, IRIN 2003a; and Z. Sukati 2009.

19. See Muwanga 2004; Nattrass 2004, 162–167; and IRIN 2009a, 2011.

20. In *An African Aristocracy: Rank among the Swazi*, the best early ethnography of Swazi peoples, Hilda Kuper (1980 [1947], 193–195) evocatively describes witnessing the return of a group pilgrimage at a royal palace from the country's three royal groves (*embilini*), burial caves for deceased princes, princesses, and queens hidden in dense forest thickets, each grove with a ritual guardian who keeps watch and demands animal sacrifice from trespassers. Gabby Dlamini (2012), as an insider anthropologist (Obbo 2006), writes about how funerary specialists for contemporary royals reproduce and maintain their social and symbolic separation from commoner or ordinary citizens. See also Njabulo Dlamini's (2005) news coverage of a royal funeral at which a twin sibling was prohibited from attending because of Swazi Cultural stipulations.

21. Smith 2014, 6. See also, for example, Fassin 2007; Biehl 2007; Susser 2009; and Nguyen 2010.

22. See also Treichler 1999; Rödlach 2006; Feldman 2008; Thornton 2008; Becker and Geissler 2009; Dilger and Luig 2010; McNeill 2011; Wilson 2013; Thomas 2014; and Parikh 2016.

23. He notes that all people's lives are cultural in the sense that they are "deeply embedded in a space of conventions historically situated" (Fassin 2007, 23).

24. Fassin's (2007) "historiography-based ethnography" recounts people's memories or "biographical narratives," which trace their histories of violence, mobility, and inequality as much as they do AIDS-related illnesses. It is a narrative that may also be confessional, taking shape in South Africa's Truth and Reconciliation Commission, the Treatment Action Campaign's activism for access to ARVs and AIDS support groups. For Nguyen (2010), a constellation of institutional, governmental, and technological forces evinces a kind of biomedical sovereignty over people's lives in whether or not they take on this confessional imperative as a way to access treatment. I return to this issue of sovereignty briefly in the book's conclusion.

25. See, for example, Booth 2004; Susser 2009; Mojola 2014; Fielding-Miller et al. 2015; Rhine 2016; and Wyrod 2016. In addition, women's and other's feminized domestic and nursing work becomes central for sick people's survival (Klaits 2010).

26. See chapter 1 as well as M. Nxumalo 1999, UNAIDS 2006; UNDP and CANGO 2007; McNeill 2011; Fielding-Miller et al. 2015, 2016; and Golomski and Nyawo 2017.

27. See, for example, Leclerc-Madlala 2001; Reis 2008; Barz and Cohen 2011; McNeill 2011; Wilson 2013; Black 2015; Parikh 2016; and Okigbo 2016.

28. See, for example, Beemer 1937; Matsebula 1976 (1972); Bonner 1983; Levin 1997; and T. Thwala 2013. A significant point in this history was in the 1950 Native Courts Proclamation when Sobhuza II, under the British colonial authorities, was given license to establish courts based on "native law and custom" (Matsebula 1976, 176).

29. See, for example, MacMillan 1985; Obbo 2006; Mbembe 2015 (2001); and Olukoshi and Nyamnjoh 2011.

30. These include *Khala Mdumbadumbane*, formerly hosted by Bongani "S'gcokosiyancinca" Dlamini, *Nasi ke siSwati* ("This is Swazi"), and *Inhlonipho* ("Respect").

31. See, for example, Kuper 1944, 1945, 1980 (1947), 1972b, 1973a, 1973b; Gluckman 1965; Beidelman 1966; S. Nxumalo 1976; Apter 1983; de Heusch 1985; Lincoln 1987; Astuti 1988; Motsa 2001; Kamera 2001; Ndlovu 2007; B. Dlamini 2007; Reis 2008; Masango 2009; N. Dlamini 2009; and Ebewo 2011.

32. On the postcolonial development of tourism, see Harrison 1995.

33. Levin (1997), Sihlongonyane (2003), and Debly (2014) frame tradition as manifestations of royalist hegemony. See also Forrester and Laterza (2014) and Forster and Nsibande (2000).

34. See, for example, Nhlapo 1990; IRIN 2003b; Mthethwa 2007a; Timberg 2004; Wastell 2007; Motau 2013; and Gwebu 2013.

35. See, for example, Borofsky et al. 2001 and Robbins 2007.

36. The citizens and government of Swaziland under kingship are authoritatively repressed by many conventional economic, political science, and human rights indicators.

37. In ritual-based accounts of Samburu marriage, sexuality, and ethnicity, for example, Meiu (2016, 228) describes such historically situated dynamics as ethno-erotic economies: "Approaching *lopiro* [ceremonies] through the framework of ethno-erotic economies, rather than as instantiating an essentialized, dehistoricized 'Samburu culture,' points to the inherent cosmopolitanism of ritual, that is, to the multiple geopolitical scales involved in its making." Comparatively, ideations of culture can be wielded politically. In the Pacific, *kastom*, an English cognate for "custom" emerged in the Solomon Islands as a way for diverse

communities to define and claim collective representation to face British colonialists and missionaries (Akin 2013), and more recently, Samoans marshal "culture" to their advantage in transnational migrations (Gershon 2012).

38. Barbara King (2013), for example, shows how recognition of death and subsequent mourning is evident for elephants, ravens, and chimpanzees.

39. See, for example, Susser 2009; Mojola 2014; Meiu 2016; and Saethre and Stadler 2017.

40. Wastell (2007, 325) writes that "most Swazis are uncomfortable with the implicit proposition inherent in the discourse of human rights that they must choose between their rights as humans and their responsibilities as Swazis, since the latter is not conceived of as a sub-level category enveloped by the former."

41. I also take ordinariness in Lambek's (2010, 2) sense of people's everyday ethical lives, which by and large are "relatively tacit, grounded in agreement rather than rule, in practice rather than knowledge or belief, and happening without calling undue attention."

1 Reckoning Life: Dying from AIDS to Living with HIV

There was always work to do in the chiefdom of Madulini. If you did not get up by your alarm, crowing roosters or rustling cattle outside your bedroom window might wake you instead. Life at the Matimba family's homestead there was busy. Two days after I first came to stay in 2011, we burned the remains of a cow that had died of an injury. When the family's hired herder did not show up some mornings, we moved the nine remaining cattle, the family's newly received bridewealth, a kilometer away to the community grazing area.[1] We took shovels to the iron-rich red earth, weeding a clearer path to the pit latrine. We helped their children with schoolwork. Two of us began working at faith-based non-governmental organizations (NGOs) that were running projects in the community. Nokwenza, the mother, tracked orphaned and vulnerable children (OVC)[2] sponsored by World Vision. I accompanied careworkers (*banakekeli*) from Shiselweni Reformed Church Home-Based Care (SHBC), a grassroots group aiding sick and dying neighbors. At the end of a day, with a cup of tea and typing notes, I was doing two kinds of work: one ethnographic and the other, for the Matimbas, to cooperatively "grow their home" (*kukhuleka ekhaya*). To not help in some way was not the most ethical thing to do.[3]

At the time I moved into their home, they were using a woodburning stove to cook. I boiled an egg on the stove one morning to eat before going out to do a round of interviews organized by my colleague the anthropologist Robin Root. That day, we were speaking with dozens of SHBC clients about their experiences with their careworkers, research that would later tell an incredible story of surviving HIV/AIDS in this community and beyond.[4] Forgetfully, I left the egg in the pot. When I returned, I looked around the kitchen for it, but it was gone. It was of no regard to me that someone might have eaten it, but Nokwenza looked concerned when she saw me looking for it. Her daughter said that Nik took it; he was Vuyo's sister's son. "I will talk to him," she said, annoyed.

Nik was thirty years old. His father was a traditionalist Dlamini, part of a family living the tenets of "Swazi Culture," and Nik grew up with his mother, a Matimba, and her family at Madulini. Nik came back to live with the Matimbas because he had lost his job at a casino. He loved the work; it was rewarding, exciting, and cosmopolitan, characteristic of the independent life he wanted to live. But wanting to be free from others when they depend on you is a challenge. Earlier in life, Nik had gone to several secondary and technical schools but was kicked out of a few or did not complete the courses. Some family members told me he was careless. At Madulini, Nokwenza saw this pattern being clearly retraced. Nik slept a lot and seemed shifty and irritable to her. Twice in three months she called him out in front of others for not doing some kind of work: once over not herding cattle and another over not chopping firewood. He did clean his own living space—a round, single-room dwelling with a thatched roof, sometimes called *kagogo*.[5] He mostly kept to himself when he wasn't hanging out at one of the small shops in the community.

One morning I woke up to the sounds of shouting. It was Nokwenza and Nik. Nik had used some soap but had not yet brought it back to the main house for use in the kitchen. The egg incident had already agitated Nokwenza, and this last incident was all she could take. In the middle of the argument, she quickly called her husband, Vuyo, on the phone to say that Nik was being difficult. Telling Nik's mother's brother made Nik angry. Nokwenza accused him of being lazy and abusing their kindness. Leaving his ironing, Nik went to see her face-to-face in the kitchen. They swung at each other. "Don't hit me," he said. "You will regret it from the day you were born!" "What does that mean?" she retorted. "I won't regret anything. You will regret all these terrible things you do and be judged from the moment you do it! You are a selfish person," she ended, her eyes watering. As he left the house, he stammered that he had to leave this craziness behind him.

The craziness would become worse than a disreputable work ethic and spats with his mother's people. We later learned Nik had been ill for some time. After a traumatic injury in 2014, he was diagnosed with a disease he identified only as "that *thing*," one that disturbed him behaviorally and affected him physically. In his case, experiences of ailing from an undiagnosed illness and being work-less for a while—in formal unemployment and not doing homestead chores—portended a kind of personal inertia. It was also a kind of social death amid others who expected him to lend a hand. *Tandla tiyagezana*—"hands wash each other" in mutual help—goes the customary siSwati saying.

The ability to work is often valued as foundational for human dignity and as a fundamental human right. Cross-culturally, ideations of work may focus more on work as an independent undertaking, whereas for others, productivity may be predicated more strongly on interdependence or mutuality. When a person is unable to work, regardless of whether it is his or her "fault" or the result of something beyond the person's control, including HIV/AIDS, this change affects social relationships. Some may step in to care for a person when he or she becomes sick and cannot work. More dire circumstances are where families may give up their relations with sick people, abandoning them altogether. Alexander Tsai and colleagues (2013; 2017), for example, show how Kenyan people's inability to work because of HIV/AIDS is a source of stigma—they are sometimes rendered "worthless."[6] In Swaziland, stigma may also derive from fear, misinformation, or caregivers reaching the limits of empathy in *inhlitiyo lembi*, a "hardened heart." In cultural cases where the value of a working life is strong, one's inability to get by on one's own is a paragon of indignity. Being alone then cruelly compounds this.

I learned most about what it meant to live a disrupted or compromised life due to HIV/AIDS from people such as Nik and the careworkers and clients of SHBC in Madulini. There were many other groups like SHBC across Swaziland and sub-Saharan Africa with related, community-minded caregiving, educational, and development goals. I also met many people who worked for or used such programs. Their experiences of surviving HIV/AIDS and others' deaths from it foreground human interpretive struggles to answer existential questions: What is the meaning of death? Can we die without suffering? If I am twenty, for example, what do I do knowing I am expected to live to age forty? Practically, surviving, understanding, and living with HIV/AIDS necessitated a kind of social work that was ongoing and, in the best cases, restorative from sufferable situations.

Robin Root tellingly used the term "reckoning" in her longitudinal study of the SHBC careworkers' life-extending interventions, written with the organization's founder, pastor and theologian Arnau van Wyngaard, and health economist Alan Whiteside (2015). Community member clients we spoke to on that day I forgot the boiled egg, along with more than fifty others in neighboring communities, made it clear that their careworkers shared with them an "unconditional love that restored [their] desire to live and adhere to treatment" (Root, van Wyngaard, and Whiteside 2014). Importantly, careworkers were informational and confidential as well as Christian, and they were as much spiritual as they were palliative. More than half the clients we spoke to told us they would have killed themselves or died without SHBC's visitations.[7]

Calling this ongoing carework and its effects "reckoning" is powerful. It hearkens to care's calculative, estimative actions pertaining to medication adherence—in other words, making sure that antiretroviral (ARV) medications are taken daily at the same time, at the right dose, and with proper food. Reckoning in this sense also refers to the ways people with varied education or health-related knowledge make sense of HIV/AIDS information such as disease epidemiology and population-level effects—what do such figures mean for people's personal and families' lives? The international scale-up of ARV distribution and treatment since the turn of the millennium has been transformative insofar as to suggest a prospective "end of AIDS" (Kenworthy, Thomann, and Parker 2017). No longer are the majority of people living with HIV dying from the opportunistic infections marking the onset of AIDS. Through ARVs as part of broader antiretroviral therapies (ARTs) and synergistic care interventions, overall life expectancy has increased as people live longer on medication.[8] This recent history also involves major cultural changes globally for people's perceptions of death, dying, and risk.

Still, medical anthropologist Eileen Moyer (2015) critically points out how such before-and-after depictions can overshadow the epidemic's practical and conceptual continuities: AIDS and HIV are still treatable, but new treatments and programs are often envisioned on what is a receded horizon for populations in poorer countries. For example, preexposure prophylaxis (PReP), now relatively common for at-risk groups in the United States, is not yet widely available in Swaziland, and some people still do not have the means to access what treatment is available. These means are actually quite basic: food, time, money, and the ability to work, among others. These issues have not been fully abated in many places,[9] yet as of 2017, Swaziland is actually leading the way in curbing new infections, a point I return to later. Future health and social work policy and interventions must be locally actionable and culturally specified to enable people to access medication.

Using the stories of Nik, Nokwenza, SHBC careworkers, and those of other HIV-related programs I worked with, this chapter traces a cultural history of reckoned life, loss, and dying in Swaziland's HIV/AIDS epidemic. It does so in three parts: the first discusses the slow emergence of HIV/AIDS on the national landscape in the 1980s and many peoples' resultant wasting from going untreated in the 1990s and early 2000s. In response to the public health crisis, communities, local and international NGOs, and the state mobilized social and pharmaceutical resources that strengthened culturally biomedical ideations of what a healthier life could be. Food, medication, and carework helped people avoid socially and physically dying from AIDS. Through these, life with HIV was thankfully extended but also portended new kinds of risks. Coming to terms with this kind of embodied experience of life at risk—a "life within limits" (Jackson 2011)—was hard work for many people, and situated as part of a longer postcolonial history and cultural production of death too.

The Age of AIDS

HIV/AIDS emerged in the kingdom in the 1980s and intensified over the next twenty years, to the point of society's near disintegration. In 1982, two years after Nik was born, King Sobhuza II passed away as the world's then longest-reigning monarch. It was a period characterized by silence, fear, and suspicion; they were dark times. The state ordered a national mourning period of sixty days as the death of the king brought *sinyama* on the nation. The state historian James S.M. Matsebula (1983, 66) documented prohibitions on plowing land; ritual haircuts for men, women, and children; and the adornment of woven-grass mourning strings. Educator Ellen Magongo (2009, 2) recalled how "the mood of the general populace changed quickly.... To my surprise such [mourning] requests were not optional but enforced by members of the police force who visited homes (mine included) and demanded that the dictates of the elders were carried out. While such acts amounted to an invasion of one's privacy, they also seemed to portend the arrival of significant change in the kingdom."[10] Vuyo Matimba, who was eight years old, laughingly remembered seeing so many people with shaved-bald heads. Nokwenza, who was seven, remembered atmospheric silences when television and radio broadcasts were periodically suspended.

The next few years were politically fractious, with internecine feuds between clans and lines of the royal Dlamini house vying to appoint a new king.[11] In 1983, an interregnum royalist council, *Liqoqo*, publicly chose Makhosetive Dlamini, the son of Sobhuza II and Ntfombi Tfwala, to the surprise of many.[12] After returning to Swaziland from boarding school in Great Britain, Dlamini was installed as King Mswati III in April 1986. The ceremony at the National Stadium included dignitaries such as Mozambican president Samora Machel, Zambian president Kenneth Kaunda, and Maureen Reagan, daughter of American president Ronald Reagan. On the day of his coronation, Mswati promised to lead as king and be king by way of his citizens—*nkhosi yinkhosi ngabantfu*. In Swazi Culture, it is said the king and kingship are the embodiments of the nation itself.

A few months later, in October 1986, a delegation of doctors from South Africa arrived in the kingdom to diagnose what turned out to be its first case of AIDS in a patient identified as "West Indian." Following up on the announcement, the *Times of Swaziland* ran a front-page headline on November 3 titled "AIDS Shockwave: More Could Have the Killer Virus" (Twala 1986) along with a smattering of misinformation about the disease[13] (see fig. 1.1). A moral and practical panic grew, at a time when public health was otherwise steadily improving and mortality rates were down due to the expansion of health clinics (N. Simelane 1987). Here and globally in the 1980s, HIV/AIDS came to the fore in popular consciousness, representing a pernicious historical conjuncture of epidemiology and political economy that would drive the disease into almost every nation on earth. Pointing out its emergence in this political moment in Swaziland, writer Shaun Raviv (2015) notes, "Since the king is the lifeblood of the nation, it is appropriate that his reign began in 1986, the same year HIV arrived." It would be almost twenty years before widespread ARV treatment slowly emerged, and thirty until the epidemic began to stabilize.

Some argue that Mswati's policies, like those of other political leaders and global economic entities, operated as structural determinants that drove disease transmission.[14] According to Jason Hickel (2012), for example, structural adjustment policies and broader market liberalization, abetted by the state in some ways, created a "neoliberal plague" of HIV/AIDS in Swaziland. In this critical perspective, a historically and economically underdeveloped postcolonial context laid the groundwork for high transmission.[15] Regionally, social life is also patriarchal: women's socioeconomic and physical vulnerabilities are pronounced, as men may often be violent in expressions of masculinity, shaping women's greater risk for HIV infection.[16] Tracing these dynamics makes up a social epidemiological approach to health and can show how wider structural and gendered processes shape disease transmission, treatment, and prevention.[17]

Fig. 1.1 *Times of Swaziland* newspaper headline, November 3, 1986.

These dynamics are more complex than kingship could singly stand in for. Linking the epidemic to the state in this way can be a serious affront to some Swazi citizens' ideations of patriotism, which Mswati as a sovereign may personify.[18] Talking about the kingship's ceremonies and the epidemic, R. Simangaliso Kumalo (2013, 120), representing the words of the late Swazi public political theologian Joshua Bheki Mzizi writes, "The focus should be on the life of the King and Princess, not on the negative impact created by HIV/Aids. When we all focus on the good life of the King, we are looking at the brighter side of our story, the story of hope, life, peace and prosperity. We know that even though we are in a valley of death and despair, the Great Spirit is with us. We shall come out and defy the statistics that we may all be wiped of the face of the earth in 2020." Dire health-related demographic projections like these would come to influence how people saw themselves as part of the epidemic and what might be done for future descendants. Even with ambitious treatment and prevention goals, HIV will likely outlive any single political figure as well as successive generations of citizens.

Test of a Generation: Culture, Demography, and Mortality

Nik was part of a generation that saw the worst effects of the disease before ARVs. He also grew up seeing strong local engagements with HIV/AIDS. Researchers, health care and public health specialists, and policymakers had lobbied for state action since the late 1980s; the Ministry of Health established the Swaziland National AIDS Programme (SNAP) in 1987. Vusi Matsebula and Thulasizwe Hannie Dlamini registered their *Emahlahlandlela* (Pioneers) grassroots AIDS support group, the first the country, as SASO, the Swaziland AIDS Support Organisation, in 1994. The year before, Hannie Dlamini publicly stated that he was HIV positive, the first person to do so in the country (Hlatshwayo 2012). Swazi women scholars Mamane Nxumalo (1999) and Phumelele Thwala (1999) were the first to write critically about HIV/AIDS in Swaziland, discussing how gender-unequal practices associated with Swazi Culture played a role in disease transmission. Nik turned eighteen in 1998, the year before Mswati publicly declared that Swazis collectively faced HIV/AIDS as a national disaster.

The effects of the epidemic by the late 1990s were wide-ranging (Daly 2001): by the time SASO opened their first office in Mbabane in 1998, the national incidence rate was estimated to be 5.5 percent; by 1999, there were an estimated 112,000 OVCs, almost a quarter of all children in the country; the Ministry of Education reported losing four teachers a week to AIDS-related illness, and business owners feared foreign investment losses due to decreased productivity in sick workers' absenteeism. The Ministry of Health and Social Welfare was not able to fully finance public treatment. Even working with the Joint United Nations Programme on HIV/AIDS (UNAIDS) and local NGOs, they were all structurally outpaced.

Around this time, a locally critical cultural consciousness also emerged regarding Swazi Culture and generational relations. Questions came to the fore of who was dying more often from AIDS and at what age, and how society could reproduce itself in the future.[19] Public health research and the media honed in on age- and power-disparate sexual relationships between younger women and older men—multiply influenced by economics, romance, and patriarchy—as potentially significant for understanding HIV transmission.[20] A coherent public cultural perception about HIV/AIDS-related demography and mortality was taking shape.

In the early 2000s, the notion of generation became a state resource of Swazi Culture in one of the kingship's major HIV prevention programs. Anthropologist Ria Reis (2008) describes how from 2001 to 2005 Mswati decreed the performance of *umcwasho* rites for the national age grade for young girls, called "flowers" (*timbali*). The rites mandated that participating girls abstain from sex. For five years, thousands of girls wore woolen tassels the colors of Swaziland's flag to symbolize their chastity. Chiefdoms meted out customary cattle fines to transgressors—girls, boys, men, and their families—for underage and premarital pregnancies and reported sexual encounters. Reis writes that *umcwasho* makes up the kingship's attempts to restore the nation during times of social disruption by ritually controlling young women's sexual vitality.[21] This time, the aim was to create a generation of HIV/AIDS-free youth.

LaGija's youngest sister told me that in 2003, members of her chiefdom's council organized girls in the area to recruit their peers. When the recruiters came to her home, she lied, telling them she was pregnant and disqualifying her as unchaste. She chose not to participate in what she felt was an undue commitment to this iteration of Swazi Culture: wearing customary clothes that boldly told everyone around her whether she had sex or not. *Umcwasho* was marred by what many saw as contradictory actions by the king. Mswati himself took five new young wives during the five-year rite, some younger than eighteen. The first, Nontsetselo Magongo, was seventeen years old in 2001. Mswati customarily fined himself a cow following criticisms that he violated his own ritual decree. Magongo named their first child, a boy, Mcwasho.[22]

After *umcwasho* ended in 2005, the state's ceremonial promotion of Swazi Culture as a form of HIV prevention continued through the end of the 2000s. HIV/AIDS-related programming was featured at the related *Umhlanga* national rites for young girls. Developed during the colonial period, *Umhlanga*, the Reed Dance, is a weeklong ceremony ritually summoning the same young girls' age grade to the country's palaces. Annually, the government shuttles nearly fifty thousand girls to march to government-owned marshlands to cut reeds and later present them to the Queen Mother. At the week's end, they dance in formation at the National Stadium before hundreds of the girls' family members, local and international tourists, and dignitaries. The king and his retinue pay them appreciation.

When I attended the 2010 Reed Dance, a woman announcer described the scene over loudspeakers to the spectators, "Entering the arena are the regiments, who are to showcase their dance skills to show their pride in being virgins and their pride for being in the Swazi nation. They are part of the campaign to suppress the HIV and AIDS virus by keeping themselves pure and abstaining from sexual intercourse." Before a large sign featuring the Queen Mother with the slogan "We are a Nation of Arts and Culture," the girls marched across the field, singing songs—lyrics such as, "we are going, we *lobola* (give bridewealth), we *lobola* for Swaziland." Nokwenza never sent her own daughters to the ceremonies after hearing that some girls who were away from their parents used the opportunity to drink. Nik's daughter was too little to go. The event is strongly exoticized and criticized abroad.[23]

These age related ceremonies are potent examples of state-produced Swazi Culture. They show how postcolonial states organize and give meaning to social (and here generational) relations in the production of culture, and how ordinary citizens may redefine culture's value amid disease and demographic stressors. Almost ten years later, the major program message for multilateral and global health entities UNAIDS and PEPFAR (US Presidential Emergency Plan for AIDS Relief) is "working towards an AIDS-free generation" (UNAIDS 2016). Their focus on mothers and children promotes the prevention of mother-to-child transmission (PMTCT), children's adherence, and social protections for children "in the first two decades of life." As a way human societies organize themselves and cache health-related messages about our lived social relationships, generations are catalyzing.

Yet prevention programming at age-related national ceremonies for older generations is comparatively smaller.[24] These people in their productive and reproductive prime were most likely to contract HIV and die from AIDS-related diseases in the late 1990s and 2000s, when the epidemic was more severe. The 1997–2007 census data showed that the crude death rate for people ages fifteen to forty-nine increased sixfold (2.8 to 16.8 per 1,000); in the 2000s, men and women in their thirties died more hospital AIDS-related deaths than other age groups (van Schalkwyk et al. 2013). From 1999 to 2001, registered funerals for people ages twenty to forty-nine at the country's largest mortuary increased from about four hundred to nine hundred (Desmond et al. 2004). Between 1994 and 1999, the number of newspaper obituaries for those ages twenty-one to forty increased from an average of fifty every six months to about two hundred (Whiteside et al. 2002). Young and middle-aged adults were dying more than people in old age and youth. By the early 2000s, AIDS-related mortality rates in some areas of the country breached the threshold status of a humanitarian emergency (Whiteside and Whalley 2007), and some policymakers (UNDP and CANGO 2007, xx) warned that Swaziland faced a potential demographic if not existential "extinction of the nation."[25]

Slow Death

These figures speak to the time before ARVs became widely available in 2003–2004, when AIDS-related illnesses drew out long, slow deaths.[26] HIV symptoms may manifest up to ten years after seroconversion, and without treatment, they worsen in debilitating ways. People with stage three HIV or AIDS experience fever, delirium, sweats, soreness, fatigue, nausea, vomiting, diarrhea, and pain. Some people become physically transformed by weight loss, rashes, and lesions. Bodily deterioration was a source of stigma, and fear of confirming HIV status often stopped people from going to test, thus foregoing a gateway for initiating treatment.[27] Over time, AIDS-related illnesses took horrible tolls in stifling uncertainty about what to do about sickness and its ruinous aftermath. Coming to terms with these generational aspects of dying from AIDS was burdensome too. At funerals, speakers and pastors encouraged the bereaved to "work" on themselves and each other as older parents laid their adult children to rest. Families faced the matter of how to care for orphaned children. Most examples they gave of this work surrounded being respectful to elders, protecting risky youth, overcoming hardship, and "going well along the way" in life, *kuhamba kahle endleleni*.[28]

I met many people in Swaziland who told me deeply personal stories of slow AIDS deaths. Stories of people having to take off from work or losing their jobs over illnesses that would not go away and would frighteningly worsen. Stories of neighbors who locked increasingly sick family members in bedrooms or out of latrines or took away their eating utensils out of fear of contagion or anger. Stories of personal inabilities to bear witness to the agonies of others, the stench of decay, and the fact that they had no medical resources to alleviate suffering. Stories of orphaned children's movement into homes of distant relatives who were reluctant to accept them—perhaps out of spite, or because the children were uncomfortable reminders of the dying process. Stories of finding neighbors in their homes who had died alone, or whole families who died over time, their empty, overgrown homesteads, unplowed fields, and tombstones remaining as silent material testaments to lives lost. Stories that cannot be retold here fully—a decision I made along with those who first told them to me, for to do so would force an account of death in ways that would be too painfully direct or reductive. Telling such stories could never fully convey what had been sacrificed.[29]

When I saw Nik again in November 2014, he was again living in the round house at Madulini. He had gotten a new job at another casino in September of that year, but this time he was on unpaid leave. After getting his first biweekly paycheck, he went to visit his daughter and her mother in the nearby town. The mother's new boyfriend got angry that he came over, and he stabbed Nik in the side of his head. Nik fled to a local hospital and stayed in Madulini to recover. He tried to go back to work in October after his stitches came out but did not have the strength. After dinner the second night of my visit, we sat at the dining room table and ran our fingers through torn bits of the lace tablecloth, preoccupying ourselves as he complained about his health.

He had nightmarish poor sleep. He looked thinner, had a gaunt, ashen face, and bore a scar running several inches behind his ear. In an interview with me in 2017, he told me that the end of 2014 was one of the hardest times in his life. Following the attack, the hospital staff had asked him to take "the test." "That's when I found out my status," he said. "At first I did not think about [it] seriously, for a couple weeks or month. Later though, I said, *I will die from this thing.*" From there on, getting well became a form of survival for Nik.

Reckoning Life: People, Food, and Pills

Surviving or reckoning HIV/AIDS meant strengthening one's life, *imphilo*. *Kuphila* means "to live" in siSwati and related languages. *Ngiyaphila*, "I am alive," is the ordinary way to say "I'm fine" to someone asking, "How are things," *Kunjani*? For Nik and the people of Madulini, surviving HIV/AIDS meant allowing others to look after or care for you, *kunakekela*, and to enliven or make you better, *kuphilisa*. Over time, a strengthened life emerged in giving oneself over to others, letting them "work" on you, in a way, so that you could do the same for yourself. Survival was a social production, a kind of interdependent formation of care that enabled one's capacities to go on living. Of course, survival also took great medical intervention; ARVs are essential, as are the other basic functional means of shelter, water, and food. Through Nik's and others' stories, I trace how caring, respectful people and vital means such as food and pharmaceuticals became materially instrumental in reckoning life and rebuilding a sense of dignity in HIV/AIDS-affected communities.

People: Careworkers, Coworkers, and Good Hearts

With respect to people, reckoning meant being part of supportive caregiving, familial, and clinical relations. These relationships imbricated people suffering from or living with HIV with pro-social others who could measurably help them. SHBC careworkers (see fig. 1.2), for example, did not abandon the sick when others did and were not indignant toward them. Careworkers and others with these sentiments were considered people with "good hearts," *tinhlitiyo letinhle*, who were willing to "freely" give compassionate love, *lutsandvo* (Root and van Wyngaard 2011). The idiom of a good heart manifested in somewhat unremarkably ordinary but powerful acts: talking and listening to, praying with, feeding, and bathing the sick, and educating those who were neglectful or misinformed. Careworkers also encouraged visits to biomedical facilities and daily intake of medication.

A redeemable goal for many newly diagnosed individuals as part of their relationships with careworkers and clinical staff was affirming a life with HIV. A range of faith-based, social justice, and development-related

Fig. 1.2 Careworkers of Shiselweni Reformed Church Home-Based Care organization (SHBC) at the community *gogo* center, Madulini, 2011. Photograph by author.

HIV support groups, such as SASO and SHBC, grew up in the 1990s and 2000s that enabled this goal.[30] Some groups linked to or created new organizations under SASO's National Network of People Living with HIV/AIDS (SWANNEPHA), founded in 2003. Groups in Swaziland also have a range of names invoking *imphilo*. For example, the 2009 support group master list of the local communications firm Lusweti includes *Imphilo isachubeka* (Life Continues), *Litsemba lekuphila* (Hope to Live), *Sesiphilile* (We Are Still Alive), *Emiphilweni* (In Our Lives), *Sicabangelimphilo* (We Think about Life), and *Kuphila lokuhle* (To Live Well). Clinics and hospitals can also be called *umtfolamphilo*, combining *imphilo* and *kutfola*, meaning literally "to get" or "obtain life."[31] Overall, careworkers and support groups helped sick people get well and, for many like Nik, get back to work.

For Nik, recovery was a desired path back to independence in returning to work at the casino. Still, he could not do it alone. In the wake of the attack, Nik's relationship with the Matimbas was on the rocks, and he felt too weak to farm, tend for animals, and do yardwork. Madulini was saturated with careworkers and outreach programs, but because he stayed there intermittently, he did not connect with a specific group. The quietude of country living and being careful not to offend his relatives coupled badly with what turned out to be HIV/AIDS-related symptoms. Life felt painfully stifling. In a 2017 Skype interview he told me, "I thought I was losing my mind" while healing from the stabbing attack, "but [the clinicians] explained to me that these things would happen because the CD4 count was very low. When they gave me the first rounds [of ARVs], I had 4. It was very, very low."[32] With his immune system seriously compromised, his recovery took several months.

After Nik initiated ART at the small-town hospital in September 2014, he began to feel physically better but continued to have nightmares.[33] He learned about this symptom in an early post-testing counseling session. The side effects of ARVs are varied and classified on a spectrum of mild to serious. Vomiting, diarrhea, and nightmares are considered milder side effects. Despite careworkers' or clinicians' encouragement, these symptoms drive some people to stop taking ARVs altogether. Sometimes, the side effects are subjects of public scrutiny on social media or in newspaper op-eds with titles like "ARVs (not HIV) are killing Africans" (*Times of Swaziland* 2013). In our interviews with SHBC clients, Robin Root and I found that some family members of people living with HIV discouraged them from taking ARVs. Some felt "disgrace" for seeing their family members take the medication in public places such as funerals. Others denied ARV's efficacy in comparison to customary medicines and that their relatives' illnesses were in fact HIV/AIDS (Root and Whiteside 2013).

Two months later, in December 2014, Nik felt well enough to travel to Mbabane to stay with his mother's younger sister Nomvula, a school principal. For him, the city's cooler climate was refreshing; referring to the limited aftercare for his stab wounds, he said, "Madulini was a bad place for someone who was sick like me. The clinic was not as strong as hospitals in town." Nomvula eventually encouraged Nik to report his attacker to the police. The man was arrested, convicted, and sentenced to three years in prison. Over time, *make lomncane*, "small mother" Nomvula, became his closest family confident on health matters. "Mostly I feel alone in talking about these health things. Even in my family," he said, "when I go home to visit and we are all together, no one asks me about my health. I know that they know my status. *Make* Nomvula asks me how I am doing, though, and I like that."

Living in town with Nomvula was advantageous. "I don't need caregivers [to] come to see me. Because I live closer to the hospital," he explained, "I can just go there when I have a question about something with my health." Also, he now lived closer to his casino job. After the attack and test, he went to Human Resources and chose to take unpaid leave over the sick leave option, telling them he needed more time to recover from his injury. So as not to identify "the other thing, ... I just showed them my scar, and they accepted my time off. I didn't have to show anything from the doctor, which would show my medical information." Nik felt that his employers respected him for taking the unpaid option—some workplaces notoriously fired people for being chronically sick[34]—and a year later he was promoted to work on the main casino floor. Happily, he now got to deal with all kinds of people as customers and deal cards in all kinds games: Hold'em, Raise'em, and Ultimate poker; Blackjack; and Baccarat.

Nik was relieved to have Nomvula's confidence at home, as he felt he could not talk about health matters at work. Some of his colleagues were uninformed about HIV/AIDS. Whereas SHBC careworkers consistently educated people on such matters, there were fewer opportunities in the workplace for people to learn more about a disease that affected everyone. "During our training sessions, they put a bit of that information in lectures for us, normally at the end of the year in September or October," Nik said. When the topic of HIV/AIDS did come up in coworkers' conversations, "we go with the flow. I put in my ideas, and I don't have a problem, but some people think differently. When I usually hear them when they talk at work, I see that these people are still 'in the forest'"—from which hard truths eventually come out, *itawuphuma ehlatsini*, writes Thoko Mgabhi (1998) in her siSwati tragic novella. "*This thing* does not determine human beings," Nik continued. "Some [coworkers] even say they can't use the same cup or the same utensils [as someone living with HIV]. It can be difficult to teach or show someone. But when *they* get that thing [themselves], or we all start saying our status, it's much simpler to talk about. I have done it, and I can help you to help yourself," he said, showing a markedly more cooperative stance compared to his time in Madulini.

Some major employers in Swaziland, such as Coca-Cola, construction firms, and textile factories, as members of the Swaziland Business Coalition on Health and AIDS (SWABCHA), run local, award-winning worker wellness initiatives. Yet more than 40 percent of people in the kingdom who are able to work are unemployed, and 13 percent cannot work due to illness or disability.[35] The reach of such workplace programs may be limited to the few who can find wage labor. Outside of these programs, people generally learn about HIV from the news, global and public health programs in their communities, and as students in primary and secondary schools. LaGija and her teacher sisters complained jokingly that HIV/AIDS had been done "to death" in the curriculum. Clinical staff, counselors, and careworkers educated people living with HIV on how to get tested, be adherent, use contraception, eat healthy, and reach out to others if they felt unwell or afraid.

Nik concluded that he was alive and well today because of his work: "What kept me going was that I knew I had a job. If I didn't have the job, I don't think I could survive." Low wages, however, made going to work every day somewhat undignified. People wanted and needed to be paid well in order to provide for both themselves and others. Surviving AIDS and living with HIV was also about having a "livelihood."[36] A job paid money, although comparably not as much as he could make in South Africa, and getting a worker visa to go there was the big challenge. His job enabled him to provide for his daughter and her mother, which he continued to do even after the attack. It also gave him the ability to repay debts to Nomvula. Later, he could cover living costs of transportation to work, phone airtime, and rent for his own apartment nearer to the casino. Work gave Nik purpose for daily living and a way to valorize his strengthened life, more than being part of a clinical or careworker program or national ceremony did. Through the help of other people like Nomvula, his clinicians, and colleagues, returning to work bore for him a sense of dignity. What compromised his life most, he felt, was the meager wages he was paid for his efforts. There were, however, other job perks that aided him with respect to his health.

Food: The Ethics of Eating and Feeding

When Nik first started at the casino, he worked in food and beverage services. He was happier being part of the business's main entertainment of gambling. The busiest time of year began in late August and early September, during *Umhlanga* and Independence Day, and concluded after the summer Christmas and New Year's holidays. "The best part of the job is interaction with the customers, meeting and sharing new ideas with people from different places," he told me, mentioning tourists from South Africa, Spain, and Ireland. "You find out what they like and how to treat them well." But his least favorite part of customer service was when some some customers became aggressive. "They get complimentary drinks which makes them spend their money. That is to our advantage," he laughed, recounting how customers get "eaten up at the gaming table because they are too drunk to play and can't concentrate." But when they didn't follow the rules of the games because they are drunk, he admitted, they cause "chaos."

Drinking and eating are indulgent vices as well as ethically entangled material actions important to reckoning a life with HIV. Known formerly by his relatives as a wild drunk, Nik mostly gave up alcohol about a year after his diagnosis, only drinking a few beers every couple of months with colleagues. As nutritious foods strengthen a body's immune system, giving up drinking is a standard clinical recommendation for people living with HIV. "When taking ARVs, the most important thing is the food," Nik explained, "and at work I get two meals a day. They debit the meals from our salary. They give us a voucher, so if you don't take it today, you can take it tomorrow. Sometimes I have to take other medications, [so] getting the food is good. At work I eat chicken stew and rice and some vegetables. We also have salads and desserts and fruit, a balanced diet that is fine, then during break we have bread with ham, cheese, lettuce, and salads." "No beans?" I asked. He laughed at my joke, saying "No beans! I hate those things! I don't want them anymore. I ate them for a very long time," referring to the school- and community-based feeding schemes that has provided plain meals of beans and maize meal to him and other food-insecure children nationally for a generation.[37]

Indeed, many households in Swaziland have a low dietary diversity and are food insecure because of macroeconomic and environmental factors and lost productivity from AIDS-related illnesses.[38] Both practically and culturally, eating in households had high stakes. It was also commensal and complex, involving gendered and age-related forms of giving, preparing, and consuming. Chapter five shows how these acts changed as part of funeral feasting. In daily life, when people living or working together did not get along, their mealtimes could turn into uncomfortable social dramas. At Madulini, Nokwenza normally made enough food for all of us: herself, her husband and daughters, me, and Nik. Around eight in the evening, she dished up plates for us to eat while watching the soap opera *Generations*. Sometimes, however, she plated for all of us except Nik, leaving his portion in the cooking pots and pans. Nokwenza did not hesitate to say she did this because Nik did not help out around the house. He often came into the main house about five minutes after we got our food and waited until Vuyo invited him to eat: "*Hawu*, Nik, you have no food," Vuyo would say disapprovingly. "Go serve yourself!"

Nik tried to be respectfully deferent to the Matimbas, all of them aware of Nik's difficult history with food and his mother's family. When he was a teenager living at Madulini, he and his friends once stole packages of chicken from a small shop to barbecue. He was disciplined for it by his late uncle Muzi, Nokwenza told me, snapping her fingers to sound a beating. When she and Vuyo lived in Matsapha in 2006, Nik came to their home one night asking for food and shelter after having dropped out of technical school and losing his rented flat. Again at Madulini in March 2011, when I was living there too, he angered his grandmother's sister after taking her ward, his younger cousin, to town for a few days to look for work without telling anyone. Nokwenza said Nik felt ashamed after returning from this trip. His relatives chastised him, and he chose not eat with them for a week.

Eating (or not) showed strained social relations surrounding unshared work and love. I have known Nokwenza for many years. She is a wonderful, loving mother and strong household head. But she made no money as a volunteer and had too much to do to manage the homestead alone without the help of another adult while Vuyo was at work. To her, Nik's inactivity showed he did not care. Feeding him was a basic means of giving love and life itself, and when he put in little effort to cooperatively grow the overall well-being in her home (*kukhuleka ekhaya*), it made her upset. Indeed, food could be weaponized as a way to protect one's own well-being and engender remorse in people who had perceptibly transgressed social boundaries. Withholding food or serving it separately and with different utensils were some of the most painful actions some families took against people living with HIV (Root 2010; 2011), as Nik also noted his casino colleagues talking about. These actions were slow starvations of food and sentiment, configured as part of a broader relationship between sociality, food, and ART that many people found difficult to parse.

Pills: Body, Form, and Time

The national scale-up of ARVs in Swaziland began in late 2003 in collaborations between the Ministry of Health, SNAP, NERCHA, the Global Fund, UNAIDS, and the Elizabeth Glaser Pediatric AIDS Foundation. Since then, PEPFAR, Doctors Without Borders, and MaxART have also been crucially involved.[39] Their demonstrable successes in curbing HIV infections and AIDS-related mortality over the past fifteen years are incredible, despite intermittent drug shortages and ongoing funding issues. Today there is much to celebrate. Swaziland's second nationwide HIV incidence survey that concluded in March 2017 showed a 44 percent decrease in new infections. Impressively, 87 percent of all people living with HIV who knew their status regularly took ARVs, and 92 percent of those were virally suppressed.[40] These are amazing testaments to ongoing, collaborative local and global public health prevention initiatives that took on one of the worst epidemics in the world.

Anthropologically, state and private health communication programming and cultural perceptions of disease etiology mutually reshape the value people attribute to pharmaceuticals such as ARVs (Nichter 2008). ARVS are now common and widely talked about, though often discreetly and most openly in supportive health- or carework-related settings. Taking ARVs is also part of many people's daily embodied experiences, as one in three people in Swaziland are HIV positive. Everyone knows someone who has HIV, though not everyone takes the same combination of medications, nor do they have the same reactions.

Earlier in the epidemic, thinness and cancerous skin lesions (*Kaposi sarcoma*) were visible symptoms of HIV/AIDS, and deaths due to wasting were common. With ARVs, some people living with HIV cleared their epidermal matters and noticeably regained weight. Unfortunately, some ARV drugs like stavudine and zidovudine, still commonly used in Swaziland (Parker et al. 2015), can cause the side effect of lipodystrophy, a syndrome of abnormal fat redistribution and loss. Over a period of eighteen to twenty-four months after starting ART, fat may accumulate in the abdomen and the upper back and recede in one's arms, legs, and face (Baril et al. 2005). People with HIV-related lipodystrophy also report "reduced satisfaction with their body image, self-esteem and social relationships, less confidence about their health and embarrassment due to body changes" (Finkelstein et al. 2015). Obesity also complicates HIV/AIDS-related lipodystrophy and is prevalent in Swaziland.[41] Even with the prospect of ARVs prolonging life, people living with HIV, as with most people regionally, face chronic food insecurity. In this regard, the material effects of ARVs played a role in the way people revalued their bodies in weight over time and, despite hunger, hid their recovery in plain sight.[42]

In 2010, a public controversy about a beloved food item—chicken—brought questions about the relation between the value of ARVs and their bodily effects to the fore. At an international development conference, the former minister of Sports, Culture & Youth Affairs, Hlobsile Ndlovu, said a government hospital nurse told that her chicken wholesalers were feeding crushed ARVs to their fowls, supposedly in an attempt to fatten them up. The Ministry of Health rebuffed her, but given the obvious ongoing consumption of both ARVs and chicken and the culturally novel relation between them, the story resonated in the news media for almost two years.[43] Reactions to this matter were somewhat two-sided: either such medications were good enough to enliven formerly thin HIV-positive people and thus good enough to fatten poultry, or ARVs were not fit for intended human consumption at all and thus were "for the birds." In the latter case, it was better to toss them off to animals as waste-like food.

Taking ARVs on a balanced diet was one challenge to adherence. Another was taking them consistently. Here, reckoning life was also a matter of time. Getting people to take pills—day to day, week to week, year to year, for the rest of their lives—is a primary focus of adherence programming. HIV-positive people learned from clinicians and careworkers that strict scheduling was critical for healthy living. Nik took his medication twice daily, at midnight and noon. "Because I work the night shift at the casino, I know to take them at 12 at night. During the day I set my cellphone for 12 and that reminds me," he explained. "Do you always do it on time?" I asked, and he answered, "not every day. Sometimes I miss the time. I'm not that accurate. It's very difficult, but I go every six months for a checkup to check what's going on. Since the last time I went, I haven't had a problem."

Technology-aided reminders such as phone alarms are commonly promoted and framed as independently minded tasks for adherence. Lusweti's widely distributed 2009 instructional guide, "Life on ARVs," for example, offered bullet-point reminders to start: "Planning ahead for weekends, holidays, and any changes to your usual routine; keeping a diary of medicinal in-take in a daily planner and ticking off each dose as days go by; using phone timers, alarm clocks, or pagers to remind you when to take your medicine"; and, acknowledging that perfect planning may not be always be possible, to "develop plans for how to overcome problems faced in the future." Altogether, these culturally biomedical pointers prompted HIV-positive people to develop tight schedules to take their ARVs.

People also developed familiarity with their medications' material form, sometimes discerning them by color and shape along with their pharmaceutical name as a way to talk about them indirectly. In our SHBC interviews, HIV-positive status was a sampling criterion, although we did not directly ask clients about their status. Yet in response to opening questions about how they felt generally, many would quickly and quietly say that they "took their pills," *-natsa philisi*, or they took a "blue pill" and that "things could be better," *kuncono*.[44] Recalling these tacit disclosure encounters, I asked Nik in our Skype interview if he took such a blue pill. He understood the meaning of what I said. "Let me check. At first they gave me pre-ART," he replied, and put down the phone. I heard a rattling, what sounded like a full bottle of pills being picked up. He then read a string of letters and numbers—"TDF3TC" (tenofovir disoproxil fumarate/lamuvidine)—saying he was not sure what it meant exactly, but that it worked well.

In Madulini, the SHBC careworkers were instrumental in helping their community member clients adhere to a schedule for taking ARVs and other medications. Reiterative encouragement and ART guidance helped them go on living (Root and Whiteside 2013), and it manifested careworkers' love. As in other rural communities, Madulini's chiefly council permitted several organizations such as SHBC to work with their residents. World Vision, the United States' Peace Corps, the World Food Programme, the Ministry of Health and Social Welfare, and Doctors Without Borders all maintained a regular presence in the chiefdom with their respective HIV/AIDS-related programs. Most did some combination of public education forums, food and aid distribution, and intermittent home inspections. While I was staying there, Doctors Without Borders revived a bimonthly educational meeting aimed at men's health issues. Their contracted local health educator, Mr. Magagula, had found success in drawing in older men to the sparsely attended meetings. He did so by organizing *sidlanhloko*, a customary men-only meal and popular get-together to boil up a cow's head to satisfyingly share. To Mr. Magagula, having people learn and eat together seemed most effective for getting his point across.

The topic for one mid-May 2011 *sidlanhloko* was ARV adherence. Mr. Magagula wore his usual bright-red vinyl jacket with an appliquéd message on the back saying "Save Swazi Babies from HIV." Mr. Sikhondze, a former contractor for the Ministry of Health, joined him, and the two spoke to a group of both older men and women at the new community center, *kagogo*. The men sat inside the open-air building, and the women sat nearby under a cluster of trees, resting from weeding the chief's fields. Their lesson first focused on each person's own timely task of taking medication. Following up on a previous meeting, Mr. Magagula said, "I've explained to you all how the pill works in the body. When you take these pills, you must commit to a time. If you choose 7 (o'clock), it must always be 7." One man asked if it was dangerous to take the pill "even ten minutes late." "It is better to do it by 7," Mr. Magagula firmly replied, but "maybe if you remember at 9, you can still take it. Do not put it off for five minutes, because later you'll put it off for another five minutes. The pill must work in your body." Mr. Sikhondze explained that for it to "always be 7" meant, in most cases, that a person took their ARVs twice daily, at 7 a.m. and 7 p.m.—"This thing works like a wheel from one to the other." Taking medicine twice daily was, of course, not everyone's regimen, and he qualified that people should ask at the clinic if they had questions.

The lesson soon turned to the social work of adherence, namely the relationships and everyday practices that might enable—or disrupt—taking ARVs. "It happens sometimes that you forget to take the pill," said Mr. Magagula, "say, maybe when you wake up and go to the fields. Maybe you only remember by 9 for some reason or because you feel the effects of not taking it. The virus is clever, and once it says 'nothing is stopping me,' it begins to affect you." Mr. Magagula echoed Nik's phone alarm tactic as well as the tactic of listening for the start of one's favorite radio show to mark the time to take the medication. He then suggested that others help remind a person, too. "It is important to commit to yourself and your time, and then tell someone to remind you. I use my children at home to remind me at 6:30. By the time the alarm rings, they give me some water to drink the pill. You need to commit yourself and not forget, even for a day." Mr. Sikhondze was also adamant, saying, "Do not think that you cannot take it. Maybe because you are going to a night vigil you won't bring it with you. No. The pill must be in your pocket."

With the smell of salted, boiled meat wafting into the center, Mr. Magagula concluded by speaking about longer-term matters: "Taking HIV pills is important. Remember, we have told you that you must do this for your whole life. There is no cure, so we are supposed to take the pills. HIV is a big problem, so we have meetings like this one at the chief's compound. Remember too [that] it is not good to run away from those who are sick, because we are trying to teach one another that life continues, and a person who has the virus who is sick is still a person like all other living people. This is a disaster, and we are living in difficult days." The residents affirmed that they better understood the stakes of missing treatments. A brother to the late chief, in respectful decorum, graciously thanked him, using the Magagula praise name: "*Mtfombeni*. You've given us knowledge to eat. We thank you, *babe* (father)."

The men ambled to the cooking pot behind the center. The women, having eaten bread and juice concentrate served by the late chief's daughters-in-law, walked back to the nearby fields. For these community members, it was clear that ARVs as individually mandated prescriptions were not materially separate from the social world. Growing food to sell and feed families, paying respect to and remembering the dead, and meeting with one's children were not preoccupying excuses for missing a pill. They were timed opportunities to sync up to medication schedules and orchestrate the prolongation of life.

Medical anthropologists are questioning what it means for people taking ARVs to be increasingly labeled as having a "chronic illness."[45] Innovative research on matter, they note, requires collaboration (Hardon and Moyer 2014), and much of this has been done among ordinary people living with HIV in Swaziland. In Madulini, it meant appealing to customary foodways to educate people better on taking pills. It also meant letting neighbors support, encourage, and talk and listen to each other in their roles as SHBC careworkers. For Nik, a more independent person, it meant letting Nomvula help him out for a while—no small task, given his lifelong issues with his mother's family. While he did not have a caregiver himself, Nik knew he could take on that kind of work if coworkers ever disclosed their status.

No one can go it alone to cover all bases of a disease of such epidemic and sociohistorical proportions. Narrowing in scale from structural and policy matters, we see that daily practical matters easily disrupt the ability to undertake best adherence practices. ARVs may expand one's horizon of being in the world, to use existential terms, as people envision themselves living longer by taking medication. They now measurably do so by twenty years or more. This life, however, is not without inevitable disruptions. People still get sick. Illness can be episodic, or more desperately, some may be unable to get medication altogether. In these ways, HIV/AIDS as a chronic illness portends a less-than-seamless lifespan, one under constant threat. Strengthening one's life is not easy, and it prompts people to work on themselves and with others to get the job done.

Conclusion: Sudden Death

Good-hearted others, medication, food, and the chance to go back to work were materially transformative for the lives of seropositive people. They were tangible, everyday cultural manifestations of broader state and global public health HIV/AIDS-related interventions. Over time, perceptions of AIDS-related illness and dying changed as ARVs became available. People discerned physical changes in others' pharmaceutically enlivened bodies, and communities reincorporated people from near-physical and social deaths. Reckoning a longer life through biomedical treatment also meant reconciling new forms of self-care and aspirations with ongoing obligations to others, allowing oneself to be cared for or be interdependent. It meant accepting a lifetime of taking medication, working through chronic illness episodes, and putting the concept of *imphilo* as health at the center of one's life. To live life in the wake of AIDS was to reckon its potentiality, to enumerate the promise of another tomorrow.

Still, despite surviving AIDS, people living with HIV continue to face persistent stigma. While individuals' restored abilities to work could mitigate HIV-related stigma, Nik's workplace situation and nondisclosure shows this was still a challenge. People also now faced the interpretive question of what it meant to die later in time but *with* HIV. Many people I met told me death, in general, was sudden. It could happen at any time, snappily appearing "just like that, *nje*," a perception that I think derives from recent popular knowledge of disease epidemiology. I take a cue here from medical anthropologist Mark Nichter (2008, 53). Using several examples of global health interventions in India, Thailand, and elsewhere around the world, Nichter shows how "exposure to information about risk can trigger a sense of vulnerability and in some cases lead a person to adopt an 'at-risk role.'" While risk communication at its best would lead people toward prevention efforts, it likewise produces a heightened risk sensibility that one's actions or life is under threat. I finish this chapter by showing how people thought about life at risk with HIV.

Being an educator, my friend LaGija had many books in her house. Amid copies of African literary classics such as Ngũgĩ wa Thiong'o's *The River Between* and Chinua Achebe's *Arrow of God*, I found the 2009 edition of the *Guinness Book of World Records*, a hardcover trade publication with a holographic fuchsia cover. Inside, the "Human Amazements" section cites a 2005 statistic that Swaziland holds the world's lowest life expectancy at thirty-one years, a factoid LaGija herself had mentioned to me when I stayed with her family in 2010. "What does that even mean for how you would live your life?" I asked one night after dinner. "*Mxm*," she clicked, tongue-in-cheek, likely for hearing a question that I myself probably would not know how to answer.

The number in the flashy book was the lowest I found in a litany of life expectancy statistics cited in health policy documents and news media, all of which said Swazi citizens had the "world's lowest" life expectancy because of HIV/AIDS.[46] The polarity of "world's lowest" and "world's highest" pricks attention as two extremes implicating our common humanity and shared ecological domain. With varied understandings of demography, what people make of such figures for their personal and familial lives is telling. UNICEF ambassador and white *sangoma*[47] James Hall recounted a conversation with an expectant mother at a Manzini clinic that echoed the numerical frustration I heard from LaGija:

> "I will outlive my baby. They say so," she explained. Who said so? Her doctors? "They said so. The UN people. The government. Babies born today won't live long as adults. They won't grow up to be old people," she said fatalistically.... The year she was born the life expectancy for a person residing in this country was in the late sixties. It, therefore, follow[ed], in her mind, that when she is 60 and with several more years left to live, her baby will be 40 and at the end of his or her lifetime. "I will love and raise my child, but in the end I will bury my child," she confided. (Hall 2010)

Her vision echoed wider generational concerns about social reproduction and burial obligation I noted above. Others felt they could prevent these obligations from going asunder. In *Inyandzaleyo!*, a collection of first-person accounts of abused people living with HIV in Swaziland, SASO cofounder Hannie Dlamini told Hall about the transformed horizons of life on ARVs: "If a person with HIV receives treatment, he or she will live longer. The longer people live, the more they can do for themselves and their families. They can do the good deeds of living. It is a religious view. But I also saw a lot of people dying who were not prepared for the deaths. I wanted to come out to make them live, so they can plan for their future and they are not unprepared dying tomorrow." (Hall 2002, 9)

Bearing witness to these figures is a reminder of life's limits and the way biomedical knowledge shapes the value of life beyond the individual. While acknowledging life's continuities, both of Hall's interviewees also show concern for how things could go on: Who or what would survive? Both register a graven sense of uncertainty about what could happen in the future with respect to their health and inevitable death. Culturally, uncertainty is a disruptive if not creative condition, and is perhaps a defining feature of what it means to be human. For people taking ARVs, the promise of a longer life twins to a life of routine uncertainty in recurrent illness and ongoing social work to strengthen one's being.[48]

Nik, LaGija, Hannie Dlamini, and others' diverse perspectives on longevity, I think, reflect this sharpened cultural consciousness about changing meanings of death after AIDS and life at risk. They also show the struggles to reckon what Didier Fassin (2007) calls the "practical ethics of life,"[49] namely the struggle to be confident in life after an HIV diagnosis, and to hold a prospective stance: what comes next for me? The next two chapters consider the religious and financial ways people moved through and went about securing at-risk lives which, in many ways, were also about assuring dignified deaths.

Notes

1. These cattle were for the husband Vuyo Matimba's older sister and were kept at their parental home in Madulini. Contemporary bridewealth (*emalobolo*) is cattle (historically ten) or money that is called "cattle" (*inkhomo*) given by a betrothed man's family to his fiancée's family. The first customary marital rite is formal betrothal, *kuteka*, where man's family provisionally accepts the women as part of their homestead. The second rite is bridewealth exchanges or promises thereof, marked by a day-long or weekend-long ceremony of slaughter, feasting, and gift presentations. When bridewealth is finally paid off—an indebted process that may take years—a final, grander party-like ceremony called *umtsimba* is held, and the woman's family reciprocally pays the man's family dowry (*umhlambiso*). See Golomski 2016b; White 2011; and James 2015.

2. OVC refers to children who have had one or more parents die (Golomski 2015a).

3. My use of "work" as an ethnographic description for this case echoes conventional humanist conceptions of a capitalist work ethic, one that interrogates compensation, quantity, and personal and cultural qualities of work experience. Bähre (2011) and Ferguson (2015) trace the potential for alternative, more equal relations of interdependency through redistributive economies in Southern African societies. In the conclusion, I put forward some thoughts on humanist and political implications for an endogenous theory of work.

4. See, for example, Root 2011; Root and van Wyngaard 2011; Root and Whiteside 2013; Golomski 2013; Root, van Wyngaard, and Whiteside 2017; and van Wyngaard, Root, and Whiteside 2017.

5. This kind of dwelling, with plastered walls and thatched roof, is called a *rondavel*, derived from an Afrikaans word to describe its round shape. It is a Westernized architectural form, a formerly completely thatched beehive-shaped dwelling. Rounded dwellings like these became rarer throughout the twentieth century and were increasingly re-valued as culturally

significant sites within homesteads (White 2010). The spaces are also called *kagogo* and are associated with grandmothers and ancestors. See chapter 6.

6. See Tsai, Bangsberg, and Weiser 2013 and Tsai et al., 2017. I thank Rebecca Fielding-Miller for pointing out this research.

7. Based on responses from seventy-nine individual interviewees, Root and Whiteside (2013) estimate that 53 percent would have lost their lives had a careworker not intervened.

8. Public health practitioners more often use the term ART to signal the complexity of HIV treatment—it is more than just taking pills (ARVs). It is more common in Swaziland for ordinary people to talk about ARVs or pills (*emaphilisi*), and I follow their usage.

9. Hardon et al. (2007) showed how food insecurity, along with transportation to and long waits at clinics—resulting in lost work hours and wages—were deterrents to ARV adherence. Telemedicine and transportation reimbursements show promise to improve adherence (Chimbindi et al. 2015; Siedner et al. 2015), as do faith-inspired initiatives (van Dijk, et al. 2014; van Wyngaard et al. 2017) and livelihood interventions (Tsai et al. 2017).

10. "Elders" connotes authority and is a colloquial term for grandparents and older relatives, pastors, chiefs, and senior politicians. See Kuper 1950; Werbner 2011; Golomski 2014; and Golomski 2016a.

11. See Daniel and Vilane 1986; MacMillan 1985; Levin 1997; and Magongo 2009.

12. His mother, Ntfombi Tfwala, initially refused to take on the position of Queen Mother, citing her own participation in the national mourning. Dzeliwe Shongwe was appointed Queen Mother after Sobhuza died and was implicated in *Liqoqo* council proceedings. The council suspended mourning for Tfwala and sought to depose Shongwe. Shongwe kept a sacred red feather crown to prevent her deinstallation. The council rebuffed her, making a python-skin headband as the new sacred royal accoutrement for Tfwala. Mswati was flown home from Sherborne boarding school in Great Britain to be publicly shown as the king-in-waiting in 1983. Tfwala ruled for her son until he turned eighteen in 1986 (Magongo 2009, 73).

13. This date also marked the end of Swaziland's state-ordered two weeks of national mourning for the death of Mozambican president Samora Michel, who had been at Mswati III's coronation and died on October 19 in a plane crash across the border in South Africa (*Times of Swaziland* 1986).

14. See Physicians for Human Rights 2007 and Hickel 2012.

15. Regionally, colonial administrative and capitalist development policies effectively created impoverished, fractured households reliant on subsistence-level farming and labor migration (Parsons and Palmer 1977). These policies stimulated migration and reshaped sexual networks to drive HIV transmission (Thornton 2008; Crush et al. 2010). Illife (2006, 44) asserts that "infection by diffusion across a long, much-permeated northern frontier"—connecting southern Africa to central Africa, the arguable geographic origin of HIV—"and through individual contacts in many sectors of a mobile, commercialized environment," imbricated Southern Africa in the epidemic. The early 1980s saw the highest levels of Swazis crossing the South African border in migrant labor, totaling some twelve thousand by 1985. Following initial seroconversion, HIV is marked by a dormancy period, and symptoms may not appear for up to ten years. The growing scale of the virus across the region manifested in the mid- to late 1990s. Simelane and Crush (2004, 6ff.) suggest that mine owners became increasingly aware of rising HIV infections among Swazis and aimed for cost-effectiveness by employing others from areas with lower infection rates. Despite continued

retrenchments in this sector, the fall of Nationalist Party rule liberalized border crossings, which nearly doubled to 800,000 per year heading to South Africa. Health economists urged Swaziland's government to consider the implications of a future epidemic, and as early as 1992 the government included HIV in discussions of future national development.

16. See M. Nxumalo 1999; Jewkes et al. 2011, 2015; and Fielding-Miller et al. 2016.

17. See Farmer 2006 (1992) and Krieger 2013.

18. This caveat is not meant to extol the charisma of leaders like him but to acknowledge how postcolonial rulers and some citizens are often inextricably entangled in mutual forms of dispossession, despite ongoing performance of cultural or ethno-nationalism (Mbembe 2015 [2001]).

19. Similarly, Whyte (2014) traces the effects of AIDS and ART in Uganda through the concepts of generational consciousness and "biogeneration." In her account, groups of people come into kinds of biomedical, social, and cultural knowledge about their collective relationships with the disease, medication, and each other as people. These generational concerns are part of what medical anthropologists describe as crises of social reproduction (Reis 2008; Golomski 2014; Mkhwanazi 2014).

20. See Leclerc-Madlala 2008; Susser 2009; IRIN 2009b; Jewkes et al. 2011, 2015; Mojola 2014; Fielding-Miller et al. 2015, 2016; and Stoebenau et al. 2016.

21. Previously, *umcwasho* was performed in the 1980s when Sobhuza II passed away and in the 1940s when soldiers returned from fighting for British colonialists in World War II (S. Nxumalo 1976; Kuper 1978, 1980 [1947]; Reis 2008).

22. In 2002, royalists took the second of these young wives, Zena Mahlangu, from her school to become a bride-in-waiting for Mswati. Her mother filed a lawsuit against the state in the High Court to reclaim her daughter, but Mahlangu later married him. In 2005 Mswati married Noliqhwa Ntentesa and Nothando Dube, both chosen at previous Reed Dances, and was betrothed to seventeen-year-old Phindile Nkambule.

23. Girls wear belts, tassels, and jewelry made of grass, sisal, dried cocoons, and other natural and sometimes percussive materials. Some international news media grossly describe girls' *imvunulo* as "bare-chested." The state was implicated in a horrible traffic accident that killed between thirteen and sixty-five girls at *Umhlanga* in 2015. The state newspaper the *Swazi Observer* reported the deaths of ten girls and three male chaperones (Lobamba 2015). Social media users, human rights organizations, and other reporters in and outside of the kingdom estimated between thirty-eight and sixty-five people died (Associated Press 2015; Monareng 2015).

24. These ceremonies include *Buganu* for married women and *iNcwala* for adult men

25. In this report, the claim was not supported with stochastic modeling, but similar population-level predictive models for Swaziland did make strong impacts on HIV/AIDS-related health and development policies (Whiteside and Henry 2011).

26. Becker (2014, e39) also uses the term "slow death" for HIV-positive people living outside of modernist health bureaucracies in Tanzania.

27. Across the South African border in Mpumalanga province, Niehaus (2005; 2007) describes how dying of AIDS at this time was gruesome. Some families denied their relatives had AIDS, yet hid them from sight because they were also dying horribly. Some people associated AIDS with leprosy or zombies, lamenting that ill people were like "living corpses." Niehaus's (2013) fieldwork assistant, "Jimmy," died a dramatic death of comorbid diseases that were likely HIV/AIDS.

28. See Golomski 2013, 2014. Rasmussen (2014, e220) notes a similar metaphor in Uganda of "journeying" to describe dying amid AIDS.

29. My approach here stems from my own ethics and practices of doing ethnography. Others are perhaps more strong-willed than I to tell these stories. In her ethnography of HIV-related cancers in Botswana, Julie Livingston (2012, 28) calls us to bear witness to the repulsive, graphic aspects of dying "to establish the stakes of illness and medical care, the disorienting immediacy of bodily experiences, and the forms of bodily consciousness that are produced through profound illnesses and practices of care." Ida Susser's (2009) South African consultant Sibongile Mkhize describes her own family members' wasting deaths from AIDS in a chapter-length account, evincing a "polygraphic" approach (Whyte 2014). None of my consultants, informants, or friends died in such a way during my research. When I began fieldwork in 2008, ARVs were increasingly available for almost four full years. When people did share such stories of wasteful AIDS deaths with me, I felt I had to take such stories in profound confidence. The ethical board that cleared my research did not obstruct me from writing about such deaths, but I knew I personally could not. To maintain what I perceived came to be strong intersubjective relationships between me and people I met in Swaziland (Jackson 2005; 2011), rewriting the story of a painful death in detail would rend asunder the bonds we had forged.

30. These groups embody what Mark Nichter (2008) calls the "politics of the possible" in improving health through advocacy and collective action when states cannot do so.

31. The siSwati word for hospital is *sibhedlela*, and the word for clinic is *likliniki*.

32. CD4 is a protein on the surface of T-cell lymphocyte white blood cells that, in part, regulates a body's immune system. An average range of CD4 T-cells is 500 to 1500 per cubic millimeter of blood. HIV infects CD4 T-cells to disrupt the immune system's response to infection, rendering treatable diseases such as influenza and hepatitis B, for example, potentially fatal.

33. The latest ART treatment guidelines (Ministry of Health 2015, 38ff.) mandate that after a test, patients are given HIV information in simple terms to "clarify misconceptions and myths." They are also counseled on good nutrition, risk reduction, and where to get more information about HIV. If they test positive, they are reassured "that they can live a long healthy life." ARVs are immediately commenced with seropositive patients who: have CD4 counts of 350 or less; are over age fifty or under age five; pregnant; have tuberculosis; and/or have a serodiscordant partner, namely a partner who is HIV negative. Opportunistic infections are treated before ART.

34. In February 2011, I attended a Lutheran church's Sunday worship service with the Matimbas. A man gave testimony that he had gone to a funeral the night before for a young man who had died from a horrible illness, having been fired for being sick by a Chinese-owned factory he worked for in a nearby town. He cried at how unfair sick people were treated at workplaces like these. Nokwenza worked for another Chinese-owned factory in Matsapha and told me about managers going to the gate to hire people after firing others who called in sick.

35. The Ministry of Labour and Social Security (2010, 15) estimated 43 percent of the population were "inactive workers"—students, the elderly, the ill, the disabled, people who "lack capital" or "look after" their own "need"—and not part of the formal labor force.

36. See: Masanjala 2007; Tsai, Bangsberg and Weiser 2013; Tsai et al. 2017; Weiser et al. 2017; and Bähre and Rodima-Taylor 2014. Comparatively, Dominik Mattes (2012, 80) met

a man named Joseph in Tanga, Tanzania, who was happy to find a new job after losing his previous one to AIDS-related illness. Despite this and having joined a support group, Joseph was set back by economic stressors and illness after being overworked in his new job.

37. See IRIN 2002; PANAPRESS 2003; J. F. Dlamini 2016; and G. Simelane 2017.

38. See DeWaal and Whiteside 2003; Naysmith, DeWaal, and Whiteside 2009; Tevera et al. 2012; Fielding-Miller et al. 2014; and van Wyngaard, Root, and Whiteside 2017.

39. MaxART is a collaboration between the Swaziland Ministry of Health, Clinton Health Access Initiative, and the Dutch Aids Fonds organization.

40. SHIMS2, the second Swaziland HIV Incidence Measurement Survey, was conducted nationally between August 2016 and March 2017 and ultimately interviewed and tested over ten thousand individuals from more than five thousand households (ICAP 2017). ICAP's (2017) figures successfully embody the 2017 UNAIDS initiative of "90-90-90" and "treatment as prevention" (TasP) initiatives (Vernooij et al. 2016; Cohen 2017; Fielding-Miller 2017). By 2020, UNAIDS's treatment targets are for 90 percent of people living with HIV to know their status, 90 percent to be on ART, and 90 percent to achieve viral suppression. Interestingly, the 90-90-90 initiative also comes branded as a potential "end to AIDS" (Kenworthy, Thomann, and Parker 2017).

41. See IRIN 2007; Zulu 2015; and Neupane, Prakash, and Doku 2016.

42. On disclosure and secrecy, see Mattes 2012; Hardon and Posel 2012; Root 2014; Smith 2014; and Rhine 2016.

43. See S. Sukati 2010 and Ndzimandze 2010, 2011. Becker (2014, e46) notes similar ARV and chicken-feeding rumors in Tanzania.

44. Children often take ARVs in the form of syrup or powders to mix in drinkable fluids, forms attesting perhaps to the siSwati word used, *kunatsa* ("to drink"). "To drink" medicine may also echo forms of customary medication ingestion. See chapter 2.

45. See Manderson and Smith-Morris 2010; Hardon and Moyer 2014; and Moyer 2015.

46. See Golomski 2013, 82ff. Calculating how long a person is expected to live, life expectancy, is found by using data on its demographic obverse: taking death rates for age-specific cohorts within a population for a period of time. Alan Whiteside, in particular, and others brought to light the severity of the epidemic through these figures (Whiteside and Henry 2011), noting that mortality due to HIV/AIDS, "almost tripled over the past 10 years" (Whiteside et. al 2006, 10) and that the "fall [in life expectancy] has been most pronounced in Swaziland, from a high of 60 years in 1998 to 31.3 years in 2004, the lowest life expectancy in the world" (Whiteside and Whalley 2007, 15).

47. *Tangoma* are customary diviner healers who diagnose affliction. It is more rare for a nonSwazi or nonblack African to be a *sangoma*. See chapter 2.

48. On general human uncertainty, see Jackson 2005, 2011. On HIV-related uncertainty, see Morris 2008; Mattes 2012, 2014; Hardon and Moyer 2014; and Whyte 2014.

49. Fassin (2007, 262–263) identifies these ethics as needs, pleasure, and virtue. Namely, "living once death has been announced means ensuring the continuity of the living body (by being careful, by watching what one eats, by taking certain medicines and not others); it also means enjoying life (by limiting pain, looking out for the simple pleasures, surrounding oneself with loved ones); it means, finally, being virtuous in the remaining time (being faithful to one's spouse, caring for one's children, saving up for one's funeral expenses; showing consideration for those who will be left behind, sometimes still participating in the collective life such as a patients' association or a support group)."

2 Religious Healing and Resurrection: "Faith without Work Is Dead"

THE DAY BEFORE New Year's Eve in 2009, I began to experience what I felt to be a recurrence of an injury I had sustained a few years earlier. I told LaGija, with whom I was staying at the time. She sympathetically asked me what I needed. Because the previous injury had required surgery, I now made arrangements to go back to the United States sooner rather than later. I told her that I wanted some explanation about what I was experiencing and confidence that I would ultimately be all right. Later that night, LaGija said simply, "The prophet will come tomorrow at 9 a.m. and pray for you." The week prior, she had told me about a man named Blessing, who had miraculously foretold her acceptance into a masters degree program overseas.

I woke up early the next day to wash and dress nicely for the prophet, because I did not know what to do for such a meeting. The rest of the family stayed in comfortable sleepwear. Blessing arrived on time, impressively dressed in embroidered jeans and shoes shined like black marble. LaGija recounted Blessing's accolades and that he had recently received a tourist visa from the United States Embassy for a month-long trip to visit Baptist churches there. After a round of introductions, the prayer began.

Blessing first asked me when I had obtained the injury. I told him when it took place and how it was remedied. "Do you believe you can get healed?" he asked, wiping his face and lowering his head. "I believe I can get healed," I replied, thinking to myself that I was not specifying by whom or what method. "I believe you will be healed. After five days, it will change you, it will be totally changed, everything, gone. Yeah," he said lowly, "*Somandla* [God]. When will you go home? What kind of sickness [is it]?" I had changed my reservation to leave the following day, and I explained the injury to him in biomedical terms. "Okay," he said, "I want you to believe that you will be healed; to hear the words that I say and believe; to hear me. My God, Jesus, *mmm*; thank you, my God." He then commanded us to stand and raise our hands. LaGija shut her eyes and began praying aloud, her rapid voice reverberating against the walls of her small living room. Blessing pressed his hands against my ribcage, saying, "My God, Jesus, I pray, in the name of Jesus. I am coming against this sickness, in Jesus's mighty name, the son of the living God. *Lose him!*"

He shouted—a gutteral *sforzando*—and I broke into a sweat in shock. His hands accompanied the shout with a quick, forceful tremor that rattled my ribcage. *"Fire!"* Then he began speaking in tongues, uttering an indiscernible language that, for them, could only emerge from his mouth through the power of the Holy Spirit. Later I tried to transcribe what was said from a digital camera recording of the encounter: *"ra dos la sha ka man di ra ra dos, shi man di ra ra so dos, kra dos sem shi ka la si kam re ma ta ram."* My hands still raised, he thrust his palms into mine, again shouting *"Fire!"* and returned one hand to my ribcage, the other still raised. The spirited language continued for another four minutes, interspersed with sudden shouts and nine more forceful hand tremors. Eventually, he turned back to English, commanding the sickness to again "lose" me and for me to "live according in Jesus's name."

My eyes had been shut the entire time, and at this point he asked me to open them. We stood eye to eye, his finger pointing at my face as he spoke in seriousness, *"I command this sickness to leave this body right now, by the name of Jesus Christ, the son of the living God."* He formed his other hand into the shape of a pincer and began to move it toward and away from me. Blessing then circled me, stood at my side, placed his hands on my lower back and stomach. *"Keh bro soto mundo shekala ba shianda ma dolo seka,"* he continued in holy tongue. We began a small call and response. "Say 'thank you, Jesus.' 'Thank you, Lord.' 'In Jesus's mighty name,'" he said, and after each statement, I repeated it back to him. He concluded: "Thank you, Jesus, this sickness is gone; by the name of Jesus, I pray. Father, there is no one like you, no one like you; stand against him. *You sickness, you will never come back to this body* in holy Jesus mighty name, I pray."

With that, he asked me to jump in place three times. Then he invoked the biblical figures of Mary, David, and again, Jesus Christ to bless me and "everything" that I would want. LaGija and I sat down on the couch. She had been walking around the room the entire time, hands raised and praying aloud. Her daughter had her head down at a table, looking at her phone. After resting for a bit, we stood up to undertake another round of laying hands and speaking in tongues. The prayer lasted twenty-two minutes altogether.

Five days later, I was home in the upper Midwest Unites States. I consulted a specialist, who told me my previous injury was not exacerbated—I was fine. While I felt encouraged by the specialist's assessment, Blessing's prophecy and the experience as a whole resonated with me as something profound. The prayer healing tuned in to powerful medical and existential questions: Can an injury be healed for life? Can diseases be rendered curable? People living with HIV, for instance, can live virally suppressed as "undetectable." What happens to people in visceral moments of contact with phenomena such as God and the Holy Spirit?

How do they feel or know they are healed? After the prayer that New Year's Eve morning, and before he left, Blessing said:

> Now the Lord says I must tell you this, *eh. He is going to use you.* You need to know that when you go back to your country, you will immediately come from the pain. The power of God will come upon you and look, *then everything will change.* Your lifestyle, everything is going to change.... He will tell you what you are going to do, and as I said, I am saying this because He says that I must say this to you, so now says the Lord, you're going to get helped, *but wait for Him, keep on waiting.* And then it will come. Pray, *because you will meet Him.*

With that, he said goodbye and went off to church—it was Sunday. Truthfully, it has been a long time coming since the big "change" he predicted for me. I do not feel that I could qualify a change in my health or well-being generally because of his spiritual induction that morning. But many others, such as LaGija, could and did. Christianity in Swaziland is incredibly popular. Ninety percent of people there claim to be Christian in some way, although not all practice what Blessing did.[1] Churches are in almost every community, and many people grow up in Christian families or go to mission-originated schools. Christian worship services and forms of prayer and healing are ecumenically diverse and powerfully transformative for many people as a resource of nonbiomedical healing, prospective insights, and ethical guidance for everyday life.

I witnessed many prayerful healing sessions like this one in a variety of places such as homes and churches (see fig. 2.1).[2] They were not as common at funerals, but like funerals, prayer healing and other religious rites were evident points to learn about perceptions of death, dying, and the afterlife. They were also a means to see how a major religion shaped funerary cultural production. LaGija herself was a pastor who prayed like Blessing. While staying in her home, I saw such healing on a daily basis, either when she herself performed it for afflicted colleagues and kin in her living room or as part of global televangelist programs, which we watched almost nightly. My host family at Madulini, the Matimbas, were also churchgoers, at more mainline Protestant mission churches such as Lutheran or Swedish, and their daughters sometimes went to Sunday school.

Trying to document prayer healing ethnographically, however, was not so easy. At first I tried to get literal transcriptions from recordings of healing sessions like the one Blessing did to me. Yet four young women I hired as transcriptionists, including LaGija's daughter and sister, would regularly not write down what we agreeably understood to be prayer including marked moments of glossolalia (speaking in tongues) and thanksgivings to and invocations of divinity. These parts of prayer were not so important to get down word for word for the young women. "Do you really need that stuff? They're just praying at that point," said LaGija's sister Banele. For them, what was actually said mattered less than

Fig. 2.1 Public prayer session at Jubilee Park, Manzini, 2011. Photograph by author.

the action of speaking itself as the practical grounds for healing. This suggested to me to focus more directly on healing events and the build-up to them such as the one I had with Blessing. In Birgit Meyer's (2010) terms, much of this healing was incredibly "sensational." By this I mean healing involved sensual actions like touching, moving, and singing at people's bodies, consumables, and the material world in which people lived among phenomena such as spirits and God.[3]

It was tough to discern whether such healing specifically treated HIV/AIDS, because the disease itself was rarely spoken about at the many worship services and rites I documented.[4] The relationship between Christianity and HIV/AIDS in Africa is well studied, and as the case of SHBC in chapter 1 showed, Christianity was critical for both public health and existential interventions in HIV-positive people's lives.[5] Still, in terms of broader religious healing in Swaziland, HIV/AIDS was a part of a panoply of life's general maladies, "bound up with wider experiences of suffering within which the pandemic is set" historically (Becker and Geissler 2009, 3). As such, this chapter's focus is not limited to HIV/AIDS-related illnesses specifically or the sensational religious healing of one specific Christian church.

While not focusing specifically on ARVs or HIV/AIDS, the religious rites and stories I document here contextualize how local pharmaceutical saturation of "life-prolonging drugs has affected individual and communal understandings of life, death, healing and stigma" (van Dijk et al. 2014). One affect common to all of these is time. Such life-prolongation through ARVs carries kinds of presumed and explicit "temporal rationalities" (Benton, Sangaramoorthy, and

Kalofonos 2017)—in other words, how people make sense of time and illness and live out their lives amid culturally predominant medication schedules and life course expectancies. With respect to religion, I follow other anthropologists who posit that neo-Pentecostal forms of Christianity may mutually influence these biomedical and socioeconomic processes in shaping people's expectations for life in the present and future.[6]

Altogether, I describe in this chapter how these cultural and religious changes strengthen sensibilities about waiting for aspired healing outcomes. For remedies for various afflictions, including but not limited to HIV/AIDS, they compel people to be patient. Despite the tangible immediacy or felt shock of some of the healing rites such as the one I experienced, people I knew said a state of being healed came about only later. In other words, one was not healed right after the ritual, but in the future: "Keep on waiting" for it, in Blessing's words. Being healed thus depended on faith that at some moment in time, a state of being healed would come about. It was affirmed yet effusive and indeterminate. It also mapped well onto the culturally biomedical logic of HIV as a chronic illness: a disease was still incurable yet supposedly manageable in the meantime. It took work to strengthen life in the interim.

Faith without Work Is Dead: How to Heal and Be Healed

The everyday matters of religious healing are well framed in a Bible verse I often heard people recount in church, Bible study sessions, and funerary night vigils. It was a New Testament verse from the Book of James (2:14–17) and was always read to resounding affirmation by the listeners. One preacher, for example, a middle-aged man, read it verbatim from a tattered New King James Bible at a funeral outside of the community of Siphofaneni I attended in October 2010: "What does it profit, my brethren, if someone says he has faith but does not have works? Can faith save him? If a brother or sister is naked and destitute of daily food, and one of you says to them, 'Depart in peace, be warmed and filled,' but you do not give them the things which are needed for the body, what does it profit? Thus also faith by itself, if it does not have works, is dead."

More simply put: "Faith without works is dead." Being Christian took more than lip service trust that things would turn out because they were in God's hands. One had to *do* something, both for oneself and others. As I saw it, being saved and healed were aspired-for conditions that people worked on to cultivate over time while waiting for these miracles to manifest. It echoes what Becker and Geissler (2009, 6) write: that Pentecostalism, Islam, and neotraditionalism in Africa are powerfully "prescriptive" in compelling religious practitioners to focus spiritually on daily, "mundane" tasks of living amid HIV/AIDS. Faith and church-based rituals were important, but it took a series of daily acts and rites to strengthen life overall.

After a brief overview of the religious landscape of Swaziland, I trace two such mundane tasks meant to enliven others, *kuphilisa*. First, spiritually discerning the value or qualities of people's medication, food, and other things in the material world to use and share with others who had less. And second, speaking and singing in religiously embodied ways to disclose suffering and heal others. Practically, this work brought people into continual contact with transformative powers of the Holy Spirit, God, and in some cases, the dead and ancestral shades. Sometimes people did not agree on what worked, depending on denominational differences or subjective preference based on past experiences of what they felt worked or not. Yet with death looming, sensational forms of healing offered a wide practical domain for ongoing experimentations in extending life.

Combining Forms of Sensational Healing

Globally, the responses to HIV/AIDS by Christian churches have been varied, ranging from condemnation of people's immoral sexualities to activism, community building, and faith healing. This goes for Swaziland too, where there are several types of Christian churches with diverse responses to the disease (Golomski and Nyawo 2017). In general, there are African initiated and independent churches (AICs), mainline churches derived from Western Christian missions, and newer ministry churches. Despite theological and political differences, some churches, especially ministries and AICs, combine healing practices that may be seen as altogether sensational or elide with forms comparable to customary medicines and practices. Indeed, the histories and interpenetration of religious healing practices in sub-Saharan Africa are complex if not impossible to ever fully disentangle.

In Swaziland the most popular churches are AICs. These churches, like mainline ones, were born out of nineteenth-century colonial mission encounters. AICs are pronounced in their overt practices of healing in comparison to other locally longstanding mainline Christian mission churches. They incorporate nonbiomedical healing phenomena deemed to represent precolonial cultural practices. These include purification, consumption of special substances, the embodiment of spirits, and variations thereof. AICs also align with state promotions of Swazi Culture.[7] The Jerikho Zionist church, for example, claims organizational "marriage to kingship" (*bayaganwa nenkhosi*).

Over the last twenty years and coincident with the rise of HIV/AIDS, there has been a broad and major increase in Christian religious activity. In the 1990s too, according to the Pan African Christian AIDS Network, registered church groups grew at an estimated 350 percent (Root 2009). Most people I met said there were more churches of all sorts today than in the past, especially Pentecostal-charismatic Christian, or "ministry," churches. This form of Christianity has been one of the world's most widely expanding religions since the end of the twentieth century.[8] Its rites take shape most commonly in the example of Blessing's prayer healing for me. In Swaziland, it emerged in the late 1980s and early 1990s through televangelism and visiting pastors from Nigeria, the United States, and other countries in southern Africa. Divine Healing Ministries and Jesus Calls Worship Centre, which accommodate hundreds if not thousands of attendees, are examples of these, and newly dot the urban neighborhoods of Mbabane, Matsapha, and Manzini. They inspire many people to be "born again" as part of joining, and in turn, change the way they go about their everyday lives.

My own colleagues at the University of Swaziland (UNISWA) considered the recent regional wave of sensational healing to represent something "neo-Pentecostal" in form.[9] Some African scholars of religion see the rites and theologies of AICs surrounding HIV/AIDS paralleling those of newer Pentecostal-style churches.[10] In both, there is a strong emphasis on spirituality, evident for members in the ability to speak in tongues, heal, claim existence of miracles and evil forces, and prophesy future conditions. Pentecostal churches also focus heavily on tithing, or giving money to the church, as a way to bring about miraculous health and wealth. LaGija explained that her own church had a "storehouse that we give to, and it can be distributed to those who need it. Faith without such works is dead." These religious practices point to new ways of understanding a world divined by God, and for my colleagues, a new point in the kingdom's religious and cultural history.[11] The fact that Pentecostal-charismatic Christianity's prayer healing emerged around the same time as the rise of HIV/AIDS and that it emerged from outside the kingdom lends itself to a historical sensibility of cultural novelty: that sensational healing can treat millennial problems of affliction.

"Discerning" Forms of Medicine

Scrutinizing or "discerning" (a term derived from Pentecostal language) one's position and elements of the material world was a common religious practice. People in Swaziland have long been careful about what they put on and in their bodies or exchange with others, and "discernment" is the newest way to talk about it. In customary marital rites, for example, food or drink first sampled publicly shows it is safe to consume. Jokingly, someone presenting beer "takes out the poison," *khipha butsi*, by drinking a bit before giving it to guests. In its Pentecostal variation, discerning means carefully assessing whether certain conditions are the result of the power of Satan or God or one's own ability to get by. At one evening Bible study session I recorded at a technical college in Matsapha, a young male student asked the instructor, "Must we accept poverty? It sounds like we are saying whatever your life outcome is, it doesn't matter what it is, I should accept oppression, sickness, poverty, and circumstance because I'm tested [by God to persevere in life]." The instructor, a man younger than the student, quickly replied, "You should discern, discern, discern!" Another student said, "To determine [if it is] God or the devil, assess what we have with God in terms of weapons. Satan led Jesus into the wilderness, [but] He didn't go by himself, suffering in hunger and fasting. The devil attacked him, but He already had the Word." In their estimation, suffering was not avoidable, yet a faithful person worked at *discerning* the source of life's challenges.

Discernment also nicely characterized the process of evaluating potential healing resources and their effects. In doing so, people tasked themselves and others to assess what might work in immediate or long-term projects to alleviate suffering. Contemporary questions about what worked as part of sensational healing often went straight to some of the most recognizable figures of Swazi Culture. Diviner women, *tangoma*, and herbal medicinal specialist men, *tinyanga* and *tigedla*, have long been the first healers a person visits when he or she is ill. They address spiritual, social, and physical ailments through the application of indigenous pharmacopoeia, *mutsi* or *muti* (meaning "medicine," "shrub," or "bush"), and or by communing with the dead or ancestral shades, *emadloti*. Most people I met claimed they had never visited *tangoma* or a similar healer.

Yet Oluwole Amusan (2009) of the Swaziland Institute for Research in Traditional Medicine, Medicinal and Indigenous Food Plants suggests that 85 percent of people in Swaziland use various forms of *mutsi* as a primary health care resource. One can purchase these medicines without the help of a healer in places ranging from open-air markets to established pharmacies. The country's largest funeral parlor, Dups, also runs several "Dups Muti" shops, although they were rebranded in the early 2010s as "Dups Herbal." This name change followed a police raid that found a former employee trafficking in certain coveted animal skins (Maziya 2010a) and was also a likely attempt to attract more Christian and nontraditionalist clientele. People in many communities, such as LaGija's mother and her neighbors, also grew herbal medicines and prepared them in their homes.

Healing with *mutsi* can be empowered by the help of a religious ritual specialist. In divinatory séances, *tangoma* ascertain whether or not *emadloti* are the cause of a person's affliction and compel *emadloti* to leave the sick person or ask the person to appease *emadloti*. A chronic illness may indicate an ancestral calling for the sick person to become a healer himself or herself. To do their work, *tangoma* speak directly to *emadloti* on behalf of their patients. Like *tinyanga*, *tangoma* may burn certain *mutsi* mixtures called *tinyamatane* as prophylactic medicines or cultivate ancestral presence for later healing. In monetary payments or chicken, goat, or cattle sacrifices, *tangoma* and patients encourage ancestors to withdraw affliction and restore well-being. Similarly, Hylton White (2010; 2013) describes how, in neighboring KwaZulu-Natal, South Africa, ancestors may afflict individuals to compel them to make similar animal or material sacrifices, like building commemorative customary homes, the kind in which Nik resided.

Tinyanga and *tigedla*, such as LaGija's own father, traffic in the use of *mutsi* that patients are prescribed to ingest, apply, or consume to get better. Like biomedical pharmaceuticals, *mutsi* have to be taken in healer-prescribed dosages, and if used incorrectly (or nefariously), can be harmful. The most negative example of this was *mutsi*'s use to hurt or kill others, something people saw as the ultimate ethical transgression: *butsakatsi*. The term is also often translated as "witchcraft." In the early years of the epidemic, HIV/AIDS etiologies and related deaths were sometimes attributed to *butsakatsi*. Local careworkers and public health and development experts, however, thought this was less about belief and more of an "'escape route' to avoid pointing a finger at the real problem" (UNDP and CANGO 2007, 9), which people felt they could not otherwise name because of stigma.[12] Before ARVs, the physical effects of untreated AIDS were horrible, making *butsakatsi* apt to describe an affliction perceived as altogether inhumane. In nonbiomedical practice, healers and their medicines remain powerful figures that popularly reference what is cited as part of Swazi Culture.

Still, healers' diagnoses, therapies, and overall cultural value have changed over time and in response to changing global economic conditions.[13] From the late nineteenth century on and during the period of settler colonialism, the biomedical and religious technologies of Christian missionaries were driving forces in the transformation of local healing practices. New communities and social movements expanded around the charismatic healing powers of new AIC prophets who profitably drew on existing healing practices. Some AICs today, for example, use herbal and liquid mixtures called *tiwasho*, a cognate for washing or cleansing, for sick people to ingest or inhale. Christian ritual specialists, sometimes called prophets, may administer *tiwasho*, as do *tangoma* and *tinyanga*, who find *tiwasho* used by AICs to be spiritually powerful. *Tiwasho* can be composed of elements such as leaves, minerals, roots, skins or scales, feathers, shells, salt, animal blood, water, isopropyl alcohol, and ashes. They are used to purify places and bodies from affliction by malevolent forces and are sometimes consumed by church members to open themselves up to better embody holy spirits.

The perceived efficacy of *tiwasho*, *mutsi*, and other kinds of herbal and natural medicines is strong enough to suggest to many people that they might be complementary to or more useful than ARVs. Robin Root and I found this perception in Madulini and other communities (Root and Whiteside 2013). The elements of these medicines have also been transformed and sold as life-giving quasi-pharmaceutical substances in smaller stores and large pharmacy chains.[14] Arguments about how best to use nonbiomedical treatments are often sensationalized in the media. In one case, four teenage brothers from an AIC died after consuming a poisoned batch of *tiwasho* at a funerary night vigil (Golomski 2016a). At a sister church's Sunday service I attended a few weeks after the incident, a senior pastor called on the worshippers to discern a particular "kind of spirit for healing," claiming that healing was not secured by "making some kind of herbal concoction of *tiwasho*, but praying for a person using bare hands." Like the healing done for me by Blessing, the laying of hands is a standard Pentecostal ritual and is also a sensational form of healing. Despite the criticism, the pastor went on to explain that his colleague testified before the church bishopric that "healing water" would also suffice.

Pastors and members of mainline and Pentecostal ministry churches often decried such nonbiomedical forms of traditional healing but still engaged in their own comparable, materially rich healing practices. Theirs involved using household substances—usually water, grape juice, and olive oil—and rendering them extraordinary in religious ritual. Like *tiwasho*, these substances were not inherently efficacious. Also like *tiwasho*, their purported power lay in the ability to heal bodies because they were vectors for the Holy Spirit. For members of these churches, these substances materialized an "anointing" and were justified with reference to the Bible. Oftentimes preachers invoked the New Testament verses of a sinful woman who was redeemed when she anointed Jesus's feet using expensive perfumed oil and her own hair. A few of my more ardent Christian consultants kept bottles of olive oil in their homes for such healing or in case someone like Blessing came over. Still, one had to carefully discern the qualities of these substances. For example, in October 2014 at a community hall in Manzini, hundreds of secondary school students were taking exams when teachers discovered what appeared to be smeared olive oil on the doorways. Despite its acknowledged healing potential, no one was sure who actually put the oil there and why. The exams were canceled, and the police were called to investigate (Shongwe 2014).

Based on her studies of epilepsy in Swaziland, Ria Reis (1996, 2002) argues that new medical forms and systems were evaluated toward a compatibility with Swazi tradition. The immensity of HIV/AIDS and Pentecostalism's pervasiveness, diversification, and ways of driving radical culture change, however, may complicate any unidirectional evaluation toward Swazi Culture. These historical conditions open up possibilities for more selective appropriations or rejections of healing substances and practices. Indeed, ARVs tend to work well; it was hard to deny and not marvel at an AIDS-affected person getting better with pharmaceutical medication. Yet ARVs have not made other healing practices irrelevant. As the case of the ARV-fed chickens showed in chapter 1,

ARVs themselves are subject to critical discernment. HIV/AIDS has culturally recharged conversations among a broad array of healers—pastors, doctors, traditional healers—to discern treatments for facets of afflictions that biomedicine may not provide. Healers are compelled to reposition and revalue what they do and use at the "ends of biomedicine," to use Jessica Hardin's (2018) words. Discernment was a religious way that people could routinely assess multiple potential healing sources.

Feeling the Word: Religious Healing in Language

In addition to religiously empowered medicine, people's own bodies and voices were powerful material conduits for sensational healing. Religious language, in its physically spoken, chanted, or sung utterances and topical content, is understood to be a material force for Christians across southern Africa.[15] Blessing's own method lay in a complex orchestration of hands, voice, and physical gestures. It was a method that could enable the "presence of the Holy Spirit *with* and *in*" people's bodies (Meyer 2010, 742) so healers could direct spiritual power to the afflicted. This kind of language helped strengthened people to live. Anthropologist Matthew Engelke (2007, 22) describes it as "a presentation of the divine that eclipses a material form" because it derives from voice, "but which is nevertheless a materialization." More simply, religious words were powerful sounds and brought some *thing* or condition into being for its speakers and listeners: a miracle, a change, relief, or a temporary cure. This language was "live and direct," meaning it was understood to transform people and things to which it was directed and had animate qualities. This transformative power was often construed as "the Word." Prayer healing involved openly calling out names of divinity: in English, the Word, God, Jesus, or the Holy Spirit; in siSwati, *Livi, Somandla, iNkulunkulu, iNkosi, Babe, Jesu Krestu*, and *Moya loyingcwele*. One could make contact with and emit this power through the senses: to see, hear, touch, or "feel" it overall, *kuva*.

The Word Embodied

These powerful spiritual entities and sensations manifest in prayer, and most people I met told me prayer was the most common thing that Christians did for those who were sick. Based on a survey of one hundred households I conducted across five urban and rural communities, out of eighty-four self-identified Christians, seventy-one agreed that Christians cared for sick people. The majority (fifty) said that prayer was the most common form of care, followed by home visitations (forty-two), such as SHBC carework.[16]

Many people told me they prayed alone, but prayer healing was most visibly a collective undertaking. It was out loud and often a public event. People prayed together and for one another almost everywhere: at funerals, church worship services, schools as part of daily morning announcements, workplaces including clinics, meetings to open and close the proceedings, and in public places such as parks and markets. Official pastors and ordinary people who were talented public speakers could most effectively initiate prayer and lead others to participate.[17] Themes of prayers derived from biblical symbolism relevant to the situation—such as getting healed from an illness or reminding the bereaved at a funeral that they too might get into Heaven—for which people were praying. While not often mentioning HIV/AIDS-related illnesses specifically, prayer healing was an opportunity for people to openly disclose general suffering, of not being well. In turn, this gave others a chance to show their concern and love to the afflicted in shared Christian idioms. A person's individual problem thus became everyone's matter.

Ministry church services often included sessions in which pastors called up members of the congregation to receive healing power by the laying of hands. Some instances were more muted, but usually the experience of laying of hands was intense. Pastors and prophets sometimes spoke quietly and intimately to afflicted people, who stood very close to the healer, explaining that God or the Holy Spirit would restore them. Like Blessing, healers could suddenly shout, shake their hands, or push or press on the afflicted at key moments. The afflicted usually felt an experiential charge and fell away or collapsed on the floor. Ushers, who passed around money collection baskets, also helped by standing behind the afflicted as he or she fell away from the healers, making sure the person did not get injured. Sometimes, ushers covered up those who collapsed or rolled on the floor so as to protect their modesty. Sometimes the ushers pushed more spiritually animated people toward the healers at the right moment during the service or would take them out of the church if they were too disturbing overall.

In some AICs, prayer healers laid hands on the afflicted, but church members were also able to bring spiritual power into being themselves through their own bodies. In the Jerikho church, for example, members facilitated the presence of holy spirits by wearing uniforms of red or multicolored robes with appliquéd astronomical insignia. They were often adorned with colorful braided ropes, keys, whistles, chains, or animal skin prints. This sensational clothing was inspired by members' dreams and visions of religious phenomena and were empowered in ritual action. In the Jerikho church, this was done in a common church rite called *siguco*, a derivation of *kuguca* or *kugucuka* ("to alter," "change," "kneel down"). *Siguco* occurred at the beginning and end of every church worship service and involved a counterclockwise march around a central pole sometimes known as *iladi*, referencing the biblical Jacob's ladder. Members chanted "Amen" while circling the pole, first in a modest walk and

Fig. 2.2 Running *siguco* in a Jerikho church in Matsapha, 2010. Photograph by author.

then intensifying to a quick, collective run, abetted by other members who watched on the side and also chanted (see fig. 2.2).

The dizzying run lasted for anywhere from ten to twenty minutes, culminating in a sweaty, shrieking blowout, in which running members induced spiritual embodiment. In the services I attended, members feeling the spirit staggered outside and sometimes collectively shook, danced, or wrestled with each other while whistling or shouting. Holy spirits were then perceived to be present in the church and affected members in beneficial ways. Usually, at the closing *siguco*, afflicted members or visitors could kneel at the pole in the middle of the running circle. Doing so, they could absorb the powers of the Holy Spirit or Word as it descended into the church and was cast off through the runners' bodies. The afflicted could also be given *tiwasho* at the service. Other AICs engaged in slower versions of *siguco* but with the aim to achieve the same healing effect.[18]

In ministry churches, pastors and lay members could embody the Word through the Holy Spirit and specially manifest it in glossolalia. For example, in 2015 I attended a worship service in Mpumalanga, South Africa, for a neo-Pentecostal church based in Swaziland. The pastor, a government official in the Ministry of Agriculture, reminded us that in Genesis, the first book of the Bible (which recounts the origins of everything), "God spoke the world into creation." Before reading 1 John, 4:4, she explained: "Words become things. God spoke things into being. We remember that He spoke the world into being in the beginning of everything. Thus what is spoken as the Word can become real in our own lives." By her interpretation, religious language brought things into material existence. Religious language was productive.

The preacher that followed her, a vibrant man named Mancoba, more fully described this material formation of language. He gave a sermon based on a reading of the Bible's Second Book of Kings, in which an infertile Shunnamite woman acted kindly toward the prophet Elisha. Elisha prophesied the woman would give birth to a child, which she did, but the child died. Elisha subsequently came to her house to resurrect him by her good faith in God's works. First, Mancoba explained how the woman's infertility was an impoverished, sufferable "situation," but that such situations should not be the basis of one's aspirations for change. For Mancoba, someone in such a situation as this should not focus on her own needs by talking about how she is poor and unwell. Rather, changing one's "situation" occurred by focusing prayerful talk on how one *wants* to live. God "speaks it" into existence, and "we get it because it is His blessing," he explained.

For the Shunnamite woman, this task was intense, for what was blessed into existence through Elisha and God's word, her child, was taken away in death. "She had a dead body in the house!" Mancoba exclaimed. "This is not what you would do these days when someone dies, brethren. You don't keep the dead body in the house. You take it to the undertaker. But this woman"—a faithful Christian, he reminded us—"took her child to the 'uppertaker,'" meaning that she called the prophet to resurrect the dead child by the power of God. Mancoba elaborated on how the child was revived by Elisha's physical actions of pressing on its body, holding it, and warming it up, and he called up a member of the church on whom to pantomime this pressing action. Elisha did this, he explained, until the child revived through a sneeze. Mancoba then asked us all to repeat the word "sneeze," emphasizing the sensational form of the child's resurrection. "Sneeze! Sneeze! Sneeze!" we chortled. "It is like those who work in the hospital," he concluded. "They pat a newborn baby a bit until it sneezes! Life and death is in the power of your tongue!"

Life in Song

Singing was also used in such a way as to bring about the Word's healing power. More broadly, music was a powerful form of sentimental expression and cultural production amid HIV/AIDS.[19] Fraser McNeill (2011), for example, shows how South African Venda people's musical rituals incorporated popular perceptions of the disease and became grounds for Venda kingship to claim cultural authority. Louise Mubanda Rasmussen (2014) notes that Ugandan Catholics wished to sing to an AIDS-afflicted person at the moment of death. In Swaziland, popular, beloved religious songs had similar functions. Historically, they derived from a standard repertoire of mission-originated Christian hymnals.[20] They were usually sung based on the appropriateness of their themes to the event at hand or a sermon's content.

Religious singing was used to materially enliven or restore an afflicted person during healing events. One of the most powerful moments of this for me was at a Jerikho service I recorded one balmy October Sunday morning in 2010. A man whom I had not seen before was present in the church. His dirtied, bright-blue UniTrans worker uniform had several tears in it. As he sat on a low wooden bench, his large stomach lay over his knees. A tall, thin man who sat more erect and stared straight ahead accompanied him. The large man spoke quietly, his words coming out with great care.

> "It has been so long since I've been to church.
> The Lord delivered me from the demons that tormented my life.
> Me,
> I died."

A few small gasps were audible. "*Nkosi yam*'" said several women—"My God"—less an exclamation of fright or anger than one of affirmative empathy. From the back of the women's side of the church, three seconds later, a voice called out, "You will live." At that moment, another woman cried out in song, cutting the man's testimony short. In chorus, for several minutes, we sang the same few verses repeatedly: "We carried what we received: the yoke of death."

The man sighed and thanked the church for the song, explaining how his life had been commandeered by demons. He identified himself as a womanizer and a murderer, akin to the biblical David who coveted and had a child by Bathsheba, the wife of Uriah the Hittite. In this Old Testament passage, David orders his soldiers to kill Uriah. For this, the prophet Nathan rebukes him. Like David and Nathan, the man said, he was reminded by a pastor in the church to "remember God." Before he could, however, the man claimed that he first "passed from this world"—a way to say he died—from his suffering. After his passing, though, he regained strength through God to live again. He also spoke about his financial and social ills: "I don't work. My son is dead and buried, but God didn't let me bury him in pain. I have no money, but I do work for God. I put my all in God, who gave me strength to do the funeral."

A woman repeated the song about the yoke of death. At the end of the service, the man's thin companion and several male members escorted him out of the church. "You will live," *uyophila*, they assured him. Someone fetched a bunch of bananas from a nearby flat while they slowly escorted the man to a church member's truck to give him a ride. The church's pastor patted the man's hands around the bananas and then shut the truck's door. The man looked at us through the window as the truck peeled away from the churchyard, and he nodded.

At this church and others, members often went beyond the confines of the building to heal the sick through song. Though not always couched in precise terms of singing, these veritable mobile healing trips involved singing as a powerful public intervention of a person's illness. Similarly, church choirs were often conscripted to sing at funerals, a practice showing support for the bereaved that likewise contributed to the production of a memorable, dignified event. Sometimes church choirs did not even need to have a member be directly related to the deceased person but might be tied instead through a more distant social relation.

I attended several funerals in the company of friends who were collectively members of a single church but of which the deceased was not a member. One night I drove LaGija's sisters to a funeral in southern Swaziland to meet their mother and several other members of the small ministry style church they belonged to in their mother's rural community. The funeral was for a brother of a pastor who sometimes visited their church. The deceased was not a member of their church, but the relationship between the visiting pastor and his congregants engendered an obligation in the latter to show sympathy and shore up numbers at the funeral by their attendance. The sisters' mother's church members had no special uniform, as women's leagues at some churches do, and we did not show our membership to their church in any specific way. Our presence of almost ten people in total, however, showed an ecumenical effort to remember the deceased and prayerfully sing for the bereaved. Indeed, at Roxanne's funeral, one of LaGija's sisters told me that being a young person of twenty-nine years of age, she and others like her didn't know what to say at events like this. Speaking at funerals was understood to be an elder person's prerogative, and they would otherwise do their best by just singing.

The Jerikho church was widely noted as being particularly good at traveling en masse via minibus to sing at funerals. One such call I took part in happened in December 2011. The worship service was sparsely attended, with only about twenty members out of the average forty. In the absence of the head pastor, an associate named Dumisani, a guard in the Royal Police Force, led the service. After reading from scripture, he relayed instructions from the head Pastor Lukhele that the congregation was to go visit and check on a sick elderly woman, *gogo* Hadzebe. What this check-up entailed became clear as a few women brought forth a "Christmas hamper." It was a stocked bucket available at grocery stores around the holidays that included many nonperishables such as spices, dehydrated stew mixes, baking ingredients, and other goods valued around SZL50 (US$6).

The brethren pooled an additional SZL174 (US$22) in cash, and Dumisani had two young men fetch *tiwasho* medicines—a bag of salt-like substance—from a nearby flat. Before leaving, Dumisani commanded the church members to undertake the *siguco* rite to both complete their brief worship service and strengthen themselves for their assigned task: "Don't hesitate when you all enter the *siguco*. It sickens the power. Give it vigor and intensity when you get into it." After the rite closed twenty minutes later, we all piled into vehicles, including mine, and made our way in the rain to inspect the ill woman.

After a half hour of doubling back from going the wrong way, we came across a male relative of the old woman when we asked for directions at a carwash. The man led us to a house where the woman was staying, near Zakhele in Manzini. Alighting from the cars with the food, we entered the house, immediately singing in a chorale-like wail. Two young teenage girls stood in the kitchen stirring a pot, looking neither surprised nor interested in the fact that a group of more than twenty red-robed church members had just shuffled in, singing at full volume.

The relative led us into a small room in a back corner of the house. An elderly woman lay diagonally across the bed, her eyelids flickering slightly. She was draped with a large fleece blanket, and beneath her was a strategically placed plastic sheet to prevent a mess from her incontinence. Dumisani began a new song, and the sound in the room swelled into a cacophony that rung against the peeling ceiling and plastered walls.

The lights were off, and it rained harder outside, the thunderous sound on the roof nearly drowning out our voices. The women placed the food hamper at the foot of the bed. No one had yet made a formal introduction to *gogo* Hadzebe, but as we sang at her, bit by bit she rolled from her lying position and began to rise to a lounging position. She made no sound and did not look up at anyone. Dumisani cut us off after ten minutes of singing and spoke prayerfully: "Let us dream nicely, Lord. We pray for the recuperation of this old woman that she may be well and have rest in her life. Let the Lord of lords help her, agree to heal her body, even where it is painful. Let it get better and make her well, Lord, unto all the Words and toward the setting sun, for your son, in your name we pray, for all eternity, amen."

After we sang for another five minutes, a pastoral associate addressed *gogo* Hadzebe directly: "Peace in the congregation. We are from church, *gogo*. We are here to inspect you, as the pastor sent us to come leave a prayer. Let us open the prayer." "Recall James [5:13]," said a male church member, "that if there be a sick person amongst you, let the sick person call the church leaders to lay hands on him, for the prayer of the righteous prevails." Another five minutes of singing preceded a kneeling prayer, where everyone in the room recited individually and out loud their own personal prayer on behalf of *gogo*. We eventually silenced ourselves, letting a single male member continue praying out loud as a representative voice.

Three women crawled onto the bed to be nearer to the old woman. She was still silent, and her eyes fluttered, downcast. "Can you see us, *gogo*? The church is here to greet you. What can you say?" asked one woman. Sitting on the bed next to her, she pressed her ear to the old woman's mouth. I saw and heard no response. "She says, 'Thank you,'" the woman reported, and we mumbled in agreement. Someone began a monetary collection, and a plate circulated the room, picking up less than SZL15 (US$2) in coins.

The women draped the blankets back across the old woman's lap. She straightened the plastic sheet, and repositioned her by pulling her legs and torso so that she lay straight across the bed, then propped her up against a pile of blankets so that she was sitting upright. The same woman asked the old woman if she had any favorite songs we could sing for her. This time, the woman was not able to report *gogo* Hadzebe's answer. This time, her silence and immobility were taken to be a nonresponse. "Do any of you amongst the women know *gogo*'s favorite song?" asked a male member. "Where is the one who stays with *gogo*?" asked the woman. The two teenage girls were beckoned from the kitchen but shook their heads, not knowing. "Let us lay hands," suggested a man. Dumisani spoke up, saying: "Today, here is this *gogo* who we are singing for. May she be taken care of. The Holy Spirit told me that she must be washed with water, methylated spirits, and salt. She must be bathed in hot water. It will help her bones and arteries when she has no strength. The hot water will give strength and enliven all of her bones. The Spirit will strengthen her because she has heard our prayers and prayer gives someone strength. She will apply salt to her feet, too."

At that point, the relative who helped us find the home interrupted us by switching on the lights. Dumisani stopped speaking, and the man declared that he did not want the old woman to undergo *siwasho*, saying that the teenage girls would not know how to create or obtain more for further washings. The relative was not part of the Jerikho church and was an otherwise skeptical man. I had previously seen him at a union's burial cooperative meeting, where he voiced criticism and distrust for a financial services company pitching their management plans (see chap. 3). Now we agreed to his request and conducted a second small monetary collection of less than SZL5 in coins (US$0.09). We sang our way out of the house. The rain had since lifted, leaving a grey, warm winter sky overhead as we went our respective ways home.

In the case of healing for *gogo* Hadzebe, the actions of singing and praying out loud had aligned with the material support of the laying of hands and the (hopeful) application of blessed substances. The voices and hands of the members, divinely strengthened in their earlier *siguco* rite, had moved the old woman. The members had caused her physical body to rise, sang at her, and spoke for her when she could not. The women who sat closest to her veritably gave her a voice through which they could converse. Their attempts to sing for her via her favorite song showed a concern for what she found memorable and drew on her existing social relations—the potential knowledge of the two young girls—to empower her. Even though the relative forbade *tiwasho*, the other resources of the collected money and food would sustain her for a while longer.

In these ways, singing and embodied, prayerful language in this church as arguable neo-Pentecostal examples of religious language was enlivening. Healing through prayer was a practice that rode a line between the immaterial and the material, a sensational form that had to be worked on by a healer, an afflicted person, and others who were present to engender experiences of bodily transformation. More extremely, this practice could also induce resurrection. As the pastor at the Swazi church in South Africa explained theologically, "Words become things" and brought things—such as life from the brink of death—into being. The question of when such healing manifested, though, was another matter.

Resurrection: Patience for the End

I once heard a pastor at a ministry church near UNISWA preach to its members that "healing was already a done deal." While healing often involved tangibly immediate contact, as with the cases of Blessing and *gogo* Hadzebe, the hoped-for outcomes of the healing encounters were described as being delayed. If there was anything certain about the outcome of such work, it was that one would be blessed and free of suffering in the afterlife. In other words, the ultimate state-of-being healing in neo-Pentecostal eschatology could be death itself—freeing one from this world to move toward a heavenly afterlife and millennial resurrection. Comparatively, there are very few studies, besides a few ethnographic notes, about changed perceptions of the afterlife itself in the context of HIV/AIDS.[21] As I heard it pronounced at church worship services and funerals, this afterlife was not predetermined or predestined. One had to wait, be patient, and work faithfully in the meantime to eventually get there.

The rhetoric of delay and transformative life-and-death encounters was especially popular in ministry churches. The prophet of a church in Mbabane, wearing a diamond-checkered tie and dark suit, explained to us in a Sunday sermon in November 2010 how outsiders came to see the awesome healing potential that was accessible to church members. He explained how curious outsiders would want to learn more about how or whether members actually received "amazing blessings" of health and wealth from God. "You don't have to say 'no'" to these outsiders, he explained, instead "you say you are waiting for it. We have been waiting for God's blessing, but no matter how hard it is to wait, what you are waiting for is from God. You say, 'We [at this church] are working on it.'"

The prophet went on speaking animatedly about waiting and an eventual powerful release of God's power to heal, referencing Psalms 29:3–9, which recounts how God's power "splinters the cedars," "thunders," and "strips the forests bare" in apocalyptic fashion. God's power, he claimed, would work against evil "demons," "devil worshippers," and "enemies" in people's lives that would cut those lives short or render them "sick." This power would flow "like a river," he emphasized, an outpouring that we all should anticipate. Healing was *in potentia*, and in the meantime, the afflicted had to "cull," "request," and "invest" in it prayerfully and practically in daily life to make it an eventual reality.

For the AIC Jerikho, a very different kind of church, eventual healing from current suffering could also be prayerfully realized in the afterlife. As at the ministry church, at the Jerikho, sickness was something people had to bear in the meantime, and healing took shape in godly death. Pastor Lukhele preached one Sunday morning in October 2011 that "a believer will not die if she or he is amongst believers in church. You should bear with one another"—*kutfwala*, to carry a burden—"so that the way to Heaven will be successful. You will not die and just die. You will go to Heaven." Between now and being on "the way" to a future good death, in Lukhele's words, one's life might still be burdened. Working cooperatively with others would alleviate pain in the present.

Acknowledging worldly suffering as a pretext for a dignified afterlife was profound, especially at funerals where such claims were laid bare. In May 2011, I went with the Matimbas to the funeral of one of Nokwenza's World Vision colleagues, Mr. Sibiya. He was extremely beloved in the community for his charity and good heart. In a graveside testimony, one woman wept as she recalled that he once gave her daughter a luxury item of body lotion. Several women were screaming grievously. The scene was emotionally wrought. A preacher then took the microphone and began speaking to calm the situation, reading several Bible verses from 1 Corinthians 15 to explain how the deceased would come to live again:

> Sibiya family, we all loved him while working with him here on earth. Hallelujah. But today, the Lord has chosen him from us as He has taken him. Jehovah is good. Sibiyas, you are not all alone. He will be raised from death when the trumpet is blown. Those who will hear it will be raised. To us who are still alive, we will be resurrected, and we will meet them in the firmament for our Lord. Jesus is coming back. Everyone, look at yourselves and look at your relationship with the Lord. We will see him very soon. Hallelujah.

A few minutes later, the emotional outpouring subsided. A man of the chief's council closed the service, thanking "the pastors for their wonderful job of putting the bandage of the Holy Spirit during this sorrowful time." Consolation blended the practical and the cosmological. Divinity manifested its ultimate power on the dead in a place that was beyond this world. For the dead and the living (who would eventually die), preachers located a miracle of resurrection in a future time. Importantly, they reminded the living that the dead person was in the presence of God, the ultimate life-giving force. A month earlier, Nokwenza had attended the funeral of her brother-in-law's relative, Mr. Kunene. His death left behind two widows and several children. She recorded a similar exegesis for me that spoke to Mr. Kunene's spiritual healing via contact with God. In the transcript below, the words in italics were spoken in English:

> At the end, God will represent us! In these times, He represents women and the youth, and there is no need for them to go to the tomb without faith. Even the children who He represents and everyone and all his chosen people, He gave them strength. To be men, women, and daughters of Christ! *I know my redeemer lives* in the end *when it comes for the Judgment* he will arrive and say "I know you." Go to the everlasting life. We are sick, we are sick and the doctors cannot cure us, *but He is by my side*, what will our savior do, Kunene will live.

In these cases, illness was part of both a physical and an existential dying process and was undone after death. Resurrection was a potential reality both in this lifetime, as with the UniTrans suit-wearing man at the Jerikho church, and in the next lifetime, as with the funerals mentioned here. I am not denying the subjective reality of resurrection—that one claims to have died from an illness or traumatic experience and lived to tell about it. For most Christians I met, one's future death would not entail suffering and actual mortal expiration but rather ascension. A good deal of social and caregiving work went into preventing the former. Inevitable passage from the world was a process in which God was inherent and in which the pain of death would be ameliorated.

Conclusion

Healing through religious language and medical discernment foreclosed local Christian ideations of life with chronic illness amid HIV/AIDS.[22] In simpler terms, prayer healing pointed to ways people understood how their own health and well-being were shaped in time and at a critical historic moment in popular religious percepts.[23] Like the biomedical and humanitarian resources that prevented earlier death as described in chapter 1, prayer healing and perceptions of a healed afterlife became a material resource for the extension of life itself. Yet in the meantime, in everyday life, people needed to work on their and others' lives as Christians and in particularly material ways to show faith in the production of healing. It allowed them to religiously participate in the production of their own long-term healing, some from incurable yet virally suppressed diseases.

In some ways, because God was involved, this work was not their duty alone to materialize. By this I do not mean that people skirted their health-related responsibilities or to suggest that they did not adhere to what was prescribed to them. Rather, healing was in many ways already a "done deal" as part of God's providence. This was something I heard at a Mbabane church in 2011 and what other (neo-) Pentecostals worldwide say in relation to their health. For example, Jessica Hardin (2016) writes that such Christians in Samoa living with metabolic disorders "sought to develop a temporality of faith, which included practices like prayer, developing intimacy with God, learning to depend on God for healing, and drawing strength from God to change health practices."

When people were facing the immensity of epidemics such as obesity, opioid addiction, and HIV/AIDS, an eternal afterlife free of suffering seemed like a good prospect. Being reunited in Heaven with others who cared for them along the way was assuring. In Swaziland, self-identified Christians did not mind giving their afflictions, HIV/AIDS-related or not, over to God to handle for a while. With life at risk for episodic illness, religiously discerning disruptions and ways to prevent them were actions valued by Christians as work that constituted faith in the overall healing process. Working on oneself and others materially in the interim was the task at hand, but it was also a burden, given that the conditions to do so were sometimes limited. It was best then to have faith in something that would divine well-being and a good death over the long term.

Notes

1. The United States Department of State's International Report on Religious Freedom (2011) cites that 90 percent of the population belongs to diverse Christian sects. See also Golomski and Nyawo 2017.

2. In 2008, 2009, and 2010–11 I attended and documented more than sixty Christian worship services, nonfunerary night vigils, and Bible study or Sunday school sessions in close field notes and audio and video recordings.

3. Meyer's (2010, 742ff.) approach to religion considers "the value attributed to bodies, things, texts, and gestures, so as to make the divine tangible in the immanent." For her, sensational forms are sensual material media and practices "through which born-again Christians are enabled to sense the presence of the Holy Spirit *with* and *in* their bodies, wherever they are, and to act on such feelings" (original emphasis). Sensational forms operate "as a necessary condition for expressing content and meaning and ethical norms and values" and "are authorized modes for invoking and organizing access to the transcendental." Finally, they "emerge over time and are often subject to contestation and even abandonment" and reveal "processes of religious transformation" and are apt for ethnographic descriptions of cultural change like the Swaziland case here.

4. Most of my closest friends, informants, and consultants were Christian and not HIV positive (or did not disclose their status if they were).

5. See Becker and Geissler 2009; Prince, Denis, and van Dijk 2009; Klaits 2010; van Dijk et al. 2014; and Burchardt 2015.

6. See Guyer 2007 and Hardin 2015. This approach to time is summed up by Guyer (2007, 411): It "aims to understand how such templates may be created, how framed,

how transposed from one practice of life to another. How do they, then, refer to and refine each other across the experiential horizon: from praying to budgeting, from gesturing obedience to making payments, from imagining devotion to providing emotional care and material sustenance?"

7. On the synergism between customary religious practices, sometimes called Swazi Traditional Religion in this context, and Christianity, see Fogelqvist 1987; Mzizi 2005; Ndlovu 2007; and Golomski and Nyawo 2017. On the cultural history of AICs, see Comaroff 1985; Meyer 2004; Tishkin and Heuser 2015; and Cabrita 2018.

8. Pentecostal-charismatic Christianity has taken root especially in North and South America, sub-Saharan Africa, Oceania, and parts of Asia, becoming part and parcel of local communities all the way up to national politics.

9. I am indebted to Hebron L. Ndlovu and Sonene Nyawo in this regard. Luhrmann (2012, xx) calls the mostly white, upper middle-class Vineyard Churches in the United States neo-Pentecostal because of their "adoption of a Pentecostal ethos" and "flamboyant emphasis on the direct experience of God." Neo-Pentecostal churches also focus on "spiritual warfare" against evil forces (van Wyk 2014). In contrast, Vineyard church members eschew intensive laying of hands and spiritual embodiment deemed characteristic of neo-Pentecostal forms in Africa. See Dilger 2007; Ukah 2008; and Gifford 2014.

10. See Togarasei 2010 and Tofa 2014. While AICs and Pentecostalism remain analytically distinct in most scholarship on African religions (Meyer 2004; Tishkin and Heuser 2015), the immensity of HIV/AIDS and its effects may both shore up and break down such differences (Becker and Geissler 2009; Burchardt 2015; Golomski and Nyawo 2017).

11. Wherever it travels, Pentecostalism tends to pose itself in strict opposition to forms of local religious cultures, despite the fact that Pentecostalism tends to also reconfigure local forms in its own terms so as to prove its necessity. For example, local evil forces might be revalued as ungodly demons, or purgative function of customary herbal medicine may be transposed as a Pentecostal fasting rite (Meyer 2004; van Wyk 2014).

12. Early on, anthropologists documented the complex associations of AIDS and "witchcraft" in local communities as well as the way Western clinical and public health practitioners made problematic assumptions about witchcraft to the detriment of their own interventions. See Green 1994; Niehaus 2005, 2007, 2013; Rödlach 2006; Thornton 2008; Ashforth 2010; and Green and Herling Ruark 2011.

13. See Makhubu 1978; Gort 1989; Reis 1996, 2002; and Golomski 2015c.

14. Some stores are similar to US pharmacy chains like CVS and Walgreens. See also Cousins 2014.

15. See Kiernan 1990; Engelke 2007; and van Wyk 2014.

16. Food and clothing donations and mourning alongside of them were also crucial. See also Nyawo, Mhlobo, and Mpapane 2009; Becker and Geissler 2009; Dilger and Luig 2010; Root and van Wyngaard 2011; and Root, van Wyngaard, and Whiteside 2017.

17. Rote prayers, where speakers used a standard set of specific liturgical texts as done in Catholicism, was less common. Prayer was mostly extemporaneous.

18. On Jerikho healing, see Fogelqvist 1987 and Golomski 2016a.

19. See Engelke 2007; Klaits 2010; McNeill 2011; Black 2015; and Okigbo 2016.

20. One song popular at funerals and beyond by singers, choirs, and music videos is "*Emagugu alelizwe, ayosal' ematfuneni,*" or "[Our] worldly goods," those things we possess in life, "are left at [our] graves." We cannot take anything with us when we die, so the

song goes, despite the ritual fact that some people were buried with some of their personal belongings (See chapter four).

21. In HIV/AIDS-related examples from sub-Saharan Africa, Beckmann (2009, 144) mentions that some Muslims in Zanzibar considered HIV-positive people's suicides as obstructing chances at an afterlife. In Uganda, charismatic Christians were more likely than mainline Christians to see their salvation in the afterlife as predestined (Christiansen 2009, 89n6). Simpson (2014, e96, e103) noted that Catholic men in Zambia vaguely imagined an afterlife but were less certain it took shape as Heaven, Hell, or Purgatory. In South Africa, a bad death amid HIV/AIDS could portend zombification (Niehaus 2005).

22. See Guyer 2007; McGovern 2012; Hardin 2015, 2016, 2018; and Benton, Sangaramoorthy, and Kalofonos 2017.

23. Jane Guyer (2007, 415) describes how global fundamentalist Christianity involves an orientation toward a "future unfolding" that is rendered practically intelligible "by waiting, by identifying, by witnessing" signs and events in the present as evidence of divine intervention and a millennial Second Coming.

3 The Secrets of Life Insurance: Saving, Care, and the Witch

"Service Beyond *Ubuntu*" is our "pay-off line." Every company has one that they use when marketing their products. Going beyond *ubuntu* means that one will do something [for another] in the same manner as one would expect to receive it, but with our services we can exceed what someone else can do for you in every single aspect. We apply the human aspect to our services. We are not just a business; we are a service for one of the most difficult times in one's life. Our services are meant to help our clients ... in death, the moment of truth is in the moment of loss.

I LISTENED AS the middle manager explained his company's main advertising slogan and what he felt was the value of their work as a life insurance and mortuary provider. We sat face-to-face in a tiny fluorescent-lit room at his suburban branch office. Behind us, tiers of fancy caskets for sale, festooned with artificial flowers, hung from the walls. At the end of the interview, he handed me a packet of glossy brochures and thanked me for visiting. "Come back to see us," the receptionist hailed as I left, "but not in a box!" In other words, do not come back dead in a coffin.

Ubuntu in isiZulu, or *buntfu* in siSwati, means humaneness or personhood and connotes principles of mutuality. As an ethical concept, it has gained considerable traction as a guiding principle of Africanist philosophies and legal reasoning, an indigenized form of social responsibility whereby people are beholden to others because they are also constituted by one another. As the regional idiom goes, "A person is a person by other people," *muntfu ngumuntfu ngabanye bantfu.* When *ubuntu* moves from an ethical domain to a commercial one, questions of value come to the fore that split along perceptual lines (Lambek 2013). Potential consumers are faced with existential questions: How can financial products be virtuous? Can a special group of experts provide the same as one's kin for a funeral? What "truths" about someone are revealed in death, as the manager noted? What is lost, and what can be gained?

This chapter shows how an emergent market of life insurance incited newer ways to prepare for funerals in Swaziland. As HIV/AIDS is sometimes called a "disease that is killing the nation," *ligicwane lelibulave,* insurance emerged mostly from outside of the nation as a financial means to deal with death. In term life insurance, a person signs up as a policyholder and lists dependents. Every month, the policyholder pays a premium to the insurance company, continuing *ad infinitum*. When the policyholder or a dependent dies, the person's family makes a claim to the company, and money is paid out to a listed beneficiary. Insurance works as a form of value production by creating and redistributing money in the contractual "moment of loss": a death. Saving and paying for insurance in Swaziland was promoted to produce "dignified" funerals in terms of insurance companies' branding initiatives.

For most people, consuming insurance was challenging amid HIV/AIDS. Going to work, making a home, farming, or raising children were more strenuous with chronic illness. People lost wages at work or were fired, and thus could not pay regular premiums. Funerals were also costly. Chris Desmond and colleagues (2004) found overall burial costs ranged between US$475 and US$700. Businesses I surveyed between 2010 and 2011 suggested that this price had increased, ranging between US$500 and US$900. Per capita income in 2016 was less than US$4,000. While costly, insurance also innovated possibilities to pay off death's compounded financial and social burdens. For many people I met, insurance was seen as a newer alternative and sometimes complementary to conventional burial cooperatives that had long provided coverage for people's deaths. Insurance was typically marketed in language and customary images of Swazi Culture and in industry-specific terms such as "risk" that uneasily moved between financial and vernacular conversations. These policies, linked to mortuary services, were culturally innovative.

In this chapter, I trace how consumers' perceptions of insurance and how they put insurance to good use produced a culture of secrecy, which in practice mostly occurred because some people kept their policies secret from their relatives. In turn, others could see this act as greedy, or *butsakatsi*-like, and policyholders close to the dead could be suspected of profiting from death. Insurance also laid the groundwork for transforming social relations by forging new ones with brokers or absconding from family altogether. In the latter, it let people distance themselves from those who might not otherwise pay for their funerals. HIV/AIDS stigma was still a problem, and with insurance, those who faced criticism for living with the disease could still assure they would get a dignified funeral through the mechanistic means of a policy. In these ways, the market rendered burial assurance more invisible and asocial. Importantly though, it also sometimes allayed the secrecy that created distance between family members by forcing transparency about saving and imbricating others in this ethical and financial action.

The bald truth remained, though, that these life-giving resources came at a life-negating moment. Anthropologist Rosalind Morris (2008, 209) characterizes

South African insurance as manifesting a "rush" for capital over the "panic" of HIV/AIDS deaths, enacting a "value-producing dimension of risk while seemingly offering the techniques with which to contain it." Her suggestion, however, that "work alone [might] interrupt the nexus of speculation and death that is the epidemic" (Morris 2008, 231) can be extended. As *Funeral Culture* shows, "work" has varied shades of meaning in Swaziland and throughout Southern Africa. It portends broader implications for understanding the cultural production of life and death in history. I show here how, at the everyday level of insurance consumption, in death's moment of loss, truths about peoples' saving and carework for each other were disclosed and the value of Swazi Culture was scrutinized.

Let Us Bury Each Other: The State, Insurance, and Burial Cooperatives

The Dlamini aristocracy under Sobhuza II strategically developed the kingdom's capitalist market by creating a national fiduciary trust, *Tibiyo TakaNgwane*, at the time of independence in 1968. In 1973, a King's Order-in-Council proposed the founding of an overarching local insurance company, and on January 1, 1974, the Swaziland Royal Insurance Corporation (SRIC) opened for business. SRIC's operational infrastructure and shareholders included several foreign pension funds and companies, but SRIC largely remained the primary insurance-selling entity operating within the country. Some industry personnel told me that several decades of SRIC dominance amounted to a stagnant monopoly. "Before, with SRIC, you would just take it or leave it," explained a brokerage house manager. A former private company executive asked me rhetorically while sitting next to his verdant poolside veranda, "Why would the shareholders or SRIC want it any other way?"

In the mid-2000s, the financial services sector broke apart the monopoly as part of the broader 1997–2022 National Development Strategy (NDS). To facilitate this process, Parliament passed two acts in 2005 that affected the insurance industry. Insurance Act No. 7 allowed foreign corporate entities to open and operate locally. The state also expanded regulatory oversight by creating the supervisory and regulatory body called the Registrar of Insurance and Retirement Funds (RIRF), now the Financial Regulatory Services Authority (FRSA).[1] SRIC quickly lost its singular presence to an influx of South African corporations that brought diverse portfolios and consumer products (see fig. 3.1).

South African traveling salespeople have long sold insurance policies across the border in Swaziland. Many industry personnel and consumers retold anxious narratives about slick brokers selling policies and jumping the border when customers claimed. This echoed the historic and sometimes violent extraction of human resources coming from outside the kingdom.[2] Indeed, one of the first field notes I wrote about perceptions of insurance was from a day I spent at the Mavuso International Trade Fair in Manzini in August 2010. There was a

Fig. 3.1 Funeral insurance advertisement at a clothing store, Nhlangano, 2011. Photograph by author.

business expo, and several insurance companies were there as vendors. I met two customer service representatives for a South African company, and we shared a bag of popcorn. A man soon came to the vendor table to make a complaint. He was angry that his claim for a local death took a long time to collect because it had to be processed in a Cape Town office. This delayed getting the money for a few days longer than expected when he urgently needed it.

This tension with South Africa as a regional economic core paralleled the relationship between the market and regulators. "We are standing between David and Goliath, but we can say we are closer to David rather than these big ones," a state regulator told me in an interview at her Mbabane office, biblically characterizing the regulators in relation to the insurance industry. "Still," she noted, "we are supportive of the business community." Insurance brokerage house managers also explained to me that RIRF defended Swazis from exterior financial predation and that they were willing to accommodate to regulatory guidelines. In the news media, the private sector also played up a general anxiety of extraction in their appreciation of state regulation: "[Zombodze] Magagula [general manager of SRIC] said they were looking forward to seeing the market fair and safe. 'There are fly-by-night companies and we are happy to have the registrar's office which will protect the interests of the customers. We want to be able to live within the laws. We can't rely on trust in the modern world, but policing which is exactly what the registrar's office is providing'" (Mavuso 2011).

The "modern world" and its markets might indeed provide supposedly limitless consumer opportunities, but it did not entail that transactions in the market would be mutual. The state, embodied in regulatory entities such as FRSA, would have to step in to guarantee "fair and safe" consumption. Newspapers regularly printed RIRF and FRSA notices warning consumers not to subscribe to particular companies that failed to register with regulators. Anxieties over disappearing brokers and unfulfilled claims from outside were mitigated by legal requirements for companies to house services in country. Yet the same oversight sometimes rendered relations between the state and existing burial cooperatives ambiguous.

Historically, a burial cooperative has been a group of people who organize with the aim to accumulate money to provide support for a member in the event of their own or a dependent's death.[3] In siSwati, a burial cooperative is called *inhlangano*, meaning simply "a group," or *umasingcwabisane*, meaning, "let us bury one another," which is also sometimes used as a vernacular term for "insurance," as well. Sometimes the English cognate *umshwalense* and popular corporate insurance brands stood in for the term, as with *i-Dups*, from Dups, the country's largest mortuary. Since at least the 1960s, burial cooperatives formed in families, churches, neighborhoods, and workplaces.[4] Membership could range from five to five hundred people. I went to several meetings for a variety of cooperatives and interviewed both members and leaders. The cooperatives have largely been the purview of women, but many men participate as well, in workplaces. Regionally, cooperatives are hugely influential. In South Africa in 2017, for example, about 11.5 million members saved an estimated ZAR49 billion or US$3.6 billion in such groups called *stokvels*, some by using mobile phone apps. Twenty-two percent of these *stokvels* focused on burial (Holmes 2017).

The other 2005 legislation associated with the insurance market was the Co-operatives Act No. 3, which compelled the burial cooperatives to incorporate.[5] Before 2005, cooperatives were supposed to register with the Ministry of Home Affairs and come under a parastatal organization called the Swaziland Association of Savings and Credit Cooperatives (SASCCO). The NDS aimed to incorporate small-scale groups such as burial cooperatives into the broader financial services sector as a means of "empowerment." The legislation was supposed to standardize the practices of cooperatives and encourage a link to a formal underwriter to provide members with actuarial guarantee.[6] This goal was compelling for most industry personnel but not for many cooperatives. Most cooperatives were, in one regulator's statement, already "self-regulating." "That is all right, they think," the regulator said, hypothesizing about the Swaziland National Association of Teachers (SNAT) burial cooperative, "but then there might be a case where all of a sudden 100 teachers die in a bus crash. Then they may not have enough money to pay everyone. Can you live up to your promises?" Such wrenching prospects swayed some cooperatives to embrace the actuarial salvation of underwriting. During my research in 2010 and 2011, however, I found that more politically liberal labor unions' cooperatives resisted this move. The state loomed dangerously in the perspective of their members and boards, as was apparent in some of their meetings I attended.

Meetings for labor unions' burial cooperatives, such as those for SNAT and the National Public Service and Allied Workers Union (NAPSAWU), often drew up to five hundred attendees. Past meeting minutes, agendas, and informational literature were passed out, presentations made, and sometimes queues formed to collect a boxed lunch and a small amount of money paid out from the cooperative for the members' attendance. Wrapped sandwiches, fruits, and cool drinks circulated outward from the meeting as members made their way to finish weekend shopping or return home, evincing the cooperative's work of productive redistribution in the form of food.[7] Several meetings I attended involved presentations by financial services or insurance companies pitching their administrative services of guarantee and management. Members usually mentioned concerns about potentially shady pricing mechanisms and past successes and failures of the company.

At one union meeting of government employees, more politically motivated members opened with cries of "Viva, viva comrades!" before listening to a sympathetic company representative try to pitch his services to their burial cooperative. He was met with a stone-faced crowd whose concerns centered on how this company would, if at all, be able to negotiate death claims through the state's untimely and circumspect payroll. In the past, when union members died and claims were made to an underwriter, the government payroll system would show no record of the unionist on file. In turn, the underwriter would not process the claim. Delayed burials fomented sociopolitical antagonism, as unions have long been persecuted for their efforts to draw popular attention to politico-economic inequalities. Even linking to the parastatal organization drew criticism, and at one cooperative's meeting, the fact that SASCCO's proposed headquarters in Mbabane still lay unfinished in construction after six years was evidence enough for members to not link to it.

Despite the insurance industry's ties to the broader goals of the NDS, the expansion of the insurance market was tied directly to the history of HIV/AIDS. Several insurance industry personnel had few reservations to admitting that the market's emergence was largely kindled by mass death. "When they see a lot of people dying, then you see a lot of businesses start popping up everywhere around here. It's really a business, and there is a big profit to be made from all of it. They know there is money to be made," explained the founder and former executive of one company. The owner of a funeral parlor who sold life insurance policies invoked a food metaphor, saying, "I do think that there is a bigger business now because of HIV.... They say that the transmission is going down and people are able to get the ARVs, but the death rate is still going out. The cake is getting smaller for the funeral industry. There are more and more mortuaries and more people are dying, but then there is less business with more and more mortuaries.... Around the early 2000s we saw a lot more business and a lot more deaths. It is probably because of HIV." There was a general consensus among insurance brokers and management whom I spoke with that within the short span of half a decade the life insurance market was becoming saturated. Yet many also noted that the market needed to diversify because the majority of consumers could not access the full range of their products. One female brokerage house manager admitted, "Life insurance is not really available for the majority of Swazis because of high premiums, lack of a market, and the fear to test." Whole life insurance policies, which provide upward of millions in monetary value, require a medical examination or "test," and an HIV diagnosis usually and immediately precludes coverage.

Some South African companies have developed life insurance products for people living with HIV/AIDS, but they are extraordinarily expensive. Medical aid schemes prohibit different rates for members who are HIV positive and are open to anyone, but these types of policies are often too pricey to join. I asked an executive-level manager about the possibility of tailoring such a whole life insurance product for the Swazi market. Laughingly, she replied, "*eish*, they are high risk! But it is true that chronic illness is manageable. People understand HIV. Education has been done to death!" Because it was so difficult to access whole life coverage, term life coverage, the industry's technical and marketed name for funeral insurance, became the most popularly promoted and purchased product.

Selling Risk, Selling Swazi Culture

One of my key interlocutors and friends was an insurance broker named Lucky. I met him at the University of Swaziland one afternoon outside of a computer lab. He had just made a product pitch for funeral insurance to an administrative assistant and was visiting several people on campus to tweak or get updates on their policies. We chatted and exchanged numbers and later became good friends. In the fall, we prowled his neighborhood for the best seasonal *marula*-fruit homebrew, and I drove him and his wife to her grandmother's funeral in Siphofaneni the following spring. Throughout that time, I made my way into research with his brother's brokerage house along with a few of the corporate companies that contracted the house to sell their products. I followed Lucky and his coworkers on the road as they made presentations to prospective policyholders. I did not see the brokers attract many new policies, despite their most persuasive and well-informed efforts—for example, the brokers usually signed up only two or three individuals from a group of forty. The presentations offered an arena to see how brokers marketed insurance through ideations of Swazi Culture, how both they and consumers revalued the notions of risk, and how that risk was related to these cultural ideations.

The brokers and I visited a wide range of places to make presentations, including a juvenile detention and reform center, military barracks, and a construction site for a post-secondary educational facility. Presentations usually took place in the morning before work or at lunchtime. Brokers contacted managers to request an opportunity to make a presentation and were then provided a captive audience of employees. Brokers made general introductions of everyone in the room—including the brokers themselves and me, the anthropologist—as well as introducing the products being sold by the different companies.

The presentations took place mostly in siSwati, peppered with a few key words in English. Many of them were technical terms related to the industry, such as "risk" and "benefits"; others, such as "challenges," were less so. Policies were usually marketed in a hierarchy of symbolic value. Companies ranked their coverage options on levels such as silver, gold, platinum, and diamond—the latter being the most expensive in terms of premium payments—or on a lettered scale from "A" onward. Such symbolism is widely familiar, given that many people have had relatives who worked as miners in the region excavating mineral wealth.

Products were also made familiar through advertising and language invoking Swazi Culture. Insurance was not marketed as something one saved for singly but rather collectively. Social forms of saving through Swazi Culture were clear in an elaborate example I encountered on a visit to the Mbabane office of one South African insurance company. On the wall, hung in gold frames, were several company advertisement posters featuring the national age grades, *emabutfo*. As discussed in chapter 1, invoking notions of generation is salient as a powerful royalist means for social and structural control amid the problem of HIV/AIDS (see chap. 1). The text on the posters emphasized "unity," "collective effort," and "harmony," and generation was overall a key symbol for social reproduction enabled through the purchasing of insurance.

One advertisement, for example, featured women's hands tying thick grasses to construct a horizontal brace for a customary homestead windscreen, *liguma*, which is also the word for the customary site for adolescent girls' collective initiation and education. In the space of the *liguma*, girls are said to learn about their sexual maturity and how men and women comport themselves so that the girls too would eventually grow to be respectable adult women. Actual *liguma* are rare, as contemporary homes are not constructed with windscreens. The limited encounters girls would have with a *liguma* would be at the National Museum, where they could see it as a heritage display, or in their participation at *Umhlanga*, where they gather reeds to bring to the Queen Mother's palace to rebuild such a screen. Despite the conspicuous absence of *liguma* in everyday life, they are trumpeted as sites of intervention in HIV/AIDS-related policy because of their instructional and cultural references for sex education. Indeed, the Education Sector Policy of 2010 drew on elements of the UN's "best practices" policies that aimed to integrate adolescent HIV/AIDS "Centres of Care and Support" and school programming that revitalized "'liguma' and 'lisango' (gender-specific huts)" (UNAIDS 2012, 5). In these cases, Swazi Culture and insurance were argued to mitigate multiple kinds of risk.

In addition to generational relations, products were based on and presented as facilitating Swazi Culture's patrilineal, polygynous kinship in marriage and childrearing. Policies fell into individual and family or group plans, with brokers pushing people to buy the latter. On family plans, policyholders could list "tribal" or "legal" spouses along with child dependents, and brokers encouraged coverage for members' extended kin.[8] "[Company C] has done research and shows that Swazis like and have many children, so there is no problem to bring in the others," explained a broker to a group of female prison warders. Policies usually covered upward of six to eight children. In a presentation to several young female secretaries of a construction company, a broker encouraged the secretaries to take out family coverage. "You can join under the family funeral plan before you're married," she explained, "but when you do get married, you bring the certificate to us.... You might be single now, but you'll marry and have children tomorrow," they were told, suggesting that they think about potential future families as a form of sociocultural and financial value.

Insurance was sold to offer benefits to families, but it could also transform families. One of the most poignant concerns voiced by prospective consumers during presentations was their obligation to care for deceased relatives' children. Several consumers asked whether or not policies would cover children who were orphaned by parents' deaths, using a customary idiom to explain how such children were "put into (their) bellies," *kufaka esiswini*, or informally entrusted across families. Brokers were eager to accommodate this concern, but according to the stipulations of several policies, children had to be formally adopted by policyholders in order to be registered as beneficiaries. Several brokers explained how consumers should take their entrusted children to the Office of Social Welfare with affidavits and legally adopt them in order to bring them under the policy. This move would show the consumer's love or compassion for the children in purchasing insurance, but it also transformed the children to being "orphaned and vulnerable" under the purview of the state. It also firmly integrated them into the legal stakes of inheritance (Golomski 2015a).

Brokers likewise used symbols of Swazi Culture to emphasize how policy payments and eventual payouts could materialize wealth and wherewithal. SRIC promoted some of its products as a form of savings at the intersection of Swazi Culture and nature. "Be as Clever as a Lilunga Bird," implored one advertisement, "also known as the Fiscal Shrike or Butcher Bird, [it] catches its pretty when times are good and hangs them on barbed wire or a thorn. Then, when it is hungry, there is always a meal waiting for it." Another prompted would-be policyholders to be as "clever as the ant," to collectively swarm and move food underground before the rainy season as a means of saving and protection. Other corporate entities selling group funeral schemes used images of mountains, dried gourds, and cattle as symbols of both cultural identity and providential resources. Brokers characterized insurance as going beyond finance to secure and sustain resources such as one's home, animal herds, automobiles, education, and bridewealth. Brokers also drew consumers to the prospect of using insurance to jumpstart these processes. Presentations were often very prophetic in that the prospect of future well-being could be bought in the here and now. Mapps, a marketing manager, asked his customers to consider how life could be transformed with insurance:

> There is not a thing that won't be helped. Insurance will begin to keep your life in order. It can start out small and work. As you continue to do your work you will be earning money.... [Company L] is there to provide for your livelihood. So when you [die] and want something for your life, nothing will be lost. You want to continue and enter into something better.... It's very good and is a secure deed. People want a secure deed.... When you take insurance, it will follow your children, all the way to tertiary level.

Term life policies did not produce tangible value in the space between policy subscription and death, but they were sold with anticipatory affect: the monthly sequence of premium payments acted to consistently remind the policyholder of value *in potentia*. It mapped the long-term project of premium payments onto the collective, familial work of caring for people across the life course. In term life insurance, death was the central transformative moment for both people and money associated with a policy. Both consumers and companies pushed for a quick submission of the death certificate for a quick turnaround time in paying out a claim, usually within forty-eight hours. For some, like the angry customer at the Trade Fair, this was not quick enough. Timely receipt was necessary to expedite the burial and save on mortuary storage fees. Some policies continued for beneficiaries or dependents after the policyholder passed on, but most were not adjusted for inflation.

Death was the primary "risk" of term life insurance, despite its inevitable occurrence. Economic understandings of risk involve expressing the randomness facing an economic agent in terms of numerical probability. Agents who cannot or do not assign or assess probabilities to alternative possible outcomes are exemplary of "uncertainty." In the Swazi market, brokers and industry personnel thought consumers found the notion of risk to be mysterious. In presentations, brokers aimed to instill concern for the concept by orienting audiences to a graver future. Playing up the inevitability of death was one way to emphasize concern for a potential hazard along with citing a lack of resources for one's family members after death. Brokers drummed on a note that without insurance, there would be no money, first for the deceased's funeral, and second for the survivors, especially the children of the deceased.

While insurance products and their associated discourses hinged on the technical concept of risk, they did not easily translate into everyday vernacular terms. Industry personnel were amused most when I asked them to define risk in siSwati. Hearty laughs followed by ponderous thought were their usual reactions. "That is a difficult one! Is there even a word for it?" asked one regulator rhetorically, "Perhaps *bungoti*?" *Bungoti* generally translates as "danger," and the regulator admitted it was not the most accurate word to express their concept of risk. A few times, people suggested the folkloric idiom, *salakutjelwa sibonwa ngemopho*, meaning, "When you do not listen to what we say, blood will be seen." For some years, SRIC advertised policies using the term *incabhayi*, which linguist David Rycroft (1981) translated as "a game of touch." One manager struggled to translate the meaning of risk but said that the word itself was not so important. Marketing the idea of risk should rather encourage one to "do something while you are still alive. You do something for your kids so that when the time comes, you don't regret not doing something," he said.

When asked to elaborate on risk in relation to consumers, industry professionals characterized Swazis as unable or unwilling to fragment or frame facets of their own actions as risky. "People are not risk takers here," one female brokerage house manager told me. "You might've walked a long ways to get from here to there and took a risk while doing it, but it's not like you see it as a risk. The content of that action is all right, but maybe you weren't really prepared for the action itself. If people don't know how to prepare, they won't grow." Similarly, a former company executive said, "Swazis don't understand risk until they experience it themselves. Then they see that they should be prepared for something. They go along just fine until they come to something bad. '*Ack! Shem!*' [they say]. Then they start to think about these things."

In both cases, consumers were seen as being perceptive, having particular objectives, and moving to accomplish them. Yet they failed to classify or critically carve out some segments of experience as more dangerous than others. For brokers, instilling a motive to critically classify experiences as risky was necessary to orient consumers to the protective and productive orders of insurance. Given the backdrop of HIV/AIDS, it is poignant to note that public health practitioners also struggled to use technical concepts of risk in HIV prevention initiatives and other work locally. For example, at a Ministry of Health research conference I attended in 2010, a physician from the Population Council reported that in informed consent education and HIV testing prior to medical male circumcision, respondents did worse on questions meant to measure their ability to comprehend surgical risk (Friedland et al. 2013).

Potential consumers, of course, were more knowledgeable about risk and better informed than brokers suggested. One day I went with Lucky after he managed to schedule a one-on-one presentation with a school registrar over the man's lunch break. As Lucky tried to pitch both investment and burial plans to him, it was clear to me that the man was not interested in subscribing to either. The registrar explained, "It is an *eventuality*, death. It is certain, I understand; no one will not die…. The only danger that I see is that you end up at such an age without any savings. This insurance attracts people who don't take care of themselves, like if I were exposed to AIDS." He envisioned himself aging to the point where what he put into a policy in total would outweigh what he would get in a claim. Death was inevitable, but other people were more predisposed to an earlier one if they lacked self-care. In a macabre corollary, a young woman I knew named Nichelle, who lived in Manzini, suggested that a person who bought insurance probably thought he or she would die an early death. Some anthropologists found the prospect of a shortened life as a reason people did not want to test for HIV, and the same reason was given for not purchasing insurance.[9] The insurance conception of death as a momentous, impinging force paralleled what some people already knew about life's finite quality and the variability of individuals.

In their sociological account of the Canadian insurance market, Richard Ericson, Aaron Doyle, and Dean Barry (2003, 37) write that "the subject of liberal risk regimes requires knowledge of risk in order to be an active consumer" in risk management markets. This speaks to Ulrich Beck's (2009) famous notion of "risk society," one in which societies become more scientifically and "rationally" concerned with future pitfalls. This is a historical process of "modernization," one that has unfolded forcibly and unevenly in sub-Saharan Africa through European colonialism but has been reconfigured on people's own terms as "active consumers." Lack of one-to-one translation for key concepts of this regime, such as risk, opens a space for creative evaluation of livelihoods, futures, and providential technologies. There has been little exploration of risk regimes as they take shape in the global South and how such regimes are felt in people's everyday lives. Ethnographic attention on how that evaluation might occur points to the salience of culture and how it is repackaged by marketers and repurposed by consumers.

John L. and Jean Comaroff (2009) argue that ethnicity and culture increasingly become the grounds for social groups to incorporate themselves as businesses or NGOs in the face of capitalist inequality. Groups' "ethnopreneurialism" in this regard redistributes new forms of value that can change the meaning of culture itself.[10] In the case here, both Swazi and South African companies trafficked in this sort of cultural production to shore up insurance's novelty and value through Swazi Culture's idioms of generation. The Comaroffs also question whether value accrues in this process for individuals or communities and note there are political stakes in the redistribution of value as profits. At the level of the nation-state, this question elides with critical concerns surrounding the Dlamini aristocracy's nonredistribution of revenue accrued in the state's fiduciary trusts (Levin 1997; Forrester and Laterza 2014). I show how on the everyday level of consumption, redistribution was likewise a political question. It involved furtive socioeconomic practices across families that rendered ambiguous marital, generational, and caregiving relationships supposedly central to Swazi Culture.

The Secrets of Life Insurance

Kwandza kwaliwa ngumtsakatsi—"Accumulation is felled by witchcraft."

At Roxanne's funeral, LaGija's sister Banele, who worked for a pension fund, jokingly said, "We Swazis don't have a culture of saving. They're concerned with the house and the cows but don't put up for other things." Many people lived with material poverty on a day-to-day basis. Saving food, goods, and most of all, money was difficult not only when incoming resources were limited but also when households supported resident members, extended kin, and sometimes neighbors who asked for assistance. Insurance fundamentally operated around a "culture of saving," namely the consistent budgeting or mobilizing of funds to make monthly payments. This also involved social relations, as policyholders might ask for a short-term loan from a friend or relative to make their monthly payment, for example. Such savings might be of eventual benefit to a wide range of the policyholder's social relations in the form of a funeral in which many of them would participate. Savings were discretely accumulated in an account over time. What became clear early on in the research with consumers and brokers was that insurance was both discrete and discreet. Buying insurance led to gendered, hushed practices whose outcomes could be read as ethically or socially suspect. Purchasing insurance and having savings produced a cultural complex I call the "secrets of life insurance."

At Swaziland's International Trade Fair at Mavuso in 2010, I struck up another conversation with an insurance company representative and her sister. "I will really tell you something you need to know," the representative explained slyly when I told her about my interest in funerals and how to pay for them. "People don't take out policies because they are scared the wife will kill them for it," she said. Shortly thereafter, a bespectacled man stopped by the booth and joined our conversation. It soon came out that he had a funeral insurance policy but had not told his wife about it. The sister asked the man why he had not told his wife, and he responded brashly, "Hey, she might be putting something in the food!" The representative and her sister looked at each other and shrieked laughingly, "*Mutsi!*"

As discussed in chapter 2, *mutsi*, or *muti*, means "medicine" in a broad sense of the term, connoting shrubs, bushes, and plants that were used as substances for customary healing similar to *tiwasho*. Herbal specialists, *tigedla*, or those who could command extraordinary enactments of the medicine, *tinyanga*, were experts at transforming such plants into powders, pastes, and other means for ingestion or inhalation to cure or prevent illnesses. There were also concoctions made to enable users of the medicine to effectively control other people's bodies, minds, and circumstances. Control ranged from ensnaring coveted lovers to killing hated enemies, and nefarious use of *mutsi* in this sense was cast as *butsakatsi*, when used to destroy people or things out of malice or revenge. No one could doubt *mutsi*'s efficacy and its use for a variety of purposes, given its continued regional salience, sale, and circulation. Historically, *mutsi* was prohibited by colonial states and missions, commercially expanded in the private market, and subject to the effects of global markets. In this instance, the man and the company reps at the trade fair cited *mutsi* in its negative sense, as a means by which one gained advantage of a policyholder by poisoning.

After the encounter at the trade fair, I used this *butsakatsi* example as a probing point for people to elaborate on their perceptions of insurance. Everyone conveyed amusement in it but did not disregard the potential malevolence surrounding insurance purchasing and investment. Witchcraft was never a tangential concern nor inconsequential. Indeed, utterance of the word usually led interviewees to speak more reservedly and quietly, indicating it was a serious issue to discuss. Lucky noted a problem of marital secrecy with respect to insurance: "People may not tell their spouses. Well, some may be more open, like Christians. They are afraid of big money, so when the big money comes, you are just asking for trouble. The women complain that husbands are no good!" LaGija at first looked surprised when I told her about it, but she agreed that revealing that one had an insurance policy might not be a smart move and could be potentially dangerous. It would be better to keep such an investment activity a secret. "That is an interesting thing you will note in your study," she said, "but hey, this thing happens with all investments. There are threats in it that everyone should be aware of. My estranged husband could even come back here and just take over this house!"

LaGija's reference to her house and husband spoke to both personal and social antagonisms between spouses in Swaziland that were easily enveloped in an explanation of witchcraft. Her husband owned their suburban house, despite the fact that he did not live there and that LaGija paid for all the municipal taxes and maintenance on it. By and large, the majority of Swazi women do not have power of attorney or decision-making powers over the allocation, use, or sale of propertied resources. For many women, property and marriage tacked uneasily between Swazi Culture and what was voiced as "modern" gender equality. It portended strained in-law and spousal relations. Indeed, in the more than half a year I spent living at LaGija's household, we had several experiences that she and others read as nefarious attempts by her then-estranged husband or others to cause undue harm. One day, after arriving home from grocery shopping, the carcass of a large crab lay on the front stoop. I had never seen a crab there outside of a supermarket freezer, and the nearest river, in which LaGija's sons told me no crabs lived, was almost two kilometers away. Several members of the household agreed that the crab must have been placed there maliciously, and that night, before and after dinner, several prayers were silently made to expel any malevolent forces remaining in our midst (Golomski 2016b).

Secrecy surrounding insurance policy subscription potentially prevented accusations of being greedy or evil, but it also prevented timely claims when someone died. If a policyholder died and had not told his or her beneficiaries about a policy, they would not know to file a claim. The owner of a brokerage house explained to me at an interview over tea, "You find that people don't tell one another about the policies they take out. You wouldn't know they took out the policy. You just have to go look through their briefcase, and then you might find it. If it is not there, maybe [the deceased] kept it at work, so you will have to go look there." Secrecy could be born from ignorance and was sometimes spoken about as something problematically cultural. At another company, a customer service representative explained to me: "There are often problems when a policyholder passes on. There is a secrecy in life that we face now where contracts are not revealed to one's family members. They end up not knowing the things that you've gone into, like investments and savings. There is nothing tangible that the relatives will know about, and they will not know about the things you've committed yourself to while you're alive. This whole thing about keeping investments a secret is common with Africans."

One company administrator admitted *butsakatsi* fears were present in adopting policies and divulging investments but saw this fear as an uncritical fallback to Swazi Culture, a move she regarded as "backward" and one that could do better through transparent dialogue. "We are here in the companies to help people learn so that they can get a brighter future," she said, suggesting educated consumption would be more enlightened and could also chart out economic decisions that could have potentially positive effects for others. Revealing and negotiating insurance policies were not limited to the members of a particular household; they involved extended relations. In one product presentation with a group of construction workers, several of the workers expressed concern over such household discussions about subscribing. One man voiced his irritation to the broker in siSwati:

> "We will then need to go and ask our wives' people [in-laws] if they ever joined [an insurance policy]. It happens that you bring bread home and yet your

wife brought it too!" "No," the broker responded. "If she thinks she has such an opportunity to work [subscribe to a policy], she would have told you she joined. This is a need, not an option, because when the person is now at the mortuary you realize the need.... When you get home, tell her you have joined here. Explain to her how important this is, and she will support you. If you go and ask her first, she will just want to pay off the debt at Ellerine's" [a franchise furniture store].

The man's coworkers laughed at his first statement, suggesting the wife or her family members had secretly taken out a policy already and not told the husband, which would mean that both were engaged in consumptive subterfuge. The broker was quick to construct a scenario of productive dialogue to her hypothetical response, even if it meant that the man or other prospective policyholder would still be secretive when first subscribing. Transparent dialogue would come afterward, and the coworkers laughed at the idea of the wife's cunning to use the money elsewhere, given the prestige value of furniture (James 2015). The broker pleaded for openness in planning for death. She tempered the laughter in the room with a final statement: "Death will come where you are just staying, and then you stand up and have to run to a funeral. It will be easy then with insurance." One of my research assistants, a UNISWA student, Sibusisiwe, initially translated the broker's words as, "Then death heats your home and you go from pillar to post!" illuminating the hectic potential of such domestic investments and conversations.

The construction worker's suggestion about his in-laws hinted at a dire situation I heard from several brokers: that of a person being over-insured across multiple policies. Regarding the intentionally and unethically over-insured, Erik Bähre (2011, 387) describes this occurrence as emanating from more avaricious tendencies, recounting a case where his research assistant Edith found out a relative had been secretively naming family members as beneficiaries and accruing upward of ZAR1000 (US$140) for each death. People in the insurance industry told me that while avarice might be present, over-insurance was more likely accidental because of secret policy enrollments. One company administrator named Lihle shared a personal story with me that summed up this conundrum. In this instance, over-insurance was accidental:

> It is really unfair in some ways. People are not advised well on these matters.... But let me make an example of [Company D] and [Company L]. As for me, my own mother died two years ago. Here was my brother. He took a policy for my mother and others from [Company D]. And then here is my sister. She took a policy for my mother at [Company L].
>
> So my mother died, and my brother ran and took the corpse to the mortuary at [Company D]. Okay, that was fine. He went to make the claim from [Company D]. And then my sister also went to make the claim from hers. You

see what happened. [Company D] was underwritten by [Company L], so our family over-claimed on my mother. I mean, you see that if you have five kids, you want to cover them and be responsible for all of them.

So we had to convene a family meeting and get together to look at these things. We all sat down and saw what had happened. One of them had to forfeit. It is really unfair, and you find that people are not telling each other where they are taking out the money from. It's better when everyone tells each other. So me, now I know, we have to sit down and discuss these things.... [Company D] gave the premiums back to my brother. But that was unfair to be paying that entire time.

In the aftermath, Lihle's family was comparatively successful by getting the refund, as I have documented other cases from brokers about policyholders who failed to make their case to companies for premium refunds in the event of over-insurance. The difference between companies and their policies, as in Lihle's case, often track back to an underwriter, the end source and financial guarantor from which insurance companies drew money to pay claims. When the market broke up the SRIC monopoly, there was only one underwriter in Swaziland. Multiple policies from different insurance companies on a single individual could all potentially snake back to a single source, which maintained a ceiling amount per person insured. As the market expanded, so did the number of underwriters, but policyholders were not always informed about where exactly the money would come from in the event of a claim.

Over-insurance problems entailed cash matters as well as the production of a funeral, as policies sometimes required the specific use of particular funeral parlors or mortuaries. Delayed communications among relatives led to costly decisions about where to take the body immediately after death. Some funeral parlors forced survivors to store bodies with them as part of their policy obligations. Ashford, the owner of a small-town mortuary who had such contracts with several insurance companies, explained how this macabre financial and bodily rerouting could happen. One day, while I was visiting Ashford, a short man came into the parlor looking shaken and inquired solemnly about his grandfather. "Was he not in the cold-storage facility?" he asked. Ashford bellowed that no elderly man was registered that week, and it came out that the man mistook where his relatives had placed his father's body as likely part of an insurance policy. Ashford explained the situation further using a hypothetical case:

> Mortuary A sells funeral insurance to Mr. Mhlophe for his father, and the plan forces them to use their storage. Mortuary B sells funeral insurance to Mr. Mhlophe's sister for the same father. Their father dies, and Mhlophe's sister claims first from B. The father dies near Mortuary B, and the body is taken there.
>
> Mortuary A may say Mr. Mhlophe is not fulfilling its policy and can withhold the claim unless Mr. Mhlophe's body is brought to them. This is because,

in Swaziland at least, competition between mortuaries can be bad. A private mortuary charges a family SZL600 [US$72] per day to keep the body if the family did not go with that mortuary's funeral insurance plan.

Ashford continued on for a few minutes, peppering his increasingly angered narrative with expletives about tactics of charging for unregistered bodies that he and the other mortuaries owners leveled against each other. He recounted how competing mortuaries sometimes called him up and demanded that a body he had in storage be delivered to their facilities so that their policyholder's obligations were fulfilled. The policyholder, of course, was forced to pay up to SZL600 (US$90) for the original mistaken delivery. In some cases, death certainly got folks running "from pillar to post," as Sibusisiwe framed it, in their attempts to pull off a funeral.

Like funeral parlors, burial cooperatives paid claims in both money and funerary goods, such as a coffin and food for a night vigil. Many people participated in several burial cooperatives in addition to subscribing to life insurance, thus maximizing potential accumulation in a person's death. In my research with several burial cooperatives, members and board members were very transparent about this multiple consumption. In a group interview with the organization that oversees one burial cooperative, the leaders were keenly aware that their members most likely had a few policies for their dependents. "People can invest in multiple burial societies and even insurance companies, as well," acknowledged the vice president. "They may invest in others as long as they get the casket from us, and then they can get the services and funds from the other groups afterwards." That same day, after the interview and during her speech to the members at their monthly meeting, she chided them to "support our business we've won here [in the cooperative]" and to not default on their monthly cooperative dues because they owed money on policies elsewhere.

There were fewer such secrets surrounding participation in burial cooperatives, which had to do with their collective form of savings. Instead of singly sending money through an ATM or bank debit to the insurance company's corporate accounts each month, burial cooperatives involved public participation. Usually, a cooperative met on a monthly basis with all members in attendance for the purpose of paying their dues and getting updates on organizational happenings and member deaths. One of the most important material forms of cooperatives was the membership booklet. At several meetings I attended, members carried small booklets with them that listed the member's name and personal details along with those of all dependents and beneficiaries. The booklets worked as publicly surveilled ledgers. Members queued with their money to meet the treasurer to turn in their dues, and they had to have their payments recorded in both their own booklet and the cooperative's official ledger. These subscriptions and payments were more social and transparent activities than insurance, ones that embodied the very names of some cooperatives that denoted forms of mutuality. One group whose members carried small pink booklets with printed crosses was *Zenzeleni*, meaning "Doing things together for one another."

Counterintuitively, the individuated nature of insurance consumption was beneficial for some, given the often highly moralized principles that governed burial cooperatives, but this sometimes played perniciously into HIV/AIDS stigma. Many burial cooperatives were located in or organized through churches, and members shored up Christian principles as a means to legitimate sharing, to advise timeliness, and to remember to make payments. Although many Christian organizations did do immense work on behalf of people living with HIV/AIDS, Robin Root (2009) notes that people living with HIV experienced stigma in some churches. She found that despite the potential liberation one might feel by disclosing to a pastor or pastor's wife, embarrassment in the church might also limit disclosure. Before the epidemic, Sophieke Kappers (1988, 169) noted that some burial cooperatives that operated through Christian churches prohibited women from joining if they drank alcohol or did not attend church. Participation in cooperatives or similarly minded Christian organizations sometimes came at a price that people living with HIV could neither easily nor ethically pay.

People living with HIV could, however, pay for a term life insurance policy and thus avoid cooperatives altogether. Because term life policies did not require a medical test for coverage and did not require perpetual public social commitments of meetings, they could effectively extract themselves from this set of social relations and still be assured that they would receive funds for an eventual dignified burial. This act trafficked in the secrecy of the person's nondisclosure of HIV status and asocial accumulation. In other words, with insurance, you pay money to the company discreetly, in contrast with burial cooperatives where you pay money at meetings in front of other members. Cooperative participation in a sense represented a social risk, where members' perceptions of someone's bodily sores or frailty might manifest in their outright condemnation of that person for being HIV positive. I never heard of a funeral not attended simply because the person had died from HIV/AIDS, yet rumors, whispers, and gossip about one's status and sexual and marital relations were enough to drive a person living with HIV from such potential encounters. The logics of investment could remove people from more intimate and public social networks of savings, and financial services administrators and brokers could help a person accumulate wealth through more confidential forms.

Conclusion: Saving as Care

The siSwati word for transparency is *kubhobhokelana*. In a study of marriage and property by the Women's Law in Southern Africa Research Trust (WLSA 1998), researchers found that transparency and love between Swazi women and their in-laws enabled women to better negotiate access to household resources and farmland. At many Sunday school and Bible study sessions I attended, pastors often encouraged spouses to talk openly with one another about their feelings, a transparency that would engender social intimacy and Christian forms of gender equality. In phone calls; dialogue; family meetings; and more innovative, culturally inflected forms of revelation, lives could be transformed and death prevented.

Robin Root told me once how this happened wonderfully for two spouses and a caregiver in a rural Shiselweni chiefdom. The wife, who was HIV positive, had disclosed to and worked with her caregiver from SHBC. The caregiver offered to mediate the woman's status disclosure to her husband. On a Saturday night, the couple met with the caregiver, who slaughtered a chicken for them to share for dinner. The woman disclosed to her husband over a pleasant, satiating, shared meal, and surprisingly, in turn, the husband disclosed his status and went to a nearby tree to unearth a stock of ARVs he had buried in the ground in hiding. In this case, transparency enabled the disclosure of further disease transmission and possible loving, coordinated efforts to care for their marriage, family, and physical lives.

Broadly, in the context of insurance consumption, one could similarly interpret transparency to be an ethical action of care that had the potential to produce material well-being. By being open about insurance consumption, spouses and families waylaid suspicions of such potentially deadly threats as witchcraft, or at least dampened the hostilities that otherwise characterized in-law relations generally in Swazi Culture. In doing so, this could have averted the more dangerous consequences of what Anita Hardon and Deborah Posel (2012) term the "embodied secrecy" of silence surrounding illness, dying, and familial violence.[11]

Transparency was the antithesis of secrecy's opacity. It enabled the production of future funerals in clearer, more straightforward consumption of policies for oneself and one's dependents. Care in this case took its form in paying toward a certain type of death. Payment was a representation of actionable intention in that one was going to undertake wage labor, save, or consistently mobilize money on another's behalf to ensure that he or she obtained a dignified funeral. Likewise, companies could exercise better transparency in consumer education and cross-business engagements to prevent conundrums of over-insurance and rerouted bodies. If they purported to value people's deaths in the name of dignity, they needed to supply a fuller account of how consumption could possibly affect consumer lives.

Caring through saving and consumption seems to be a staple of the contemporary commercial world, but people in sub-Saharan Africa have been involved in this process in troubling ways. For example, Nora Kenworthy (2017) describes how Gap, Inc., tried to bring the disease to light by selling HIV-branded T-shirts in the North to raise awareness of the disease. However, this effort involved producing the shirts in Lesotho, a kingdom whose citizens, like in Swaziland, many working as low-wage textile manufacturers, faced material dispossession and high HIV prevalence. The case of insurance shows how consumption focused on ameliorating suffering but was partially and positively revalued in cultural terms. Consumption of insurance was innovative in some regards in that its secrets skirted the critical moralized high ground of in-laws or some members of cooperatives. Yet being transparent led to a broader field of mutual recognition, where possibilities for care in the form of future funerals were realized. In the face of death, insurance facilitated the redistribution of life in the form of money, key for the production of funerals. Funerals themselves, their subsequent rites, and what goes into making them are the foci of the following three chapters.

Notes

1. The Registrar was further bureaucratized under the Financial Regulatory Services Authority (FRSA) in 2010. Regulators engaged in licensing, site and desktop monitoring of companies, technical training, and educational outreach for consumers.

2. Historically, this took shape in conscripting Swazi men to migrate to work in South African mines. I thank Mark Auslander for suggesting this early on in my fieldwork. See Parsons and Palmer 1977; Bonner 1983; Crush 1987; and Levin 1997.

3. These often operated on a rotating savings and credit model.

4. Kappers (1988) found that the earliest burial-specific cooperatives began in the 1960s, although similar groups formed in urbanizing areas and towns much earlier than that via migrant labor routes. See Kuper and Kaplan 1944; Ranger 2004; and Lee 2011.

5. As defined by Act No. 3, a cooperative was made "an association of registered people who have voluntarily come together to achieve a common end through the formation of a democratically controlled organization, making equitable contributions of required capital and accepting a fair share of the risks and benefits of the association's undertakings." The legal definition tries to harness the variability of the scale, scope, and everyday practice of cooperatives, as some centered around agricultural production and burial activities while others operated as "Christmas clubs" to save up for a holiday-time payout.

6. This is a type of insurance that a loan company can buy to protect itself in case someone who borrows money from them cannot pay it back.

7. See Bähre (2011, 2012) and chapter 5 on funeral-related food redistribution.

8. Many policies permitted elderly parents to be added as dependents or had separate plans for grandparents or parents-in-law. These add-on plans were much more expensive and classified as high risk because older people were anticipated to have fewer years left to live.

9. See Morris 2008; Oxlund 2014, e77; and Simpson 2014, e97.

10. At more intimate ritual and household levels among East Africa pastoralists, for example, George Paul Meiu (2016) shows how these processes of ethnic and cultural commodification are also thoroughly gendered and sexualized.

11. See also Root 2009, 2014; Hardon and Moyer 2014; Moyer 2015; and Rhine 2016.

4 Grounded: Body Politics of Burial and Cremation

> When the cloth covering the deceased was removed it revealed the remains of the deceased dressed in a brown suit. The suit was oversized because it looked too big for the deceased. She explained that the body of the deceased had shrunk considerably and the waist size of the trousers was now double. The face and hands were exposed. The face had turned pitch black with only holes in the eye sockets. The flesh had dried up into the bones. There was a white dust-like substance on some areas of the face, and the mortuary owner explained that this was in an effort to preserve the portions of the face that were disintegrating. The hands were claw-like, and the flesh thereon had dried completely and was stuck to the bones. It was a sad experience for me as I recalled that he was also made in the image of God and my faith was sorely tested as I beheld the horror of his corpse.

THESE WERE THE words of Judge Qinisile Mabuza reflecting on the most famous dead body in Swaziland's recent history.[1] On July 7, 2007 Mabuza and members of Swaziland's High Court went to the Mbabane Burial Society to inspect the body of Andreas Mzikayise Ntshangase, the late chief of an area called Mkhwakhweni. Duduzile Dlamini, whom other funeral parlor owners told me was the only person in the country qualified in embalming, ran the society. By this time, Ntshangase had been lying in the morgue for nearly five years. He had died in 2002.

Ntshangase's body was at the center of a dispute surrounding land and succession. His lineage traces to an adviser of Zulu King Mpande (1798–1872), and historically, some of its members have been chiefs at Mkhwakhweni in the Dlamini Swazi polity since the 1860s. At the time of his death, Ntshangase was also a member of the elite state Border and Restoration Committee. King Mswati III ordered this committee, along with other high-ranking royalist council, to deliberate on the burial. Despite the members voting thirty-one to six on a burial at Mkhwakhweni, his family's home for at least four generations, the head of the councils, Prince Tfohlongwane, upended this vote when Ntshangase's royal relative Princess Tsase claimed the chiefdom for herself. According to this faction, Mswati allegedly agreed on the matter that Ntshangase would be buried in another area, called Mpuluzi. Ntshangase's wives and several of his sons, with support from Mkhwakhweni's chief's council, filed an injunction to stop the burial.

The shock of the bodily remains was sufferable for Mabuza as an affront to his human dignity because his humanity seemed almost absent in his corpse. This was something unholy and unethical. In this estimation, care for another person in death should go on without obstruction, and the plans holding up the burial were malevolent. Mabuza's colleague Judge J. Mamba wrote in a subsequent ruling related to the case: "No one can teach you that to keep or prevent a corpse from being buried, for five years ... is wicked and evil. To know and or understand this, you need to have a heart, soul and conscience. In short, 'buntfu'—the very essence of being."[2] The shock was of cultural and legal proportions, too: an exaggerated court process crossing Western and Swazi Law and Custom due to the royal faction's "blind and inappropriate use of custom" led to an exaggerated death in Ntshangase's unburied wasting (Princess Tsase and Others 2008, 16). Ultimately ruling against the royalist councils, Mabuza ordered the burial at Mkhwakhweni. For those five years, Ntshangase's widows were secluded to mourn, *kuzila*, their plight exposed in global news coverage of the story.[3]

There were several self-identified state political oppositionist parties at Ntshangase's funeral, which was uninterrupted despite heavy police presence.[4] A grounds crew dumped four wheelbarrows of cement onto the grave to prevent someone from digging it up. Ntshangase was finally grounded. The case was extraordinary but was not unlike burial disputes of political elites in other societies.[5] By virtue of their multigenerational inhabitation of the area, an extensive set of local allegiances from area residents, and their predecessors' burials, the Ntshangases won the right for burial, and royalty was unexpectedly thwarted.[6] The tactics to get Ntshangase in the ground were extreme but were also disturbingly common for many ordinary families as part of Swaziland's changing culture of funerals.

The first part of this book shows how people prepared for death amid HIV/AIDS. This chapter opens the second part to describe what people do when death happens and in its aftermath. It focuses on the human body as a potent and political form to show how families actionably answer cultural questions about where dead bodies should go, where they should be buried, and what should be done to them. The horrors surrounding Ntshangase's corpse and the proliferation of interment disputes across the country show how cultural production in a disease epidemic happens at the end of life and how the value of human bodies is itself up for grabs.

Bodies matter materially as part of funerals—in moving, cleansing, clothing, burying, and identifying with them—and as part of a longer cultural history of death and human substances in Africa.[7] Socially, they secure a sense of belonging for survivors in a time when the volume of bodies going into the ground is alarming.[8] A host of confounding factors, including landlessness, state intervention and development, and changing gender ideologies increasingly disrupt smooth burials. These bear out an agonistic body politics, where revaluations of how to deal with death itself amid material dispossession push bodies to the political foreground. They also help explain popular pushback against the state-driven innovations such as cremation.

The body itself is a useful vantage point for cultural interpretation. To describe the carework involved in moving a body from the site of death to its resting place is to show how, in Deborah Posel and Pamila Gupta's (2009, 308) terms, "the control of corpses is always simultaneously about the social production of life." A human body, they write, is a "material object, on one hand, and a signifier of wider political, economic, cultural, ideological and theological endeavours, on the other". The dead pose a conundrum for the living in the form of their immediate material remains, to which the living must do something that reflects their value. Following David Graeber (2006, 73), value in this sense is not only about how much funerals cost overall or how much a body is worth, although these matters do come up. It is, in his words, "about the production of people," and that value is "always entirely implicated in processes of transformation" in which "families are created, grow and break apart; people are born, mature, reproduce, grow old and die."

An ethnographic focus on the dead body under particular historic conditions sheds light on aspects of funeral culture in Swaziland that are otherwise enigmatic or at first glance disturbing. My focus is not meant to suggest that people in Swaziland are obsessed with death; they work hard to make funerals dignified events. Rather, this focus shows how funerals are also material matters and today challenge tenets that Swazi Culture pays utmost respect for the dead.

Birth to Wholeness: The Incorporation of People in Burial

People become who they are by their own actions, but enduring customary practices surrounding *umsebenti* rites show how the body itself matters as a way for personhood to come into being over the life course. I call this process *incorporation*. In discussing Mende people's kinship in Sierra Leone, Mariane Ferme (2001) describes incorporation as familial negotiations of hierarchy that go into making marriages, a process that echoes local histories of enslavement. In Swaziland, hierarchies are also evident and gendered in the making of patrilines, in which men's families culturally dominate household life. Yet these and broader processes across the life course play out in deliberately corporeal ways. Through material actions in life cycle rites and everyday carework, people effectively become social beings as part of familial or other groups as well as wholesome bodily individuals. Amid HIV/AIDS, as chapter 1 showed, this carework may be staggered or strengthened.

Like funerals, life cycle rites such as coming-of-age and marriage are deemed "ritual" in local English terms, or *umsebenti* in siSwati. They take work to accomplish. For example, in customary childhood rites, children and mothers were secluded and children strengthened by being given beads to wear and burned *mutsi* to inhale. Women bearing children of royalist or traditionalist Dlamini men wore and still wear special wooden necklaces, *ematinta*, during their pregnancy. Nik, being part of a traditionalist Dlamini family, had failed to do this for his daughter's mother, and it became a matter of ongoing dissention as the child grew up. Children are initially presented to their father's people as belonging to the patriline, which Nik did do, or are otherwise incorporated later through payments of cattle, which also values the mother's reproductive work. *Mutsi* application has become more rare, given the rise in antitraditionalist sentiment linked to neo-Pentecostalism, and children are now more often part of the water-based baptismal rites of churches.

Emalobolo bridewealth exchanges and their counterpoint rites of dowry, *umhlambiso*, are materially effective in transforming people from being single to being married. Rites enacting this change include forced weeping, the anointing or smearing of substances such as red ochre and Vaseline, cattle slaughter and the sacrificial use of their blood and organs, dancing or a reserved demeanor during the event, and the consumption of particular foods, such as wedding cake in white weddings and soured milk and eggs in women's rites. Beyond these events, more mundane acts such as feeding, clothing, washing, and sheltering one another form the basis for everyday acts of incorporation. They also evidenced Christian ethics, as discussed in chapter 2. In total, these acts socially, materially, and fully enable one's humanity, *buntfu*, and show a lifetime of relational carework that has gone into doing so. The rest of this chapter focuses specifically on how treatment of the dead body grounds this incorporation and the importance of bodily wholeness for the funeral and afterward.[9]

Purity and Danger in the "Fridge"

When a person dies, the survivors undertake a process that brings to light a cultural value of bodily wholeness, or the body as a complete, integral, incorporated form. Of course, people may die anywhere—Roxanne in a road accident, Banele's child's father in a hospital, some clients of the SHBC group in their homes—and the majority of people who die are quickly ushered to a mortuary. Mortuary in siSwati is *imoshali*, which sounds like the English word "mortuary" but also situates the verb *kumosha* as a location, *kumosha* meaning to diminish, dissipate, or go down; one might say "*imosh' imali,*" meaning "the money is spent." LaGija's sister Buyiswa and a few others I knew liked to jokingly call the mortuary the

Fig. 4.1 Men from a burial cooperative renovate parts for their new morgue, Manzini, 2010. Photograph by author.

"fridge" or vice versa, laughingly telling us to put the supermarket groceries *emoshali* in their kitchen.

The Nazarene Christian missionaries opened the first hospital mortuary in the 1920s (Kuper [1947] 1969). Kuper ([1947] 1980), and Brian Marwick ([1940] 1966) recounted how in the 1930s bodies were kept at home and buried within a few days. The medicalization of death and the expansion of mortuaries led to their largely unquestioned use as the first stopping point for a person after death. From the early 2000s on, however, hospital and municipal mortuaries found themselves at full capacity because of high HIV/AIDS-related death rates and were increasingly unable to house bodies in a seemingly proper way. The deplorable conditions of some mortuaries were subject to intense public outcry.[10] Given the host of preparations needed for funerals and burial, some bodies could spend up to a week in a mortuary. Most families, though, tried to organize the funeral quickly to save money on daily storage rates and prevent the body from potentially coming into the foul conditions reported by local newspapers.

Mortuaries were important places for storage and actions that showed bodily care for the deceased (see fig. 4.1). Bodies were washed and cleaned there, an important task because of the sometimes gruesome conditions of a death. This work was formerly done at the deceased's home and divided to either older men or women according to the gender of the deceased. Today, mortuary staff can wash and prepare the body for a fee, but relatives or members of the deceased's burial cooperative can also use the site to do the washing themselves for free.

After that, the body was clothed in the person's finest attire. An eighteen-year-old man named Mkhonta, who worked as a site caretaker for a burial cooperative's mortuary, told me:

> The *talukati* (oldest women) in our cooperative are the ones who wash the body and hair and dress it nicely in clothes and then put it in the coffin. The family [of the deceased] may choose to do it, or *talukati* can be hired for E250 [US$28]. You have to wash the body because it may come from the hospital.... Let's say you were in an accident and you have a thing [pointing to and rubbing the back of his head]. They don't wash the body at all ... they just bring it here. So the *talukati* will wash the blood and make it clean. That way when we look at the body at the funeral, it is clean.

There is no recorded method of customary or precolonial embalming, and "washing" refers to the external use of water, soap, and perfumes. A good death from natural causes is less complicated in terms of how the body is treated before burial. Like Roxanne, those who died bad deaths from traffic accidents not only required special burial locales but also special handling before burial. Before dinner one evening at Madulini, a visiting husband and wife explained the rites to do if a person died in such a way. Per some clans' customs, an initial purification by slaughtering a goat was needed. The family collected the blood and organs— namely, the gallbladder, *inyongo*, also used in some marital rites, and the undigested food of the stomach, *umswana*—to anoint the deceased and gravesite. A rite called *kulahlabantfu*, literally "to leave people behind," could be done at the site of death, including hospital beds, and involved prayers or a verbal address to the deceased while sweeping the area with sacred leafy branches. Visiting the site of death was also important, as any material bits of the corpse that were left behind had to be picked up and taken away.

Keeping the body whole—that is, pure and in one piece—before burial was a grave social concern. *Butsakatsi* comes to the fore in this regard as a material and subjective reality in reported macabre cases of mysteriously dismembered corpses. Recurring stories appeared in the local newspapers about incidents where bodies were found at crime scenes, mortuaries, and funerals with parts missing, and more horrific stories of "ritual murder," where people were outright killed for their body parts. This phenomenon has been linked to state election cycles in which rivals or those who might vote against a local favorite are killed off (Masimula 2008), but body extraction—body parts going missing—happened throughout the year. While I was staying at Madulini, an eleven-year-old albino girl, Banele Nxumalo, was found decapitated near her home in a neighboring community. Residents and others I spoke with explained the head was taken by evil people likely contracted by an *inyanga* to make *mutsi*. Another story covered an incident in which the funeral of a young woman, Ncobile Vilane, was suspended after her relatives came to pick up her body from the mortuary and found parts of her legs and face missing.[11] While extraction may occur anywhere at any time, mortuaries could also be dangerous places in this regard. Mkhonta described to me how shady characters showed up once at his work asking for bodily bits:

> You see, there is a point before they bury the person, in the morning, where they call the family to come to the coffin. They open the coffin, and everyone will look so that [they] can "see one last time." You have to view the body, otherwise how would you know that you are burying the right person? What would you do if you buried the wrong person? You know, people at the mortuaries here, *bayaganga* (they are criminal)!
>
> Sometimes, *tinyanga* can come to the mortuary and say to the worker that they need the body parts for medicine and will pay the workers to either let them go take parts or have the workers do it. They will even cut off the testicles! When the family comes to get the body, they won't know the testicles are missing! But you know you need to check to see: "Hey, are his ears there? Are his eyes there?" It's best to look.... If one of them came here, I would make him wait and then go hide in the other room and call 999 [the police]!

In this economy of preservation and extraction, bodies held inherent forms of vitality that were not extinguished when the person died and could be redistributed for medicinally generative or destructive purposes. Suggestively, the vitality of bodies worked and was associated with *mutsi* because the bodies were similarly composed of natural and organic materials.[12] Mkhonta's was not an isolated explanation of this phenomenon. Other funeral parlor managers and employees described to me similar alleged cases of body part extraction or the sale of mortuary service ephemera such as tools and water, which, by proxy to the deceased body, were said to hold vital properties. A year after I spoke with Mkhonta, some newspaper reporters went undercover to seek out this *materia medica* and visited several mortuaries, including his. Allegedly, they got a male attendant there to sell the water used to wash corpses, but he first refused the request because their offered price was too low.[13] The story caused a national scandal. Police investigated the mortuary and several others throughout 2013, in response to which mortuary managers, hospital administrators, and the principal secretary for the Ministry of Health denied that such sales occurred, one denouncing the acts as "terrible and unSwazi."[14]

Funeral parlors, insurance companies, and burial cooperatives interconnected with one another as service providers dealing with bodies. Together, the three types of organizations worked somewhat imperfectly because of stipulations about body transportation and storage, of which consumers and their families were only sometimes aware. Funeral parlors and their owners had stakes in bodies as forms of financial value, and most spoke about this work as necessary and lucrative yet also under threat as part of a shrinking market resulting from competition. Over cool glasses of water, Walter, who owned a small funeral parlor in the Lubombo district, told me about the "corruption" that occurred among these service providers, pointing to the financial value of bodies, which mortuaries fought for along legal-contractual lines:

> God is great and steers you in the right direction, but this can be a bad business. You know what it is though, in the hospitals, there are nurses, orderlies, administration, and mortuary attendants who are making deals with private mortuaries. They are in the hospital, and then when someone dies, they tell the family members, "Hey, you should go over here to this place, I know they can get you a good deal." There is some corruption down here, but there is a lot in Mbabane and Manzini. I was doing a lot to show it. I called up [a former minister] because I know him and he is from around here. I called up the newspapers too, and was telling them to look into all of this stuff. [The former minister] said he would look into it, but then I didn't hear back from him for a while. I was spinning my wheels.

Turning from the point of view of administrators to that of the families, anthropologist Sjaak van der Geest (2006) describes how families exploit liminality by using mortuaries in Ghana. This means they draw out the time of the body's storage there in order to prepare for and aggrandize the eventual funeral, thereby suspending the corpse in an in-between state of death and burial. Most families in Swaziland wanted a quick in-and-out when using mortuaries, but increasingly, many bodies also faced a different kind of liminality there because of overcrowding and social abandonment. Several newspaper stories pointed out the problem of unclaimed bodies in hospital and municipal mortuaries, some of which lie in state for up to several years and compel asking existential and cultural questions. "What happened to the Swazi culture of having respect for the dead?" one town councilor asked in this respect, and "Is it really possible that Swazi moral fiber has degenerated to the extent a person would allow their relative to lie idle in the mortuary for years without being buried?"[15]

Outside of families and hospitals, neighbors, landlords, or strangers who come across a dead body first call the police, who then bring it to a hospital mortuary. Members of the Manzini City Council (2014) recently explained that the rise in abandoned bodies, especially in urban areas, derived from suburban cohabitation practices: unmarried couples lived in rented flats but did not get to know each other's extended families, possibly because their relationships were extramarital. When one partner died, the other left without a trace, fearing the family's accusations of infidelity or *butsakatsi*. Other abandoned bodies were identified as migrants, and making contact with next-of-kin was difficult. Without someone to deliberate on disposal, both the mortuary and the body itself were stuck *in limen*. Despite their abandonment, however, these dead without a home were mourned in public forums such as Facebook and the newspaper websites that reported on the matter.[16]

Going Home

Most people spoke about the dead "going home," multiply referencing Heaven, a comforting afterlife, the funeral, and the burial site. Per Swazi Culture, burial was customarily at one's natal home, and for a married woman, at the home of her husband's people. Getting the body from the mortuary to the funeral entailed payment and sometimes purification rites as part of the transaction. If not using the mortuary's vehicles as part of burial cooperative benefits or an insurance policy, a person driving the body could be paid in cash, perhaps for fuel and to clean the vehicle if necessary. Drivers could also employ *tinyanga* or Christian healers to use medicinal substances to expel *sinyama*. Some told me that in the past a slaughtered beast was used for the same effect. Even though Swaziland takes only about four hours to traverse by car, transportation was costly in terms of gasoline, driving time, and mobile phone time used to call for directions. Bodies were trundled back a few hours before the first part of the funeral, the night vigil, or if there was no vigil, the day of the burial itself.

In siSwati, a night vigil is called *umlindzelo*, from the verb *kulindzela*, meaning to watch over, keep guard, or wait for someone or something. Night vigils usually started on Saturday evenings and ran through the night, with burial taking place around sunrise. Many family members arrived in the afternoon to start preparations, and as the sun set, more and more attendees arrived by bus, car, or foot. Usually, a large tent and many chairs were rented and set up adjacent to one of the main houses to accommodate up to hundreds of people. The majority sat in the tent, listening to pastoral emcees and various speakers give sermons. Collectively, attendees were encouraged to sing or give their own testimonies too, which helped keep the whole event going. The principal mourners, usually the mothers, aunts, sisters, and wives of the deceased, sat with the body in a nearby room, accompanying the beloved and assuring that nothing went missing.

Throughout the night vigil, the body stayed secluded with the principal mourners yet was the topic of many of the speeches by emcees and others. Contemporary neo-Pentecostal eschatology suggested that the soul or spirit left the body, ideally coming into the full presence of God by going "home" to Heaven. In customary iterations, the spirit dwelled near the homestead to eventually be summoned to reside among other ancestral shades. Most sermons instructed attendees to live collectively and respectably among others—showing the "work" to realize their faith—instead of focusing on the biography of the deceased person specifically. Some pastors elaborated on Bible lore and verses that dealt with the body and death. These tended to emphasize processes of bodily decay and the body's inferior relation to soul, spirit, and other transcendent phenomena.

Many of the speeches I heard compelled people to forget the body as a dirty, foul thing or as the husk of the former person. The first example here comes from Mr. Sibiya's funeral, at which the preacher cited 1 Corinthians 15, and the second came from a sermon at a funeral for a Lukhele woman:

> When the body is buried, it is mortal. When it is raised, it will be immortal. When buried, it is ugly and weak. When raised, it will be beautiful and strong. There is of course a physical body, so there has to be a spiritual body.

> Even though you can't see where the grave is [when you will eventually die], I know that my Savior is here. But what will He do? He lives. I will see with new eyes, not anyone else's eyes, but my eyes alone. In other words, Job is telling us that when the Lord represents us, He gives us a fresh body; He gives us another life.

These statements were not meant to be disrespectful. Despite the theological stipulations and characterizations of a dead body's uselessness or dirtiness, the body was carefully scrutinized. People tenderly, visually interacted with it throughout the funeral. If flies, leaves, or other errant things floated into the mourning room, the bereaved removed them. Bereaved women described to me how important it was to visually witness the body in order to materialize the person as an enduring memory (Golomski 2015c). The vigil was the last chance to behold the corpse itself, and muted comments were made about how nice the dead looked when dressed nicely and adorned with flowers.

Usually there was a ceremonial viewing of the body in the casket before it was closed. Typically, near the end of the vigil around three or four in the morning, the emcee offered attendees the chance to make condolences in this way. The viewing was noisy and dramatic, as many women openly wept in their short condolences or bent down briefly to cry face-to-face with the sitting mourners. The viewing took several minutes and ended with some of the mourners tidying the casket linens or the deceased's clothes before shutting the lid. The principal mourners also put items of clothing belonging to the deceased into the casket itself, a symbolic act of clothing the person again.

Sometimes, in order to warm them up and shake off drowsiness, the emcee had attendees get up from their seats and dance around the tent for a few minutes. The musicians helped by playing a bit more animated rhythms on a keyboard or drum set. Most attendees took the chance to jump around for a bit, stretch, and make happier expressions after sitting dour and still in their chairs for several hours. At a few funerals I went to, these reprieves included a joyful dance line that moved around the tent and into the room where the body lay.

At night vigils, reference to the biography of the deceased and his or her particular body was more muted. Talk about the person's individual life came to the fore at the burial ceremony, *umngcwabo*, which began around sunrise. These ceremonies included the production and distribution of photocopied, folded paper programs that featured a picture of the deceased, dates of birth and death, a short description of his or her life, and an outline of the ceremonial proceedings. The proceedings revolved around designated groups and people making final, memory-laden, loving statements about the deceased. The proceedings clearly established the attendees' relatedness to the person, and by proxy, social obligations to surviving individuals across families. It was standard that representatives for the families of one's mother and father, spouse or spouses, church, and one's place of employment would make condolences, with an emcee calling forth and thanking each speaker for their words. Prayers, song, and politeness in permitting people to speak, even if out of turn, all qualified the event as dignified and helped ease people's sentiments as the event moved toward the actual burial, where some people would become more emotional.[17]

Following the speeches, pallbearers would move the body from the tent and proceed to the gravesite. While en route, the body might be taken to significant sites within the homestead. For example, at the burial in Madulini for Mr. Mseleku, a local liaison of a foreign-development NGO, his male relatives carried the casket to the rear of the tent and then up two steps to the door of his former bedroom, with one pastor saying, "Here is your bedroom, your home!" "Showing" the deceased his or her room was a symbolic farewell, a common rite regionally; it had long been customary to show or carry the body around the home or to the cattle pen.[18]

The cattle pen, *sibaya* or *kraal*, formerly served as the gravesite for senior and mostly male members of a family. Customary rules relating to gender and rank were implicated in the decision to bury someone there. In the past, ancestors were verbally invoked at the majority of life cycle rites to watch over the living, ensure the transformative passage of each person, and receive animal sacrifices. Like ancestors, these animals resided in or near the pens and were material reminders of extensive interfamilial and intergenerational exchanges. They remained culturally significant as a form of ritual value.[19] Yet the overtly Christian character of contemporary funeral culture led many attendees to deride ancestors or cut them out of the ceremonial proceedings. Except for the very oldest people, who lived long lives according to customary or Swazi Culture principles, bodies were no longer buried in pens and not often shown these sites. Indeed, at another funeral I attended in Madulini, the uncle of the deceased ran out in front of the burial procession, waving his arms to try to reroute the crowd toward the cattle pen before it made its way to the gravesite. The procession, led by several pastors from the deceased's mainline Christian church, steered the pallbearers and the casket away from the uncle. The crowd followed, leaving him in front of the pen shaking his head to the backs of the attendees.

The actual burial at the gravesite entailed more speeches, and the event reached its dramatic, emotional pinnacle as the body was put into the earth.

Fig. 4.2 Morning burial procession at a funeral, Siphofaneni, 2010. Photograph by author.

Again, singing helped facilitate continuity during and between rites and focused people's grief in a collective production of comforting each other and the bereaved. Mortuary employees or cooperative members prepared the gravesite with a small tent and a few chairs adjacent to the grave for the principal mourners and lined the grave with runners of faux grass along with the mechanical device used to lower the casket into the hole. The pallbearers approached the grave with the casket, as did women carrying a load of goods representing the deceased's personal items (see fig. 4.2). These items usually included several blankets or clothes and grass mats, evidence of the person's material incorporation through life cycle ritual exchanges with others over a lifetime.

Interment was completed in several layers. Uniformly cut logs were sometimes placed in the grave first, followed by a grass mat that someone had cut down the middle with a machete. The casket was then lowered into the grave, and the load of goods carried by the women was placed on top. After small condolence cards were read aloud, both they and their accompanying bouquets of flowers were tossed inside the grave instead of decorating the site itself. The emcee then invited the attendees to approach the grave to toss in a handful of dirt, an act that usually incited loud wailing from several women who approached the grave to do so but were unable to complete the task and were carried away in grief. The programs were also collected and tossed in the grave at this time.

As with many Christian church worship services and healing ceremonies, funerals involved the collection of money. Plates, hats, and other impromptu vessels got circulated for attendees to put in monetary offerings for the family. Before the attending men filled the grave, a representative for the area's chiefly council (*libandlancane*) made a final statement of condolence to the families, which also effectively reaffirmed the council's decision to allow the body to be buried in that place. Because the burial attracted more attendees than the night vigil, this public declaration was heard by up to several hundred people and grounded the deceased by the means of local political authorities.

In the end, then, the dead went home, went from this world, or into the earth, *kuhamba emhlabeni*, interred with their possessions and hopefully in a memorable, dignified way. Their position was an "earthly anchorage" of home, to use Parker Shipton's (2009) term, a material referent for the living to trace their relatedness to the deceased and their belonging to a wider social group living in the area. Keeping the body clean, purified, clothed, and all together in one piece from the point of death to placement in the ground replicated the sensual, material carework a person received over his or her lifetime. The funeral was a near end point in this process of social and bodily incorporation. In this way, the event was compassionate, relational, and dignified: the living had done their funerary duties. Burial might seem to be the last say in death, but in a time of material dispossession, bodies continued to animate sociopolitical life long after the funeral.

The Gender of Body Politics: Corpse Custody Disputes

In death, the body as a wholesome accretion of incorporative practices became a vital means by which the living could improve their lots. If people were able to possess a body and bury it on their own terms, they were often able to lay more solid future claims to the place in which the body was buried. With burial of the dead came potential rights for the living to belong there, both residentially and economically in terms of using the land for farming, cattle grazing, or further development. Possessing a body was crucial for access to resources linked to the deceased's financial assets, such as wills, pensions, and bank accounts. This is not to say that people crudely economized bodies of the deceased to get what they needed to get by. There were also deeply social and emotional sentiments in play about who would best dignify the person in his or her burial and who belonged to whom, given the work put in to incorporate the person over a lifetime. Responses to these questions were reconfigured along changing lines of gendered autonomy and inequality. Given the context of material dispossession generally, both ordinary and elite families such as the Ntshangases went to extreme lengths to get control of dead bodies.

Contemporary burials took place either in the countryside, where interment occurred in or around a family's homestead on Swazi Nation Land,[20] or in a community or municipal cemetery in town. Enduring stipulations of

Swazi Culture gave preference to patrilocal residence for a countryside burial location, although these kinship forms have been historically flexible and are so today with regard to gender.[21] Most people would acknowledge that a man, his wife or wives, and their children should be buried at the man's home or that of his parents, according to this traditionalist principle. Because of shifting claims of land tenure, suburbanization, and people's increased mobility in and out of an area, some chiefdoms have established community cemeteries, where anyone who had lived in the area may be buried regardless of lineal relations.

Burial outside of a family-specific yard in some ways interrupted relatives' ability to claim belonging to that property and subsequently to farm or build a dwelling structure there. Also, major development projects, such as fruit, sugar, and biofuel plantations and the new King Mswati III International Airport near Sikhuphe, played into crowding out small-scale land tenure in the countryside, sometimes in the form of forced evictions and mass exhumations.[22] Other times, as in the Ntshangase case, it was the royalist state's direct predation in newly placing its own princes to rule an area and upend existing occupants. Municipal cemeteries also evacuated potential claims by the living for residential belonging, as historically, cemeteries in towns were made up of non-related individuals and were colonially segregated by race.[23] Recently, the Manzini City Council encouraged residents to bury the deceased at their countryside homes because of municipal landlessness and because their cemeteries were reaching maximum capacity, leaving citizens in a bind about burial across the urban-rural divide.

The racial dispossession of land in Southern Africa is a historical fact.[24] Deborah James (2007, 22) notes that contemporary legal claims for the return of land in South Africa increasingly cite ancestral or family burials at particular plots and other "iconic tropes of localised cultural experience" as justification for land restitution. James traces this partly to a South African ANC (African National Congress) government's traditionalist discourse, which supported black citizens' aspirations for land and helped to evidence their "informal rights" to reoccupy it. Across the border in Swaziland, however, disputes about burial locale actually *subverted* aspects of state-centric, gendered discourses of Swazi Culture that would determine where people belonged, both living and dead. Ordinary families involved in corpse custody and burial locale disputes were indeed concerned with landlessness and how a body might solidify their claims to belong somewhere. The case of Ntshangase makes this clear, as the courts ruled against the state in burying the late chief firmly in his ancestral home. Yet these cases also played out with regard to gender; along shifting legal lines of patrilocal obligations stipulated by Swazi Culture; and through alternatives read through the 2005 Constitution.

In the majority of cases I documented, burial location disputes had to do with marriage and people's economic inabilities to authenticate a marriage according to Swazi Culture. In this rendering, marriage was considered legitimate when it was produced through a series of gift exchanges and in everyday acts of material care between husband and wife. Men were often unable or unwilling to do so, as seen especially in their failure to pay bridewealth.[25] In turn, some women and their families felt enabled to run around the stipulations of patrilocal burial at their husbands' homes. In this way, as men's ability to fulfill obligations of marital incorporation were rendered tenuous or absent altogether—due to illness or precarious economies—women and their families shored up gendered forms of postmortem autonomy.

This story of changing ideations of gender also had a lot do with constitutional law, as the government unfurled a national Constitution in 2005 that proffered vague language about women's economic and social equality. Many women and their families turned to the Constitution to seek recourse beyond the patriarchal bias of "Swazi Law and Custom," although the courts and lawyers struggle to determine how this dual legal system can operate smoothly. According to civic legislation during this time, a woman's family could shortcut her husband's claim to her estate if, at the time of the woman's death, the husband had undertaken the first rites of marriage in Swazi Culture called *kuteka* but had not yet paid bridewealth. In turn, her family would be entitled to receive her estate if other plans were not already deliberated in a will. As Swazi lawyer Maxine LaNgwenya (2012) writes, "This clash between legal rights and actual laws means that women continue to be discriminated against in Swaziland in ways that are fundamentally unjust and constitute an offence against human dignity." Carrying this idea into the dynamics of funeral culture, when husbands could not provide for nor dignify wives in life, wives need not be buried near their husbands in death. Wives and their families then went beyond Swazi Culture to make sure they were buried on their own terms.

Cases where this runaround took place were dramatic.[26] As with Ntshangase, they played out in macabre liminality. In one case, Nansi, one of my interlocutors from a neo-Pentecostal-style church I attended over several months, explained how corpse custody disputes unfolded both in sociological terms and through her own extended family's experience. According to Nansi, disputes generally came about when a "married" woman died and her husband, as per tenets of Swazi Law and Custom, laid claim to her estate. After citing the Constitution as broadly changing the socio-legal game of marriage, Nansi recounted her family's experience of corpse custody, which spoke to in-laws, failures to accomplish certain *umsebenti* rites, and wealth possession. She described the situation as emotionally difficult and socially "ridiculous," and like others, her family's story made its way into the newspapers and tacked between civil law and Swazi Law and Custom in multiple courts.

Nansi explained that her husband's mother's co-wife's daughter Nontsiky "came from little and had little." Nontsiky was living with and in love with a certain man for a long time. Formal plans for marriage, either civic or *kuteka*, never came up. The man died, and his family requested that she be betrothed to him in the *kuteka* rite postmortem—initiating an effective "ghost marriage"—and wear the mourning gowns like a widow. Nontsiky moved to the in-laws' homestead and undertook the ritual mourning for nearly two years. However, after that time, the husband's family had not arranged for the rite of *kugeza emanti* to take place, which would have effectively brought her out from mourning, thus cleansing her and the family from the death. According to Nansi and others I spoke with, the husband's family should have taken responsibility for coordinating the rite.

Nontsiky's family furiously extracted her from the husband's family's home and themselves organized the ceremonious removal of the mourning gowns. Nontsiky continued to maintain cordial relations with her in-laws, and she sometimes resided at their house. A few months after being brought back from mourning, however, she succumbed to an undisclosed illness and died. As she was supposedly incorporated into her husband's lineage by the *kuteka* rite, the husband's family brought Nontsiky's body to a commercial mortuary. After two weeks, however, the husband's family had not organized her funeral nor paid the storage fees. Nansi surmised that Nontsiky's body was abandoned because the husband's family saw they were not likely to receive anything substantial in terms of her personal estate. Nontsiky's own family eventually paid the mortuary and had the body released. She was buried at her own family's homestead, despite the Swazi Cultural convention that a woman betrothed by *kuteka* rites should be buried patrilocally.

A second case I documented and that Nokwenza had told me about took place at Madulini. The main actors were the husband, Mveli Mnisi, and his two wives, LaShongwe and LaGcina. LaGcina was originally from a community near Madulini. Mr. Mnisi often worked in town in Manzini, and there he met LaGcina, who was going about her own projects. Mr. Mnisi and LaGcina married in *kuteka* rites and had four children. He built a house for LaGcina near Manzini, where she stayed and worked at a small market stand. Back in Madulini, Mr. Mnisi met LaShongwe, a member of an established area mainline mission church, and they married in civic rites. The two had a daughter and son, and they lived patrilocally at Mr. Mnisi's parental home.

When Mr. Mnisi's parents both died, the property deferred to him while LaShongwe was living there with her children. The parents' original house on the property, a round-style house, fell into disuse. LaShongwe had an addition to the main house erected for herself and her children, and they used the rondavel as a chicken coop. Eventually, as a stick-and-mud house does without upkeep, it collapsed. "The house was killed by them [in their arguments]," a neighborhood housewife explained to me. "There was only a barren floor left of the house where his parents had lived." It was evident to the housewife and others in the community that LaShongwe's incorporation into the Mnisi family was also transforming the family socially and materially.

LaGcina died in 2009 from an undisclosed illness. When she died, LaShongwe thought Mr. Mnisi might try to bury LaGcina in the Mnisi family graveyard in Madulini and conduct the funeral in the house that she had erected with him. LaShongwe, along with her daughters, hired a lawyer and went to the High Court in Mbabane. Through this move, LaShongwe wanted to prevent LaGcina's body from receiving a burial that would enable property rights to LaGcina's children and be a constant reminder of her husband's other marital relationship. Mr. Mnisi's patrilineal relatives wanted to have the funeral service and erect a tent for the attendees near the site of his parents' former house and did not want the proceedings to occur at LaShongwe's house. They were supportive, however, of burying LaGcina in the family cemetery in the community, which would also bring LaGcina's children closer to Madulini and likely engender claims for their residential belonging.

Mr. Mnisi went to the chief's council—which incidentally included several of his patrilineal relatives—and was advised by the council to get his own lawyer, as LaShongwe had. Mr. Mnisi's relative worked for the magistrate and alerted him to get witnesses to testify about the *kuteka* to LaGcina and to also show his marriage certificate to LaShongwe, both of which were needed for the court appearance. "Make sure to be on time for your case," the relative said, "or even come early, or you might not have the opportunity to make your point." The housewife telling me the story laughed, recounting a joke that on the day of the hearing at the high court, Mr. Mnisi and LaShongwe had slept in the same bed, used the same blanket, woke up in their house together, boarded a bus and made the hour-plus trip and series of transfers together, only to arrive in court and argue with each other.

Like the Ntshangase case, the court proceedings for Mr. Mnisi and his wives resulted in an inspection *in loco* by a judge. Everyone in the community was highly intrigued when they heard about the judge coming to inspect the homestead to decide on the burial spot. "I remember the day the judge came," Nokwenza recalled: "Everyone wanted to see what would happen, and the whole community turned out. LaShongwe was there with her daughters, and when the judge arrived to greet her and inspect the property, LaShongwe cried out loud, 'I am all by myself! I am Shongwe and they are all Mnisi! I am all by myself!' As if they were all there to kill her, and as if anyone would miss this at all, because most people here are of the Mnisi clan and concerned because Mr. Mnisi is family to them." In the end, the judge decided that they could have the burial service in the yard, but they would have to erect the tent five hundred meters away from LaShongwe's house. Mr. Mnisi's patrilineal relatives decided to not hold the funeral in his parents' yard and to not bury LaGcina in their main family cemetery. Nearby was another Mnisi homestead where the co-wife of Mnisi's mother had lived. This homestead had its own small family cemetery, and LaGcina was buried there. "LaShongwe and her daughters did not even go to the funeral. They stayed away," said Nokwenza. After the funeral, the chiefly council called many of the Mnisi men together with Mveli Mnisi. They scolded Mr. Mnisi, saying that he must "tie the knot," *kubopha lifindvo*, meaning reconcile the situation. To strengthen what had been accomplished in the funeral and to allay future claims to his descendants' love, land, and livelihood, Mr. Mnisi built a house for the late LaGcina on the property where her funeral was held and where she was buried. Today, LaGcina's youngest child lives in the house with her own children. "I think LaShongwe was jealous," Nokwenza concluded:

> She was concerned about LaGcina's children getting their rights and support over her own children later on. LaShongwe did not want LaGcina to come to the area, because if she was buried in the Mnisi cemetery with the funeral held in Mr. Mnisi's yard and in LaShongwe's house, LaGcina's children might one day come after, say, LaShongwe dies, and try and inherit that house. They are also children of her husband, but by another wife. LaShongwe wanted to give the house to her children only. Really, if it were me, it wouldn't matter. If I were sharing my man and the other woman died, it would be fine. I wouldn't worry about that one because she is dead. I would be happy to have the man all to myself now!

In both cases, the Mnisis and Nontsiky, the dimensions of what authenticates a marriage by Swazi Culture were called into question in the wake of a death. The funerary milieu now being a site of cultural revaluation, the issue of patrilocal burial unfolded in claims about material provisioning and whether or not what had been done by the husband and his family would fully constitute the dead woman's incorporation. In trying to prevent the burial, LaShongwe sought to secure a future for her children outside of Swazi Culture through civil law, arguably preventing her from being cut to an inferior position as the second wife to LaGcina. The patrilineal relatives, going through Swazi Law and Custom, aimed to uphold the obligations associated with Mr. Mnisi's customary marriage to LaGcina and thereby secure potential livelihood for her children. For Nontsiky, her continued patrilineal incorporation even beyond her husband's death in the Swazi Cultural stipulations of ghost marriage and mourning were not enough to foreclose the avarice of her in-laws that rode alongside these stipulations.

Susan Reynolds Whyte (2005, 156) found a similar dynamic of contested burials in Uganda. As in Swaziland, her East African case of burial dispute points to ways in which people were made to belong to or become part of particular homes.

Disputes split along gendered lines, where men invoked customary principles to determine interment while women invoked arguments of sympathy and experiences of care. She suggests that together these gendered forms tell "stories about sickness and death" and the ways "social actors place themselves into relations with past, present and possible future with other people."

In Swaziland too the recent interrelated histories of mass death, constitutional law, and gender enable people to tell such stories practically in the wake of funerals. They could place themselves in advantageous positions, both prospectively—for the living in future belonging—and immediately, for the dead in placement in the ground. The story of relatedness had to do with lifelong experiences of care, the absence of which became justification for some women and their families to avoid patrilocal burial. As more and more people were placed in the ground because of HIV/AIDS, a body politics played out over the value of Swazi Culture and what a death beyond burial could mean for the living.

From Wholeness to Ashes: Cremation

In 1952, the former colonial Inspector of Education Henry Dumbrell wrote that several older Swazi men told him that cremation, or "pyre burning," was not at all common then. The men explained that only two families, the Maseko and Simelane clans, had done so. They were part of *emakhandzambili*, groups of people who were culturally and politically incorporated when the Dlaminis migrated there and encountered them between 1815 and 1830. In King Sobhuza I's attempts to consolidate royalist Swazi Culture at that time, cremation died out, although the former sites of these pyres, made of *isihlangu* trees (*Maytenus heterophylla*), were pointed out to Dumbrell on the banks of the Buhlungu River, into which people's ashes had been tossed.

A little shy of two hundred years later, cremation has returned to Swaziland as part of contemporary funeral culture and is an enigmatic topic of discussion. Aside from what turns out to be a comparably pricey endeavor to burial, cremation is locally strange because it arguably confounds the materiality bound up with personhood and burial precisely because there is no body to deal with after death. The politics of burning bodies turns out to be equally contentious, as local business leaders and municipal boards have promoted cremation as a way to deal with problems of landlessness.

Up until the turn of the millennium, if families wanted cremation, they had to contract with a local funeral parlor to secure necessary permits to transport the body across the border to have the procedure done in South Africa, then bring the cremains back into the kingdom. One funeral parlor manager named Mlandvo explained that he and his colleagues "have been doing [cremation] all along, except we take the body to New Castle in South Africa. It is not so expensive. We only charge E1000 (US$145). Of course, there is also a charge for the transport.

You have to buy the coffin with us, but we don't charge you to use the mortuary. The customers pay me, and I pay the crematorium in South Africa. We were doing that for years." Mlandvo and several other managers working in the industry, some for more than a decade, told me that interest in cremation has always been negligible and that "Asians"—referring to people of South Asian, East Asian, and Middle Eastern origin—were usually their primary customers for this service.

Dups, Swaziland's largest and oldest private funeral parlor, expanded their operations into this area by opening the country's first crematorium in 2007, undertaking lengthy environmental and social impact assessments prior to construction. Dups was aware of the potential "shock of the new," and in conjunction with their grand opening, printed a full advertorial section in the *Times of Swaziland* to frame the value of cremation for a public unfamiliar with the procedure. Titled "Crematorium: Making Plans for Today, the Future and Beyond: Modern Cremation Process," the advertorial offered some initial insight into the procedure and, of course, its advantages as an alternative to burial:

> Cremation is just one service that Dups provides and just like when cellphones arrived, they were a phenomenon, but 10 years down the line, they are the best innovations of technology. "At Dups, we believe in ingenuity and venturing into new territory. The cremation concept may be new but [with] the right amount of education and the willingness to try new things, it will be an option for many," said [owner Philip] DeSousa. The cremator used by Dups has to be one of the most modern and of highest quality....
>
> Ashes may be disposed of in any-way. For instance, over a mountain-top or over an ocean or river. The most interesting thing about cremation is the amount of space that is saved. Can you believe that 36 urns can be placed in one casket grave site? "That could be a whole generation!" said DeSousa. This ... is easier because it also makes relocation easier because no family rituals will have to be conducted in order to exhume the body. Family members may also be buried in urns or placed on a wall of remembrance. As time goes by, Dups is planning to buy land where this may be done.... Crematoriums will allow relatives to view the charging [of the body into the cremator] and ... this is done for religious reasons, e.g., Hindus. (Mabusela 2007)

The article cited wide-ranging advantages of cremation, aimed to encompass issues of commemoration, cultural newness, and interestingly, issues of size and space. In this last respect, the article invoked a hypothetical surprise about how the totality of a family's cremains could occupy so little space. It also hinted that exhumation of a body might be a concern, one that might not be so far off, given the rise of corpse custody disputes generally. In the latter point especially, the article suggested that the placement of bodies might be less permanent than expected and that cremation can cut out the problem of where and how a body gets placed.

Tacking back and forth between issues of space and commemoration, families were shown that they might not even need to have a funeral in their own homes if they chose to use the company chapel and memorial service rooms as part of the onsite cremation process. The cremains would also be taken out of families' hands and locales, as the company proposed using a future memorial park. While claiming to do away with some elements of funerals, the article simultaneously introduced a host of novel rituals that ironically implicated spaces of a different expanse, in the memorial park, mountain precipices, or ocean waters—which are not found in Swaziland, as the country is landlocked. Dups was on foreign ground here. The encouraging leading lines invited readers to consider how even though cremation was something familiar to peoples other than Swazi, it could still accommodate Swazi Culture and people's families.

Beyond the advertorial, cremation had some initial popular exposure when the crematorium first opened. The mayor of Manzini was cited as saying that the crematorium came at a crucial time when the municipality was facing a land shortage (Mabusela 2007). Likewise, a number of celebrities who passed away following its opening were cremated—with some notoriety. For example, after Miss Swaziland 2008, Tiffany Simelane, took her own life after a series of scandals and personal misfortunes, her family stated that she underwent cremation according to her own wishes (Ngubane 2009). Echoing Dumbrell (1952), the family said that as members of the Simelane clan, they had previously burned their dead, although several Simelanes I met told me they had not heard of doing such a thing in their immediate families.

Cremation was also emphasized in the 2011 death of beloved radio broadcaster Doris Sikhutsali. I remember that, while sitting on the couch with Nokwenza one afternoon in Madulini, an unfamiliar voice opened Doris's regular show by announcing her death. Nokwenza gasped. Several days later, a story appeared in the *Times of Swaziland* detailing Doris's wish for cremation. Despite a general consensus that it was a good thing that her wish was fulfilled, many of her media colleagues, including "gospel artists ... said it was unfortunate that there was no funeral vigil because they had planned to sing in honour of Doris" (M. Nkambule 2011). For them, cremation circumvented the production of a conventional funeral, where many would have been able to vaingloriously sing on her behalf. The cremation procedure cost E6300 (US$476), and Doris's cremation inspired her sisters to state they would likewise be cremated when their time came.

Going beyond media examples, most people I spoke to had a sense of either ambiguity or aversion for cremation, giving theological and cultural reasons. The reasons largely hinged on material concerns and issues of land. Culturally, they took shape in claims that cremation was just not part of Swazi Culture, namely that it had not been done before, at least not since the reign of Sobhuza I (c. 1815–1836). The newness of the procedure was clear for Dups, in both their advertisements and in casual conversation with their employees. In 2014, I visited a branch office in the Manzini district. While usually busy, the place was empty then except for a young man at a customer service cubicle with a desktop computer, the background featuring images of the Egyptian pyramids. When I asked him about cremation, he said, "Swazis don't tend to do cremation because of this culture thing." "What does culture mean?" I asked. "Well," he replied, "they would rather take the body and put it in the ground. Things are changing, but they are going slowly." He then elaborated on cremation's advantages by playing up the minimal space it involved in terms of not needing a burial plot and in the transformed size of the body. He explained encouragingly, "We provide you with a box for the ashes. You can walk out with the box even under your arm. It is small and convenient. You don't need to worry about people knowing you're carrying around a body, because no one even notices. You don't need to a buy a coffin to use when the body is burned, and there is a contraption that the body goes inside to burn. You can, however, rent a coffin or casket from us if you want to take the ashes somewhere and do a ceremony."

He confirmed with a colleague by telephone that the procedure cost E8142 (US$764), a price that included these accoutrements and use of the chapel at the company headquarters for two hours—"You can even bring your own pastor and have a service there!" As I left, he thanked me and dropped a last suggestion that if I chose cremation for myself, I might think about tacking on an insurance policy that would pay toward the event and include E10000 (US$937) in additional coverage. To the employee, the cremation was culturally unSwazi because of what was done to the body, even if the technological improvement of diminishing its size would alleviate practical burdens. Another person I spoke with, a female masters student studying economics at UNISWA, surmised that because the cremation was largely beyond Swazi Culture, those who elected to burn bodies were themselves either non-Swazi—such as the "Asians" mentioned by the funeral parlor managers—or were perhaps beyond the normal stock of the majority of citizens.

The student thought that although Tiffany Simelane and Doris Sikhutsali were Swazi, they were both particularly famous and did not do what ordinary Swazi did for a living. Their well-salaried careers heightened their ability to pay for this process. Also, the only other person this student knew who had undergone cremation was the wife of her foreign-born former Bible college instructor. Sadly, like Tiffany, the wife of the instructor had taken her own life. The student explained that the wife "chose cremation ... because she felt like her life had nothing in it. She wanted to [be cremated] ... because, how do I say, you see, it's like her life was hell already." In the student's reasoning, a tragic life and death by suicide portended the choice of cremation, which, as a form of death, was outside the domain of Swazi Culture.[27]

The masters student's invocation of Hell points also to the pervasive theological reasons people gave in their aversion for cremation. With the majority of people nominally self-identifying as Christian, biblical scripture is often cited as ethical, mythic-historical, or cultural justification for the way things are done or in explanations for existential questions such as those dealing with death. A shop clerk at a store selling school uniforms in Manzini once gave me her "personal views" of cremation:

> I wouldn't want to do it myself. The smell of a burning body would be absolutely awful. It's just the smell that would be too much, I think. I am a Christian, and we don't believe in such things, I think. How are we able to rise again as the Bible says if we are nothing but ashes? The coloreds in Swaziland prefer cremation, as I've heard.
>
> They often wish to take the remains back to wherever they come from originally, maybe Greece or somewhere, and it is cheaper and easier to transport the ashes then. As the Bible says, the bones will be joined together again, but how do you join them back when they are just ashes?

The clerk was referring to the Bible passage Ezekiel 37, which describes a resurrection in a desert where God miraculously rejoined desiccated bones of a dead person. The Bible overall does not specifically defend or support cremation. People I spoke with about cremation did not usually draw parallels with Bible verses such as Ecclesiastes 12:7, about the mortal decay of humans into dust of the earth. Cremation would short-circuit this process anyway by immediately turning bodies into this residue. Again, funeral speeches that involved the dead body generally spoke about how it mattered less than the soul, which would ultimately be the vehicle of a person's resurrection. Similarly, conversations about cremation focused on how a body transformed in cremation might not rematerialize in an afterlife, as if ashes were something that could not be divinely remade into human form.

In contrast to the clerk, the owner of a funeral parlor told me that she and her husband would like to be cremated, although she understood why most ordinary Swazi would not wish for it. She picked up on several themes I had heard from others. Like Dups did, she cited issues of land as justification for cremation, and like the shop clerk, she eventually enveloped the broader credibility of the procedure within the Bible:

> [Cremation] makes sense in that the cemeteries are getter smaller and smaller as more people are put inside. Take for example the cemetery at Ngwane Park [in Manzini]. Many of those places are not secured. The animals will just walk through and trample your grave, and there are sometimes not-so-savory people who go there at night. There is nothing wrong with cremation versus burial. I'd like to be cremated, and my children can choose what they want to do for themselves. I hope they will do it for me when I pass [on].
>
> There are problems with inflation in the prices of both cremation and burial, as it seems to have gone up. Most do not believe in cremation. Some might think that you will still be alive somehow when you are put in the fire,

and you will feel the pain of being burned. If you are burned, some believe you may not be able to come back as *lidloti* (ancestral spirit). The Bible speaks mostly about your soul, not your body, after you are dead, so it is not necessarily an issue in God's eyes, I think.

While the parlor owner desired cremation, which she hoped her children would help her facilitate, it was a desire that, while not standard per Swazi Culture, reflected the public discourse of landlessness as a problem because of mass death.[28] "Why cremate?" was more popularly subsumed to the question, "What would you bury?" In most conversations I had with people about cremation, whether they were for or against it, the issue of land came up as centrally important, and without a body, there would be no way to make a claim to a place on earth. At the Mavuso Trade Fair in 2011, one new Dups employee explained to me that "people are concerned about where they will put the remains. We show them that there is a problem with land [scarcity], and when there is ... no space to bury someone, we can solve that problem with cremation." The funeral parlor owner cited the Ngwane Park municipal cemetery in Manzini's suburbs as a case in point of this landlessness, and it was evident from the difference between my first visit in 2010 and my most recent in 2014 that the site would soon reach maximum occupancy.

That same year, the Manzini City Council (2014) reported in the *Swazi Observer* on a new initiative between the Municipal Council of Manzini, the Royal Swazi Police, and Dups to begin conducting pauper cremations rather than pauper burials. The Council claimed that they were running out of room, both for urban burial and for storage space in mortuaries, due to the sheer volume of unclaimed, abandoned bodies. Ashes would be kept for six months to give relatives time to claim the cremains before they would be disposed of in a "legally acceptable manner." Daniel Dlamini, then cremation manager for Dups, noted that people might be "scared" of cremation, although it should be viewed as a "better option." He earnestly reminded readers "as Swazis" to "cling to our humane tradition of giving our loved ones a dignified burial so that we keep our conscience clear at all times."

For dead people to be dispossessed of their bodies altogether was an unsettling proposition. Cremation effectively transgressed the enduring form of interment of grounded burial. Perhaps because the Bible is vague on cremation and that cremation has been only part of clan-specific histories, people faced an interpretive vacuum when presented with cremation as a consumer option. By presenting cremation as a novel technology in an emerging market, Dups had to take an active role in changing culture by revaluing cremation with regard to changing ecological circumstances and economic burdens. This was a challenge that consumers, who perceived cremation in terms of compromised bodily wholeness and sensorial pollution, did not take lightly. Likewise, it was a challenge for Dups, which still trafficked primarily in burial goods such as coffins, making the sale of this new service ever more complicated.

Conclusion

What is embedded in claims to bury someone somewhere he or she does not belong? What is embedded in claims to not bury someone but rather to burn them? A focus on contemporary burial practices of funeral culture in Swaziland showed that bodies were materially vital in the making of social lives and futures. Even in death, the body inhered a form of life, *imphilo*, but its material stuff of bones made up relatedness between people on and below the face of the earth. In a cultural milieu of epidemic proportions, the living got by with the resources they had at hand, and in a time of funerals, these resources were dead bodies themselves and their placement in the ground.

Driven multiply by sentiments of avarice, love, jealousy, betrayal, and flight from Swazi Law and Custom in civil courts, the dead became objects of a gendered body politics, earthly anchors for others who might gain from their particular placement. Foregrounding the body also enlivens a "pragmatic or problem-oriented" approach that Reynolds Whyte (2005) argues for in understanding burial disputes. The body's materiality was central in this way in that it presented a few last chances for the living at a funeral to show how the deceased was well cared for in life and worthy of a final, dignified passage.

Notes

1. See His Royal Highness Prince Tfohlongwane N. O. and Others v. Ntshangase and Others (Civil Appeal No. 25/07) 2007 SZSC 13 (November 15, 2007) and Princess Tsase and Others v. Lindimpi Wilson Ntshangase and Others (Case No. 4381/07) 2008 SZHC (February 15, 2008).

2. Princess Tsase and Others v. Lindimpi Wilson Ntshangase and Others (Case No. 4381/07) 2008 SZHC (February 15, 2008), 16.

3. See Mfanasibili 2007; Mthethwa 2007a, 2007b; News24 2007; and Golomski 2010.

4. These were the African National Congress (ANC) and Inkatha Freedom Party (IFP) of South Africa and the People's United Democratic Movement (PUDEMO) of Swaziland. Debly (2014) writes that Swazi state police have recently disrupted or prevented some funerals for these prodemocracy party members.

5. See Cohen and Adhiambo 1992; Verdery 1999; de Witte 2001; and Mbembe 2015 (2001).

6. The case was extraordinary for resonating as a criticism of state governance in *tinkhundla*. See Levin 1997; Sihlongonyane 2003; T. Thwala 2013; and much of the digital writing by the international Swaziland Solidarity Network.

7. See Bernault 2006; Lee and Vaughan 2008; Posel and Gupta 2009; Geissler and Prince 2010; Jindra and Nöret 2011; Fontein and Harries 2013; and Kalusa and Vaughan 2013.

8. Claims of belonging in funerals and burials also unfold as part of ethnic identity politics and globalization. See Jua 2005; Page 2007; and Geschiere 2009.

9. This description of the material forms of life cycle rites in Swaziland is slim, given that the emphasis is on funerals, and more has to be written and theorized about how Swazi personhood is constituted. On *inhlawulo* rites in South Africa, see Mkhwanazi (2014). For many Swazi people, clothing is an ethical act that prevents exposure and nakedness, and *imvunulo* situates one's identity and humanity (R. Twala 1951; Kuper 1973a, 1973b; Golomski 2015c). On material substance and exchange in marriage, see Kuper 1950; Nhlapo 1992; and Golomski 2016b. Wastell (2007) uses materiality as a vantage point for analyzing kingship.

10. See IRIN 2003b; Mzileni 2007; Maziya 2011; and Malinga 2014.

11. See Raviv 2015; Zulu 2009a; Maphalala 2009; and Maziya 2010b.

12. Ria Reis, personal communication to author, May 19, 2009.

13. They offered E50 ($5) for 100ml, while the attendant said he could score E500 ($50) for the same amount. Allegedly, they coaxed him to collect and sell the water at E100 ($10).

14. See J. Dlamini 2013; Motau 2013; and Nene 2013.

15. See Mabuza 2008 and Manzini City Council 2014.

16. In the case of an abandoned body, the town or chiefly council and mortuary must make an application to the regional administrator, an appointee of the royalist *Tinkhundla* administration, requesting disposal. If approved, the council will then consult other administrative and governing committees on where and how to dispose of the body. A "pauper burial" is seen as disrespectful and barely humane yet has long been the only option for municipalities. Recently, the Manzini City Council recently turned to Dups to cremate thirty abandoned bodies out of concerns over alleged lack of space.

17. See Durham and Klaits 2002 and Klaits 2010.

18. See Berglund 1976; Kuper 1980 (1947); and Kasenene 1993.

19. See White 2004, 2011 and James 2015.

20. Swazi Nation Land was a category of land developed in 1907 under British colonialism. Following local people's dispossession of land in the 1890s due to pressure on King Mbandzeni from settler concessionaires, the British colonial government allocated about a third of all available land in the region for Swazi settlement, keeping the rest for themselves to occupy and develop. Under Sobhuza II's Lifa Fund, Swazis increasingly bought back land from colonialists for their own use. See Parsons and Palmer 1977; Rose 1992; and Levin 1997.

21. On patrilineal kinship generally, see Kuper 1950, 1980 (1947); and Golomski 2016b. On Swazi kinship's historical flexibility, see Russell 1984; H. Simelane 2011; and Golomski 2015a.

22. See S. Dlamini 2010; C. Matsebula 2014; and S. Nkambule 2014b.

23. See Bremersdorp Urban Area Advisory Committee 1943 and Golomski 2015b.

24. See Parsons and Palmer 1977; Levin 1997; and N. C. Dlamini 2007.

25. See Hunter 2010; Smith 2014; and Wyrod 2016.

26. See Maseko 2006; Zwane 2006; and Vilakati 2010.

27. In this explanation, I am indebted to Hylton White's (2010, 511ff.) expert phrasing.

28. Landlessness has long been a problem for the majority of Swazi citizens and the Dlamini kingship alike (H. Simelane 1991; Levin 1997). King Mbandzeni signed over much of the land to Boer concessionaires at the onset of European colonialism, and the Land Allotment Act of 1907 placed most people in overcrowded "Native Areas." The state was able to purchase back much of the land in the form of Swazi Nation Land, but issues of suburbanization, development, and state predation recycle old problems in new forms.

5 Life in a Takeaway Box: Mobility and Purity in Funeral Feasts

THE WHITE RISING sun cast itself out over the land. We gave thanks for it after what had been a cold night as we walked back toward Mr. Ngcobo's house from his burial at the community cemetery. Mr. Ngcobo was the brother of the pastor at LaGija's family's neo-Pentecostal church. As church members, LaGija, Buyiswa, and their mother felt obligated to attend the funeral even though they had not met Mr. Ngcobo before. In the yard, a large group of people had already formed a near-impenetrable circle around a group of women at a folding table.

I approached the crowd with Vusi, an agricultural researcher from UNISWA and musical director at the church. He pushed us toward the table's edge. Small towers of white Styrofoam takeaway boxes came into view, some stacked ten high. One of the women caught sight of us and passed us two boxes. Gleeful from the quick steal amid the crowd, we quickly moved off and sat on the fender of Vusi's small truck to eat. We opened the lids. Water droplets from condensation ran down onto the food the inside: rice, a Kentucky-fried-style chicken drumstick, a ladling of beef stew, a few oily lettuce leaves, and a quarter of a boiled potato smeared with mayonnaise. "What are funerals like now compared to the past?" I asked Vusi between sporkfuls.

He replied, "In the past, when someone died, the family was sad, and they didn't to do anything like work or go outside. People came, and they brought food for the family. The family was mourning. They were not supposed to be cooking. Nowadays it's not the same." "How so?" I asked. "See these women. They're the family, and they're cooking for the visitors," he explained. "Why's that?" I pushed further. "I don't know why," he said smilingly, brushing a grain of rice from his mustache. The crowd encircling the table soon dissipated, as did the small mountain of white boxes. We finished our portions, and after handshakes and goodbyes, we each loaded a few relatives and church members into our cars for the drive home. Some carried their boxes with them, holding them in their laps to keep them from spilling as the cars jostled over the potholed dirt road. On the way to Nhlangano to drop off Buyiswa at her college netball tournament, a few such empty boxes tumbled along the highway, whipped up by passing cars.

A few months later, I sped down the same highway to meet Mr. Dlamini in a neighboring community in the Mamba Kingdom.[1] Mr. Dlamini was a former hospital orderly and the new owner of a small funeral parlor. We sat in his sunny, dusty living room. His wife had just left for an afternoon shopping trip, and the aroma of cooked sugar beans wafted in from the kitchen. Sitting on bouffant plastic-wrapped couches, we shared a liter of Coca-Cola as he told me about funerals. "Let's say that someone from the Dlamini family died," he began. "They would sit down and mourn. They wouldn't cook food. Neighbors would come by and bring them something to eat because they are mourning. Now, if someone dies at Dlaminis, the Dlaminis must cook for the visitors who come over. We must slaughter a cow, buy the rice, cook the food, and do all that. It's like a party!" he explained, going on to say what was cooked, how, and by whom. When I asked why funerals were now feast-like parties, he simply said "Development."

Big meals were often the first things mentioned when I asked how funerals had changed, and next, that work roles were inverted. In the past, it was said, there was not a lot of food, not like one sees today with giant roiling cauldrons to boil vegetables or the towers of takeaway boxes at some funerals. In the past, people said, members of the deceased person's household, as bereaved mourners, did not cook food for themselves or do other domestic activity in the wake of death. Visitors from the community or neighborhood would bring victuals for the bereaved to consume. To some people I spoke with, these changes were peculiar, and for others they were irritating, irrational, and potentially destructive for household economies.

Development and health economists have been fascinated by the high costs that go into funerals in this context (Case et al. 2013). Health scientist Chris Desmond and his colleagues (2004, 48), exploring HIV/AIDS mortality in Swaziland, note, "Observations relating to burial practices ... have shown very little evidence of practices adapting to a changed environment [of frequent funerals].... One could speculate that cultural beliefs and practices are a strong force in opposing change. Yet the ritual of large and expensive funerals is in fact only fairly recent and not an established custom." Concerns for funeral expenditures are part of policy research on HIV/AIDS-related food insecurity and poverty. Alex DeWaal and Alan Whiteside (2003) argue that Swaziland and other countries with prolonged HIV/AIDS epidemics face a new form of variant famine. In their account, households come to experience widespread food insecurity, and national governments remain accountable for improving the health and socioeconomic conditions of their citizens as factors in combating HIV/AIDS-related destitution.[2]

The state has also taken its own approaches to what it sees as problems surrounding consumption and death. In 2002, King Mswati III issued a royal decree banning funeral feasts. This move was already enforced in some chiefdoms because of concerns that destitute households would quickly deplete their material resources in producing meals for more and more funerals. One BBC article that year (Holloway 2002) described how people were "told at community meetings called by their chiefs, that close relatives and friends understandably need refreshments at funerals. But the modern trend was for the bereaved, already bearing heavy funeral costs, to pay for food and liquor for large crowds of visiting mourners. This was not in keeping with true Swazi culture, they were told by their chiefs." Some people I met thought it was a good idea to return to the way things used to be. Others pointed out that people bringing their own food would be embarrassing. In communities where the royal decree was enforced, any family found out to have slaughtered a beast at their home for a funeral would in turn pay a fine to chief. Whether to serve food at a funeral, how much, and for whom were big questions that came to the fore at a dire moment.

Why then do the bereaved now feed attendees when it used to be the other way around? Why are they now considered big meals? Some people I spoke with, such as Mr. Dlamini, chalked up the changes to "globalization" or "development," while most, like Vusi, said they did not know, lamenting change broadly in that what happens now is not part of Swazi Culture. Critical historical explanations for these dynamics easily expand on what Mr. Dlamini said. They show how and when certain commodities, commercial entities, and qualities of funerals such as dignity came into being through changing colonial-era economies and migration patterns (Ranger 2004; Lee and Vaughan 2008). People's laments about these matters intimate how cultural forms of consumption have changed broadly with respect to larger historical forces, including HIV/AIDS. Within this approach may also be answers to the above questions about work role inversions, the desire to provide feasts, and why funeral feasts matter.

Funerals involved ordinary actions such as cooking, eating, and washing. The effects of this work were profoundly social and extended beyond the full stomachs and subjective intentions of people who prepared and ate food at the event. In this chapter I describe who did the work of food production, how, and why, and how food was distributed in certain ways, such as in a takeaway box. I consider how changes generated patterns of redistribution, where food as a vital form of life, *imphilo*, got moved around. In this way, "beliefs and practices" such as feeding more people were not necessarily resistant to change. Rather, they were strategic cultural actions to revalue and redistribute life-giving resources that were available.

Mourners and Visitors

Who was actually a funeral visitor? Who was a mourner? These roles were presumed to carry certain duties and were ascribed to people mostly based on their age and gender. This was clear in the way people talked about who mourners and visitors were at funerals and what they were expected to do, sometimes based on Swazi Culture and other times on social or emotional relationships with the dead. These terms are imperfect and cannot fully encompass the practical and subjective fact that people are both mourners and visitors, either simultaneously while at a funeral or variably, over the course of a lifetime.

Swazi Culture tends to reify principles of patriarchy and patrilineal kinship which have long shaped mourning roles. Based on her research with King Sobhuza II and his royal family, the anthropologist Hilda Kuper ([1947] 1980) first described mourning as indicating a gradation of social rank. If the deceased was a married man, for example, he received the most elaborate mourning rites, while unmarried women or children supposedly received less ritual attention. However, she later qualified this hierarchical model to focus more on how interpersonal closeness was construed in relationship idioms such as *ligazi lami*, "my blood (relative)." Her important point that "kinship obligations depend chiefly on contiguity, on day-to-day relationships, but are fictionalized as blood ties" (Kuper 1950, 106), is seen in the shifting categories of kin that make up mourners and visitors at contemporary funerals.

Bereavement has also been a function of peoples' relationships in place, as much as of flexible principles of kinship. In the past and today, women were expected to move into their husband's home when they married. When a married woman died, the principal mourners included her family members, who had to come to her husband's or his family's home for the funeral (see chap. 4). Principal mourners for unmarried adults were siblings and their spouses, the deceased's parents, and the parents' female siblings who were "mothers" of the deceased. Unmarried adults would be buried at their parents' homestead, having not solidified one of their own in marriage per Swazi Culture. Neighbors and non-kin living close-by curried emotional and domestic support for mourners and made up the majority of categorical funerary visitors. Formerly, people beyond the homestead heard about a dying person or the death itself from messengers or runners, *bagijimi*, who were sent from the household to notify the chief. Chiefs would then spread the news to others in the area through their own messengers. The burial, taking place between one and three days after the death, would be a small, local affair.

Funerals began to grow in size because of the increasing participation of non-kin associated with Christian churches, an expansion that has its origins in the colonial and early post-colonial period. Christian missionaries from Europe and the United States have been present in the region since the 1840s, when a Wesleyan mission group led by James Allison first arrived. Many subsequent missions established new social, spiritual, and sometimes residential communities at their missions stations and beyond. Missionaries encouraged these loose communities of friends, associates, and neighbors to form new types of social relations with attendant obligations determined by the morals of the church, including non-homestead or community burial in "dignified" Christian funerals (Ranger 2004; Jindra 2005). These events often skirted conventions in the scale and complexity of local funerary production, which were based on gender, age, and social hierarchies.

Funeral size and numbers expanded too through changing forms of wage labor amid colonial-era industrialization. Geographer Jonathan Crush (1987; 1996) documents how more and more Swazi men migrated to South Africa from the late nineteenth century onward. Many were politically recruited to work in new gold and diamond mining operations there, and some went to get away from work on local white-owned farms. Workers were housed in hostels or set up lives in urban neighborhoods clustered around ethnic affiliations based on their regions of origin. Within these places, associations developed that had several social and economic functions, including supporting the funerals or bodily repatriation of migrants. New churches and new branches of older churches in cities also aided this expansion.[3]

Visitors at contemporary funerals included a much broader retinue of associates, such as members of people's churches, as well as coworkers, burial cooperative members, friends, and former schoolmates. Visitors came to pay respects to mourners in mostly Christian language and sentiments and also as representatives of members of churches, like Mr. Ngcobo. Besides burial cooperative members, women's leagues within churches, conspicuously marked by special uniforms of hats, skirts, blouses, capes, and pins or broaches, often fostered the greatest spiritual and social support. Visiting church representatives could consist of anywhere from five to more than twenty individuals going to a bereaved homestead or a funeral, thereby increasing the overall size of the event and its qualities of dignity. Today, instead of communication via runners, death is broadcast to more potential visitors through mobile phone calls and text messages.

In the past, people in Swaziland had worked cooperatively or were organized for community agricultural projects by chiefs and kings.[4] It is not clear, however, that funerals were communally or economically organized in this way. Development studies specialist Sophieke Kappers (1988) suggests that women's cooperative rotating-savings-and-credit groups in Swaziland first appeared in the 1960s and 1970s, inspired by returning labor migrants' associations. Their main objectives were economic and ethical—to borrow, lend, and save among each other—and a few offered material support for members' funerals. Money and other resources coordinated by these groups and other associations could rapidly flow back into bereaved homesteads. This was enabled too by colonial infrastructural developments such as railways, paved roads, postal services, telephones, and expanded transportation options in buses and cars. These colonial projects of development and modernization increased people's opportunities to travel to funerals for others with whom they felt interdependent or obligated, especially in new communities of church and work.

Newer funeral visitors also included more distant kin who lived beyond the homestead. These were kin on the father's side and members of related male lineages—for example, the children of one's grandfather's brother—and kin on the mother's side, such as the wives of one's mother's brothers. Some kin on the mother's side already lived at more patriarchal homesteads, but most (non-kin) funeral visitors did not live at the homestead of the deceased.[5] Increasingly, kinswomen on both sides provided food-related support at funerals as the events grew in size. In the case of LaGija at Roxanne's funeral, such visitors included siblings of a woman married to a brother of the dead person, who also ceremoniously presented food to the bereaved and prepared and served it after the burial. Families began to draw on greater degrees of kin relationships, including in-law relationships, to mobilize food-related work and to more strongly distinguish kin from diverse non-kin that were now populating the event. Kinswomen could be readily incorporated as part of the overall production of a funeral when needed. As in other cases of blood or in-law kinship in Swaziland, these relations were "flexible" or were remade under particular historic conditions as people sought better lives.[6] Families could recruit these women to help out first, instead of hiring non-kin such as a caterer, because ostensibly the women would do it for free as a culturally ethical act.

This history of increased mobility and economic and social change informs contemporary claims that mourners must now feed visitors. There are many more visitors, including more distant kin, who now show up at mourners' homes. In the past, while some food was likely available at the home of the bereaved, visitors more often brought their own victuals for their journey and to consume at the homestead for the duration of their stay. This was a function of longer travel times by foot or unpaved roads, the lack of food to purchase along the way, and ongoing cycles of household food insecurity. Visits could last from one to several nights, as prior to the wider use of mortuary storage, the body was usually buried within three days. Food that visitors carried with them in this sense is called *umphako* or *ingcamu*. It is also the term for food prepared at one's home and eaten on a journey generally, or used jokingly for a packed lunch.

The fact that today insurance companies pay out large sums of money to family members as policy beneficiaries suggests to people that there will be some material evidence of this payout at their home during the funeral. Some insurance policies and companies are specifically promoted as ones that pay for food. This money is situated firmly in the hands of the deceased's relatives, the mourners, because non-relatives generally cannot take out life insurance policies on other people. With a presumed cash windfall and more people showing up to make funerals dignified, the obligation of feeding falls to the family, who feel compelled to give thanks to attendees. There are also more mourning kin altogether providing for the funeral—relatives with insurance policies and kinswomen helping to enact policy benefits in preparing food.

Women continue to be the basis of food-related support. Despite the voiced concerns about mourning kin doing this work, it is clear that non-kin visitors are also taking up the task in critical ways. Churches and burial cooperatives to which the deceased belonged have historically also contributed. Increasingly, though, people unknown to the bereaved help run funerals in their work as employees of insurance companies, funeral parlors, and catering companies who are legally contracted to participate and provide service. David Graeber (2006, 74) argues that contributions by kinswomen in ceremonial settings such as funerals are key, often-unacknowledged forms of unequal labor that are central for human social reproduction. Tracing this labor reveals what is actually at "stake of human existence." For Graeber, what is at stake is breaking through illusions that some people—here, women—need not be automatically assigned to certain work, and that this work is in fact more about social and cultural production than it is about the economy. People acknowledge that the work is burdensome for those who (have to) do it, but working together, and less divisively, can make things taste less bitter.

Cooking Food: Cooperation and Appreciation

By working cooperatively and showing appreciation for collective outcomes—such as offering chicken drumsticks, scones, and tea—both mourners and visitors obliged each other to help out in the production of their own future funerals and those of family members. More immediately, cooking food for a funeral required cutting, stirring, scooping, and stacking, and there was a lot of it to do (see fig. 5.1). Contemporary funeral culture entailed these acts in producing large feasts that also involved long-term financial, planning, and organizational contributions. They supplemented but also went beyond what kin put in. Still, questions remained for many people over why such sizeable consumption was necessary and how to best appreciate it despite ambiguity.

After I came back to Madulini from a weekend trip to Durban in March 2011, Nokwenza told me about the time she spent that weekend helping out at a funeral. She helped cook for the funeral of Colani, a distant relative of her husband Vuyo's family. Linked to them by marriage, Nokwenza was brought in as a relative on the mother's side to do the work. On a Saturday afternoon, Colani's body arrived at his parents' homestead in southern Swaziland, having come across the border from a mortuary in South Africa, where he had worked. Many relatives who were living, working, or studying in South Africa arrived at the same time. What

Fig. 5.1 Funeral feast queue with Styrofoam plates near Bethany, 2010. Photograph by author.

Nokwenza said is a good depiction of all that goes into cooking. "We ate supper along with them and then washed all their dishes. After that, we started cooking again!" she laughed, and continued:

> We cooked rice, *samp* (hominy), chicken portions for those who don't take beef, and salads: beetroot, butternut, potato. People don't like chopping all the greens! We cooked both inside and outside the house. The salads were prepared in the garage, where they keep the *emahewu* (maize meal drink), *umcombotsi* (maize meal beer), and water. We divided into groups. We made tea in the kitchen and boiled water in a large pot with the coal stove. We had plastic bags for the *mafrezile* (artificially colored and flavored ice blocks) and different scones and slices of bread. It is easy to serve this food then at the vigil. Another person can then just pour the tea from a large kettle and another person can just hand out the cups. We added sugar and milk to the tea. Outside we used large pots over fire to cook the beef, rice, and *samp*.
>
> Around 3a.m., they opened the casket for the family members to see Colani. They really cried at that point, because it had been some days since they saw him [both alive at work and deceased at the mortuary], and now this was the last time they'd see him. After that, we brought the tea we brewed. Those who dug the grave were from the community. We gave them *umcombotsi* and *emahewu* because they need that thing to dig the grave quickly at night! Even in Madulini, those people wish to drink that while digging the grave. They say,

"Hey, we need that thing," and if you don't give it to them, they just leave you! The family brewed the drinks during the week, as it takes some days to finish. You can't do all this alone.

After [the morning burial], we gave takeaways to those who were in a hurry, but others used plates. We placed tables outside, and the people made a queue. There were also tables inside the tent where food was served and another serving area in the main house for the women sitting with the body all night, because after burial they return to the room where they were sitting. In the tent were relatives, church members, and pastors, and people outside the tent were from the community and other farther places. The food was the same for all and all from the same pot!

Anyone can go to a funeral. Many people can go … and give comfort at the night vigil. You don't cook for special people only. You will cook for anyone who comes. Well, not in those communities which are not allowed to cook at funerals. You only see at the beginning of the service that, *eish*, there are a lot of people! Maybe [the deceased] was a well-known person in the community and was known from afar. Even Colani was well known in South Africa and in northern Swaziland where his mother comes from, so there were many people from afar.

The menu was not extravagant or extra-special, she told me. The food included commercially available and ordinary homemade items. The latter were maize meal beverages ranging in degrees of fermentation from the slightly so (*emahewu*) to the alcoholic (*umcombotsi*). For the male relatives digging the grave, drinks helped energize them to work quickly, without which they would not have felt appreciated, as Nokwenza laughingly said. Items such as these have to be made earlier in the week, thus expanding the scope of the work beyond Nokwenza's own twenty-four-hour role. The men were not "special people," and her statement might suggest that with regard to food consumption, not even the bereaved get special treatment, since the food is distributed equitably: "The same for all and all from the same pot." Funerary consumption and distribution is less centered on concerns of hierarchy or distinctions between mourners and visitors and more on the ability to provide for everyone, a capacity that requires cooperation and ample resources.

Burial cooperatives and private catering companies as part of funeral insurance policies supplemented the kinwork of producing funeral feasts. The vice-president of a church-based burial cooperative in Manzini told me in a group interview in 2010 that "development brought catering, so now we have the feasts. I don't know where it comes from, but our main concern is a decent burial and not catering." My observations at the cooperative's office and mortuary, however, pointed to the importance of food in making any burial "dignified" or "decent." Over the course of one Friday afternoon I was there, members brought in six ten-kilogram bags of onions and potatoes as well as six large jars of cooking oil and mayonnaise, placing them in an already stocked back storage room for redistribution for members' death claims. Relatives still bring food for consumption to the household of the bereaved, but cooperatives can easily provide greater quantity, given their financial resources and particular allocation based on a member's subscription.

Similarly, in August 2014, I visited the windowless Manzini office of a long-standing burial cooperative with origins and headquarters in South Africa. An administrator, a senior woman with thick dreadlocks, ran down the list of membership benefits for me, which included E3000 (US$228) for purchasing meat. All non-meat groceries were provided free of charge. A woman came in with her adult daughter, who was severely burned, her face covered by large sunglasses and hidden by a pink baseball cap. She sat using her mobile phone as her mother asked questions about joining the cooperative. The mother was especially interested in both grace periods for premium payments and catering for a funeral. She recounted how some older men of her husband's household made smirking remarks at a recent funeral for an eighteen-year-old relative about the quality and lack of food. "They were making noise about it all," sighed the woman. "What do you think you can do for us?"

The administrator told her that in the previous month they had organized catering for four funerals in one weekend, including two for teachers and one for a police officer. At these three funerals, the cooperative teamed up with several teachers from the deceased teachers' respective schools and colleagues from the police department and were able to accommodate everything with ease. "There is a lot of money to buy food, and we are able to cook everything quickly," she noted. She listed several items on the menu: onions, juice, and "meat like you've never seen. We will prepare it there or else we will do it elsewhere, and it will arrive in cartons for us to dish out." "Some might complain that the meat is not enough," she continued, "but since we know we are cooking for the public, there won't be an issue about running out of food because you won't with our scheme. It is not unprepared or not well-cooked. The aunties will show up with the food. We will stir those pots!"

Ashford, the funeral parlor owner, explained to me, "Those co-ops give out the money because the family wants to make tea and scones in the night and then in the morning they give everyone a breakfast thing, too. I think the influence really came from South Africa, the same with insurance." The expansion of commercial life insurance brought with it not only diversified options for burial assurance but also new funerary commodities such as memorial flowers and wreaths, printed programs, and hired catering. One insurance company, B3, is famously known for its catering services. A branch office manager told me in a September 2010 interview: "The circumstances surrounding the death might be beyond the control of the family, and there are provisions we can work with. There is money included in some policies for a feast," he recounted, "but we can deduct that from the policy if they decide they do not want the feast after the funeral."

Catering is not part of all policies but is a bonus addition of a consumer's choice. B3 also offered a pre-funeral policy that included E1000 (US$133) specifically for a "food hamper," paid out within twenty-four to forty-eight hours of a policyholder's or dependent's death. Claims were made in-house, which, according to the manager, meant that no funds were simply disbursed outright as money but rather in the form of vouchers or food itself. The company did not employ a full-time catering staff; they solicited short-term contractors, or "tenders," to cook. These were small groups of women and small companies who otherwise did catering for businesses, weddings, and special events. Contractors purchased food from urban wholesale stores such as Boxer Superstore, did prep work outside of the funeral, and trucked it in with insurance company vehicles to finish and serve it. The manager admitted that they themselves contributed to the rise of funeral feasts and explained it as an effective and affective response to contemporary mobile life:

> The world has become a village. Before, you would go on a ship. You would take a ship across the ocean, and it would take one month. Now, you get on the airplane, go to sleep, and the next day you are in Washington D.C. You see, it is the same thing for funerals.
>
> In the past, they were village issues with only a few distant relatives. But now it is much more about the community and the transport. It attracts more people. Now when they hear about someone who died, they may drive four to five hours to get to the funeral. They have traveled a long ways, and they are coming to a place in the villages where there are no shops or anything else. The family is providing an essential service to those who are coming to the funeral. They may have left early in the morning, and they came without food, and then get there at suppertime. It is also cold at night for them to be outside, so you need to keep them warm with the tea.
>
> The food is not a luxury. It is unfortunate. In the past, food was available. Neighbors and family members would come over when I lost a relative; they would come to mourn for you, and they bring you the food in hampers. Unfortunately, that has changed, and it has become a burden for the bereaved. People lost what they had, the support structure, and the burden is heavy.

The manager said this all in a sympathetic tone, and his explanation justified the business of catering in saying that social life is fragmented and accelerated because of different mobile and transport technologies. His explanation also shored up modernization as a historical and political-economic reason for the expansion of funeral participation generally. It honed in on matters of rural communities being underdeveloped, in his estimation, "where there are no shops."

He also made a very blunt yet poignant remark that pointed to insecurity, or more heavily, a barer life: "Food is not a luxury." This resonated with what an administrator at another insurance company told me in October 2010 about the quality of food and its distribution at funerals. "It is true!" he said. "The family spends all the money on this food for the visitors, but you know that they are serving it for these people in such a way where they don't put in any salt!" Together we laughed at the hypothetical family's shrewd lack of flavoring. He paused as if he were reflecting on the statement, then continued more steadily, "The family has made all the food for visitors, yes. If a visitor goes and sees this thing [the bereaved preparing the feast] is wrong, how can you refuse the food? You can't refuse what they made for you, so you just eat it."

"Food is not a luxury." In some ways, this remark echoed the concerns of health economists and the state about reckless expenditure. Food is a form of life and sustenance, yet there may not be enough to go around. Producing a feast on a large scale, and unfortunately, being compelled to do it often, took economic tolls on households whose labor and wage-earning capacities may suddenly be cut short by a person's death. Catering and burial cooperative investment may push back against the precipice of financial oblivion by assuring that what little the family might have was on credit or not totally spent, and that food, which was scarce, may be brought in by someone else.

Of course, households spent their own money over the long term in cooperatives and insurance policies, and these groups were legally obligated to provide their services. Wherever food came from, bereaved relatives like Nokwenza were often then socially obligated to take up the task of reworking the food in acts of cooking and redistributing it. Insofar as ethical and economic value may be represented in material things such as food items (Lambek 2013), "the burden is heavy" to do this. As the first administrator said, there may be very little to work with. In this sense, food was less about luxury; its scarcity was more about poverty.

"Food is not a luxury" also in the sense that it was not about inessential or hedonistic gratification. Because it was prepared for a large number of people, where quantity might be more important than quality, it might turn out unfortunately bland—without salt. Like I heard from the insurance administrator, LaGija's daughter told me that she disliked going to royalists' national ceremonies because of the food. With hundreds if not thousands of people in attendance, provisions for the masses were usually prepared and served indelicately. She told me that at one event she attended for the parading of the royal army, along with the meat from a few dozen cattle, "they just had wheelbarrows full of carrot salad and shovels [to serve it]. I can't stand that, all of us eating from it like that."

The beads of condensation left on the takeaway boxes at Mr. Ngcobo's funeral pointed out how some food usually got cold (and then wet) after sitting out for several hours. Yet at funerals, both people who cooked it and those who received it were grateful for the food, and most would not refuse or withdraw from this exchange. Nokwenza recounted how she was once at a funeral that had run low on their offerings. "At one funeral I went to, they ran out of rice and *samp*, so they served us bread with the beef and soup," she said, "and they apologized, but they were glad to see us and gave us the food."

Food was valuable if not pleasurable, even if the quality was lacking, by being negotiated at the center of particular social relations of obligation that were critical for the overall success of funerals as dignified, memorable events. Feasts were made up of ordinary foods that one generally made for a meal at home or bought prepared from a local restaurant or grocery store, but the extraordinariness of the funeral and the excessive production and distribution of goods likewise registered something beyond the food's evident form. Rethinking the work of critical theorist Georges Bataille ([1949], 1991, 21), funerary food's ordinary quality and the expenditures for it might be illuminated in the idea of "an accursed share." By this he refers to a "general economy" of energy, material things, and humans, of which its productions always overflow their potential use. He writes: "The living organism, in a situation determined by the play of energy on the surface of the globe, ordinarily receives more energy than is necessary for maintaining life; the excess energy (wealth) can be used for the growth of a system (e.g., an organism); if the system can no longer grow, or if the excess cannot be completely absorbed in its growth, it must necessarily be lost without profit; it must be spent, willingly or not, gloriously or catastrophically."

That which we must spend that also exceeds our needs in a finite world is our "accursed share" to deal with, both existentially and economically. Still, it might be too hasty to judge the funeral feast as a "catastrophic" expenditure, as health economists or the state might, or as something uncritically "glorious." People's own reflections on the culture of contemporary funerals tended to wax critical, given the ubiquity of funerals and the material goods needed for them. Feasts produced peelings from vegetables, detritus of Styrofoam, plastic bags, and gasoline fumes from generators used to power stoves and kettles for cooking, yet I never saw leftovers or food go to waste at a funeral. Everything was consumed, sent away in takeaway boxes, or packed up and put in a cupboard or refrigerator if the household had one.

Food was thoroughly appreciated, as philosopher of health sciences Annemarie Mol (2010) uses the term. Appreciation forms at the intersection of sensorial and individual taste, social consumption, and acknowledgment of the labor or systems that were put into its creation. Because many households were likely to be food insecure, food was not a luxury; it was vital. The labor in its preparation by women and others was all-consuming, and those who ate the fruits of that labor were appreciative. These actions and their outcomes were sustaining, life-giving, and ultimately made up a form of sociability in this particular age of HIV/AIDS.

The mobilities of development and globalization are forces that contributed in different ways to present conditions of scarcity. For people I met in Swaziland, they were also central forces to the expansion of funerary participation and consumption. They effectively required people and goods such as food to move from outside the homestead back into the homestead as the site of a funeral. Food for consumption that came into the purview of a funeral was thoroughly appreciated despite concerns about its abundance amid scarcity.

Purification

Cross-culturally, eating is a metaphor for sex. As sex was the main mode of transmission in the HIV/AIDS epidemic in Swaziland, food and actions done to it took on new value. For example, the November 27, 2010, *Times of Swaziland* issue featured a public health message showing a smiling young man riding in a car saying, *Ngitofa ngidlile, angife ngidlile, ungadla lishonile phela*, meaning, "I might die and will have eaten, I might not die and will still have eaten, but cannot eat when the sun sets." The last line was in English: "and Sipho got HIV!" The message was part of a series titled "*Str'u, aw'kaphephi*," meaning "It's true, you're not protected (from getting HIV)," produced by the local health communications firm Lusweti from 2009 on.

The series used popular siSwati idioms that were often used as excuses people gave for their ongoing high-risk behavior, such as staying in extramarital or multiple sexual relations and not using contraception. The intended message was locally apparent. The idiom of a setting sun connoted death and threats against a person's life. The ad depicted how the man used the excuse, chose to have sex, and contracted HIV. The aim of the series was to encourage people to change their behavior, as was standard practice in public health—in this case, consumption without some kind of modification (contraception) led to affliction.

This section describes how food and other elements of contemporary funerals were similarly modified or transformed with the function to enliven (*kuphilisa*) consumers in processes I qualify as purgative. In other words, food and other elements at funerals came to be purifying through women's practical and ritual work. This was also an issue of place, given the closeness of the women's work to one's homestead as a site of burial.[7] Purifying foodstuffs and other elements in a funeral functioned similarly as material processes of value transformation, turning that which was brought from outside into something culturally wholesome to enliven participants. These value transformations played on enduring customary forms of ritual purification that had long been mobile and were not limited to the site of the funeral itself. The stuff that went into funerals became qualitatively better or different than it had been before by the working hands of women and others.

The most delectable and valuable foodstuff at funerals, as in most meals, was meat (*inyama*). Historically, meat for funeral consumption came from a ceremonial sacrifice. It provided substance for consumption, and in the case of customary or non-Christian funerals, indicated to ancestral shades on the paternal side that someone had died and may eventually be joining their ethereal collective. Senior relatives on the paternal side would slaughter a beast culled from the herd of the deceased person's household or given to them by other relatives. Hilda Kuper ([1947] 1980, 180) wrote that for death and burial, senior men oversaw the "killing of the sacrificial beasts" and the gifting of beasts to the deceased's mother's kin and non-kin who assisted with preparing and moving the corpse. In her book-length ethnographies and fiction covering death and burial, Kuper does not mention a ceremonial feast for the participants before or after the burial.[8] Yet in her original field notes she wrote that "all meat must be eaten and the remaining bones burnt" (Kuper n.d.) at a funeral, evidencing some degree of meat consumption as the outcome of multiple gift or social exchanges of animals and the slaughter of a few.

The blood from sacrifice was particularly important, as ancestors were said to find it tastier.[9] Spilled blood at the cattle pen was seen as a symbol of cleansing poor relations amid social disputes. Ancestors in turn blessed people, food, and items of material culture, providing protection for the time being, until an unfortunate incident might indicate otherwise to the living that the shades had withdrawn their support. Several rarer customary delicacies, *tibiliboco*, included blood as an ingredient, as in a dish Nokwenza fondly called *bubhindze*, which mixed dried cattle blood with onions and spices to make sauce for starches and enhance their flavor and quality. A meal with meat was more often desirable, and blood from sacrifice further imbued value into the meat, the sacrificer, and both living and spiritual consumers of the beast. Like elsewhere across Africa, cattle are of tremendous value while still walking on their four legs, and when killed and cooked, they transform their consumers through nourishing strength.

Historically, indigenous healers were crucial for the purification of bodies and people through food such as meat. *Tinyanga* and *tigedla* healers commanded esoteric knowledge of animals and plants as technologies to transform things to which they were applied. Some species are widely known to have medicinal properties, but healers were and are experts at combining, mixing, and discerning efficacies of substances to use for particular conditions. Healers have long been summoned to orchestrate and abet life cycle rites, and in their work carried special substances with them into the homes of community members. British colonial administrator and ethnologist Brian Marwick (1966 [1940], 223) provided some of the earliest insight on *tinyangas'* roles in funerary consumption and purification: "When the [traditional] doctor comes a beast (*inkomo yokuluma*) is killed.... When the meat is roasted the doctor puts a sort of powder on it. This is then given to the people who have taken part in the burial and all the relatives of the deceased. They eat small pieces only. When this has been done the *inyanga* (doctor) washes them with a decoction of the plant called *maguqu*. If a relative of the deceased is not present at the burial he will have to *luma* when he returns, which may be several months afterwards."

Kuluma means "to bite." Linguist David Rycroft (1981, 59) notes one meaning as to "partake ritually of herbs after the death of a relative." Biting and subsequently spitting out herbal *mutsi* medicines is common in other rites such as *emalobolo* marital exchanges and kingship ceremonies and also works as a means for purification. Here it was aligned with meat consumption and necessary for all funeral participants to expel death pollution. *Maguqu* has as its root verb *kuguqa* or its later siSwati standardized form *kugucuka*, meaning to alter, change, and make something different in its state of being. This term informs the Christian AIC *siguco* healing rites discussed in chapter 2. The space and time of purification could extend beyond the funeral itself to accommodate those who were traveling or most likely doing wage labor elsewhere as migrants.

Similarly, in her original field notes on death and "traditional religion," Kuper (n.d.) recorded a communal practice called *kuhlambulula etaleni*, in which the mourners convened in nearby fields after a burial to "eat roasted plant materials" before returning home. *Kuhlambulula* means to cleanse, clarify, make clear, dilute a liquid substance such as beer, or loosen one's bowels (Rycroft 1981; MacMillan 2010). *Etaleni* is a place for leftovers or rubbish. This may indicate purification but does not preclude a ceremonial meal that healers put together. Healers also doled out other herbal medicines and mixtures of charcoal and water to funeral visitors so as to stave off their hunger and to consume food on behalf of mourners who were otherwise prohibited from doing so.

Cattle sacrifice and meat consumption were also done at the secondary phase of mortuary rites called *umchinso* or *umbuyiso*. This rite marked the end of the mourning period for certain bereaved people, namely widows and mothers of the deceased. Widows such as Mzikayise Ntshangase's wives noted in chapter 4 were supposedly polluted by death and had to remain in the house to prevent symbolic contagion. The rite usually occurred according to seasonal and lunar calendars. Most people told me they were held one to three years or winters following the death. Healers used to abet these mortuary rites by purifying the bereaved of their pollution using medicinal decoctions. *Tinyanga* helped call the deceased's wandering spirit back to the homestead and presumptuously thank the ancestors for allowing him or her to join them as a new ancestor. The bereaved could show thanks to the ancestors, healers, and *umchinso* attendees by spilling more blood in another sacrificial meal. Again, the purification of bodies and spaces was tied to the transformative properties of substances like blood by eating meat and other foodstuffs.

Cattle slaughter or sacrifice is far less common at contemporary funerals, given that many households do not have a stock of cattle from which to cull. Meat is also more easily purchased from commercial butchers or grocery stores using funds from a burial cooperative or insurance policy payout. Relatives might also buy an animal, as Nokwenza explained was done for Colani's funeral. For that funeral, a wealthier, supportive Matimba relative provided both a cow and a goat for the bereaved household to eat during the week and for the funeral feast itself. It was first slaughtered and cleaned at a commercial butchery in Nhlangano before being given to the women to prepare. At some funerals, both chicken and beef were provided, but usually a beef stew was the main meat. Given the large number of attendees, the bereaved also purchased many bags of frozen "white-people" chicken portions, *ramtutu*, from urban wholesalers. A household's free-range chickens were too delectable and too few to slaughter and serve to the masses.

Besides the economic dimension, Christian ideologies that were introduced in the colonial period and through to the present were widely understood to have banned participants from slaughter. Indeed, thirty-eight household survey respondents out of seventy-four across five rural and urban communities said that *umchinso*, *umbuyiso*, and *kuphahla*, the rites of ancestral remembrance, were no longer performed. Many attributed the change simply to "Christians." Some neo-Pentecostal pastors, such as Justice Dlamini, rendered funerary matters of Swazi Culture problematic. He was featured in a front-page story of the *Times of Swaziland* (2010) decrying consumption at funerals on the assertion that slaughter was demonic. In his opinion, most Christians were not qualified to bless the food or could not fully "discern" its value (see chap. 2), making consumers susceptible to affliction.

Despite its derisive tensions with Swazi Culture, Christianity effectively inserted itself into local worlds by playing on material forms such as blood and purification to shore up their credibility. For example, AICs such as Jerikho and the Zionist Church of Christ used biblical metaphors of water when talking about the purifying effects of their healers' charcoal-water *tiwasho* mixtures. Several Christian funerals I attended had such a basin available for participants to wash their hands in and thus relieve themselves from *sinyama* or *libhadi* they might contract at the event or otherwise develop in the wake of the death. Prophets in these churches could become adept at the particular application of certain medicinal concoctions for bodily and social maladies and compete in popularity with religious healing resources of *tinyanga*.

A major point about contemporary funeral culture is that *umchinso* and *umbuyiso* rites have been effectively transposed into Christian secondary-phase mortuary rites called *kugeza emanti*, literally "to wash [with] water." Pastors may use holy waters and oils at funerals to anoint participants who feel they need strengthening in these rites. Water and blood are perceived to have different properties, and the Bible's emphasis on the latter opens up the possibility for congruencies between customary and Christian aims of purification. The spilled blood of Jesus in his crucifixion was often foregrounded in funeral speeches as a substance that enlivened participants from affliction and death. All blood is not the same, and of course most people knew bodily fluids such as blood could carry the virus that renders one HIV positive. In the context of contemporary Christian funerals, though, the blood of Jesus was an ultimately transformative medium.

One speaker at a funeral I attended near Mahlanya in October 2010 explained, "There isn't another blood that will save people except the blood of Jesus Christ." A month later, at another funeral near Sidvokovdo, the emcee said, "You forget that you are not worth silver nor gold, but you were brought by a higher force, the blood of Jesus Christ!" Finally, over cups of instant coffee in his Mbabane office, a life insurance administrator explained how the value of blood has changed with regard to Christianity: "There is that thing of slaughtering a cow in custom. In Swazi Culture we can spill the blood for the ancestors. They may still like to do that thing in rural areas, but me, hey, I don't even go for those things because I am a Christian and I don't believe in that.... Some will just buy the food instead. Some people may not have a cow to slaughter. In that case, you say 'It's all right' ... you can just get blood and spill that."

When contributing to a family's funeral that involved elements of Swazi Culture such as an animal sacrifice, a Christian person might have to temper his or her criticism or advocate for something less traditionalist. Rather than give up on the practice of using blood as a purifying property or vilify those who might do so at a funeral, people turned a blind eye or sacrificed their more militant position. Indeed, sacrifice as an act of giving oneself up to God instead of killing an animal was also foregrounded in funeral speeches derived from the Bible. Again, this enabled an easy congruency while encouraging people to think differently about the concept altogether. For example, at the same funeral near Mahlanya in 2010, the pastor called on participants to remember the Bible verse Romans 12, which asks believers to give up their bodies for Christ. "Sacrifice your body wholly to accept the Holy Spirit," he shouted, and continued:

> Sacrifice isn't about busying yourself in the church by being a member of a committee or the church board. Sacrifice is simply giving your body up to the Spirit during the worship service. Be there and give it as a sacrifice. God will do what must be done with what you give Him. Only in worship and the sacrifice of your body, brethren, will we go home (to Heaven).

Entrance into Heaven was contingent on a bodily person who gave himself or herself wholly to God and was unfettered by unimportant matters. Rather than using an intermediary figure such as a beast or other object of sacrifice to commune with God, Christians had to sacrifice themselves. Critically, they did so in the extraordinary place of the funeral, where God's presence was most recognizable in biblical exegeses, prayer, and human death. The division of mind and body common to Enlightenment-related thinking still justified an indictment of sacrifice. If one's mind or soul is that which ultimately transcends to Heaven, the body itself as sacrificial object can be the medium or vessel given up to commune more purely with divinity. For some Christians, this was importantly without the more bodily emphases of blood and bones.

Human bodies were culturally qualified as altogether different things from food. Yet they were both material forms whose value over time was produced in different ways in rites of purification. These transformations occurred through social relations particular to a historical age, thus customary healers and sacrificial logics had greater purchase at some times than Christian practice and HIV/AIDS messaging had at others. In everyday negotiations surrounding the value of food and bodies, consumption and purification had continually been bound up with one another in generating vitality, *imphilo*, amid death.

Conclusion: Life On the Move

In her study of funeral parlors in South Africa, historian Rebekah Lee (2011) traces commercial exhumation and embalming, which "offer intriguing solutions to some of the long-standing dilemmas posed by death on the move." Lee situates death with regard to mobility and migrancy, entrenched as part of Southern Africa's postcolonial landscape, to highlight problems that occur when people die away from home. Mobility enables life for people across many underdeveloped rural locales and cities by circulating money earned in wage labor. The return and presence of the dead at times, however, present disquiet.

When faced with the conundrum of funerary role inversion and criticisms of funeral expansion, I think interesting insights are gained when we flip Lee's notion to consider how other funerary things—bodies, blood, and food especially—are revalued and circulated as forms of "life on the move." Their mobility in Swaziland is the result of historic forces such as migration labor and the commercialization of death that put people in motion across multiple borders. The eternal problem of death, of course, persisted amid such changes in bodily storage and transportation technologies. While aiding the survivors, these forces also abetted the expansion of funerals in size and numbers of attendees as well as increased foodstuffs that built up facets of the presumed qualities of dignity at funerals.

As the world underwent "development" and "globalization," in people's own words, so did social relations within and beyond households. The fact that more people came to funerals became perceptual grounds for claims about role inversions regarding food or grounds to remind people to provide support for those shiftily identified as bereaved. For the bereaved, women's work of food preparation, cooking, and serving was instrumental. This work was predicated on reworking store-bought or donated foodstuffs and thereby transforming their value as an act of purification. The social scene of cooking may appear inimical, but it was moralized as commensal to make it a successful, dignified event. Neighbors, church members, and strangers (in the case of hired caterers) were resourceful in coordinating the delivery of food. Food brought into the liminal site of the bereaved household was initially unprepared or of differential value. There, it was physically and medicinally worked over and redistributed for consumption at both the funeral itself and potentially beyond in takeaway boxes, even if it sometimes tasted flavorless.

Anthropologist Michael D. Jackson (2011, 94) sees ritual as "a process where life-energy, in the form of fuel, food, labor and generative power, is symbolically managed—amassed, increased, stored, shared, exchanged and transferred." It is a useful definition to see how food-related elements traverse various circuits within and beyond the funeral. At the gastrointestinal level of circuitry, attendees veritably embodied the ethical and regenerative properties of food in its ingestion. After a long night in a tent or car parked in the yard, a hearty meal was well received and had the capacity to enliven consumers. Expressions of *"mnandzi"* (good, tasty, or delicious) were usually audible among laughter, sniffles, jokes, and conversation during the morning meal following the burial, even if the food was cold or without salt. Through these meals, people's bodies were provisionally energized by eating protein and carbohydrate-rich foods. This gave them strength to pack up and go on their respective journeys home by car, bus, minibus, or on foot. In this way, life embodied in ingested and digested food enabled mobility.

Another level of circuitry was one more national and facilitated in one simple transportation and storage technology: the takeaway box. Funeral attendees redistributed life-giving food out into the social world through the ubiquitous white Styrofoam plates and boxes seen at nearly all funerals. Occasionally littered and blowing along the roadsides on weekends by those who ate and ran or could not wait to get home, these storage vessels evinced a staggered but nonetheless fulfilling consumption. Some attendees may have slept through the morning burial and took their meals in the later hours of the day during transport. Most attendees, however, carried plates and takeaway boxes of food not for themselves but for others.

This food could be given to friends, coworkers, or fellow brethren picked up on the way to church worship services, given that funerals tend to conclude on Sunday mornings. It could also be given to family members at home who could not go to the funeral. Some people were too tired from the long working week to have strength for a night vigil, and some were too lazy to stay up all night to get food. Others were customarily prohibited from attending. These included children who were sometimes left at home to sleep under the care of a guardian's neighbors and friends and those, such as Roxanne's brother, who worked for kingship and could not attend because of symbolic contagion. Still others may not have attended the funeral because they were physically unable to, as in the case of ill or infirm people and the advanced elderly who could not make the journey. Going on foot would have been too difficult, as would being jostled uncomfortably in a car going over unpaved roads. Through a takeaway box, these people might later indulge in food that had been vitally revalued and thus maintain or improve their bodily conditions. Indeed, people living with HIV and taking ARVs required stable food intake, a sometimes difficult requirement, given wider food insecurities. Despite the relatively conscripted fare of a funeral meal, a takeaway box could still provide a much-needed resource for a homebound person suffering from the disease.

Anthropologists Michael Jindra and Joël Noret (2011, 24) write that "we cannot assume that the ostentatiousness or extravagance at funerals are always strategic for status seeking. There is often a hidden face of the lavishness that is generally reported, and we must take seriously this lavishness or lack thereof." Funerals in Swaziland are critical events in which shifting social relations involved in their production enabled transformations of value, including modes of purification for food and other substances that strengthen the lives and health of their users. The present conundrum of big meals is a recent historic iteration of an ongoing cultural process wherein that which may give life is insecurely negotiated and consumed.

Notes

1. Historically, the area of present-day Swaziland was made up of many indigenous polities and kingdoms, such as the Mamba, that were eventually subsumed under Dlamini control.

2. See DeWaal and Whiteside 2003; Naysmith, DeWaal, and Whiteside 2009; and Fielding-Miller et al. 2014.

3. See Kuper and Kaplan 1944; Ranger 2004; Bähre 2007; Geschiere 2009; and Núñez and Wheeler 2012.

4. See *Times of Swaziland* 1945; Kuper 1980 (1947); Atkins 1993; White 2010; Bähre and Rodima-Taylor 2014; and Ferguson 2015.

5. Matrilateral kin lived with a married woman in some polygynous instances. Younger sisters of married women could be brought into households as surrogate mothers, junior wives, or servants, for example. See Kuper 1950, 1970, 1980 (1947) and Golomski 2015a.

6. See Kuper 1950; Russell 1984; and Golomski 2015a.

7. In taking this as a form of postcolonial cultural production, I carry forward from Hylton White's (2010; 2013) ethnography. He describes how people in KwaZulu-Natal are perceptibly pulled back to their rural homes by ancestral shades to construct dwellings for them. This is a material process bound up with the dead that reinstates South African apartheid-era constructions of radical cultural difference between urban and rural places, the latter becoming the site of ethnocultural production.

8. See Kuper 1965, 1970, 1980 (1947).

9. See Berglund 1976; Ngubane 1977; Kuper 1980 (1947); and White 2013.

6 Commemoration and Cultural Change: *Memento Radicalis*

LaGIJA PUT HER phone down in the car's cup holder to switch into higher gear as we merged onto the freeway. "What do these people want from me?" she asked, "*mxm.*" There was another family affair, one over a matter she already thought was long dead—or rather, over a relative she thought was. For three months now LaGija had been receiving messages from Magdalene, her father's daughter by another woman whom LaGija's sisters jokingly called one of his "bushwives." The narrative of a polygynous or extended family through extramarital affairs was one LaGija often retold with scorn. The license her father and other men were afforded in relationships in Swazi Culture was the bane of women, she said, along with the obligations they would then have toward people like Magdalene. This time, Magdalene's messages were about spinning their web of social relationships even wider.

Magdalene had been telling LaGija she was sick. LaGija's coworkers, friends, and family often asked her for prayerful healing interventions, but this was not such a call. Magdalene was sick from a series of foreboding dreams of a shadowy yet familiar presence. In waking, she would feel a terrible, lethargic weight and had sought religious insight on what was now becoming a problem. Magdalene went to a church that tested LaGija's neo-Pentecostal patience, a church that, in LaGija's eyes, failed to disavow some particularly troubling aspects of Swazi Culture such as the power of the dead, as ancestors or otherwise. After Magdalene's further counseling and prayer with her church members, the shadowy presence was figured to be her deceased maternal grandmother, a not unholy spirit nocturnally calling on her about an important matter: putting up a tombstone at her grave.

In the wake of the revelation, Magdalene made phone calls and sent messages to her relatives asking for monetary, social, and material support to put together a ritual for her grandmother. It involved purchasing and erecting a tombstone and holding a ceremony. Of course, LaGija surmised, the ceremony would require a day's worth of travel to the original grave—"all the way out in the bush, where there is no one out there anymore at their homestead," she said—a day's worth of food preparation, interaction with relatives who reminded her of her father's infidelities, and cash to pay for the stone. To not contribute would risk a degree of social aspersion that she would not help her own family member, however distant, to dignify the dead. To contribute, though, would risk her own relationship with her God and likeminded church brethren who claimed that such spiritual calls were the devil's work. For LaGija, building a new grave for the unquiet dead would be to bring them too close for comfort.

Magdalene stopped messaging about the tombstone after LaGija suggested that her plans for commemoration would come about by the grace of God (rather than telling her flatly that she would not give the money). For the zealously faithful like LaGija, the dead as spiritual presence, dream, shadow, or phenomenon was too unwieldy to give credence to in this way. Yet even the most disciplined Christians could never be too sure about how the dead worked, so ignoring them altogether was not possible—the epidemic made this clear. Looking above the mango tree outside LaGija's kitchen window on a clear day, one could faintly see the hillside of the Ngwane Park cemetery. This municipal cemetery, rivaling the size of adjacent subdivisions, opened in the early 2000s, when the death rate was peaking. In such an age, death cascades. In this instance, the long since departed, such as the grandmother, emerge alongside the more recently deceased from HIV/AIDS, both welling up the earth in more graves, tombstones, and mortuary ephemera that spanned "the bush" to the city. It is an unsettling commercial accretion of "banal accoutrements of death" (Comaroff 2007, 203), or rather, memories. In the wake of AIDS, the dead have come to occupy the living. Criticisms such as LaGija's about how the living might best remember the dead is not a sleight to their dignity but a question of whether such a massive task is possible and why they are consigned to do so much.

This chapter covers commemoration in the material afterlife of funerals. Namely, it shows the ways the dead are differently valued through the stuff the living put up to remember them by. Customary forms of interment, I show, were long more muted kinds of commemoration. Today, an expanded commercial market of tombstones and their placements in large new cemeteries make the dead more publicly and personally known. This works alongside enduring ritual practices of keeping memorabilia, which further foreground the presence of the dead in everyday life. Their pressing density, felt by LaGija, Magdalene, and others, make up what I take to be a diffuse and radical form of public memorial to the epidemic.

Comparatively for the epidemic in South Africa, Kylie Thomas (2014, 9) sees a "monumental failure to mourn the losses of AIDS." There are fewer commemorative sites like the Gugu Dlamini AIDS Ribbon and park in Durban, which was built to honor a woman murdered in 2000 for publicly declaring her HIV-positive status. Thomas notes, though, that there has been little cultural production for a public form of mourning that redresses the sheer affective volume of loss. Public mourning is critical, she writes, because "those we fail to mourn are those whose lives are unrecognized in the political sphere. The 1,000 people who die of AIDS in South Africa each day testify to this fact, their lives for the most part invisible within public memory as their deaths." The formal works produced by prolific artists and writers, in her estimation, might counterproductively render those same lives invisible. Works made by HIV-positive people, such as memory boxes of orphans and the dying organized by humanitarian aid entities, may be too subjective to fathom.[1]

Mourning cascading death seems impossible in this regard, perhaps until commemoration itself becomes political, pressing for public recognition and action against the forms of postcolonial power that negate life. For example, funerals in South Africa for murdered anti-apartheid activists in the 1980s became regular weekly spectacles "intended to shape social memory" of the National Party's state violence against non-whites (Ramphele 1997, 107). This funerary political legacy also shaped later activism around structural violence in the delayed rollout of ARVs in South Africa and demands for recognition of citizens' deaths.[2] Similarly, Teresa Debly (2014) describes the Swazi state's recent disturbing intrusions into the funerals of political activists, such as that of Musa J. Dlamini of People's United Democratic Movement (PUDEMO), over attendees singing songs suspected to be protesting or critical of the government. Yet despite the precedents, public political scrutiny of HIV/AIDS and death does not seem to surround funerary rituals in Swaziland. Indeed, funerals are rather muted with regard to political claims for accountability concerning the epidemic. People tend not to ask who or what is responsible for these deaths and what is going to be done about them.

This relative silence at the ritual event itself, however, does not discount politics altogether. This chapter considers how these politics emerge after the funeral in the forms of ordinary memorabilia and mortuary consumer goods that ground historic consciousness of mass death. These forms force public witnessing, in the shape of tombstones, for example, in stone-faced or object permanence. Commemoration may not zero in on questions of responsibility, but it foregrounds questions of value. Why have particular forms of memory—funeral parlor goods, landscapes altered by new cemeteries, and the political and economic policies and commercial markets that produce these—come to make up what counts as dignity? What else could matter in the making of the worthiness of death and life?

I consider how the material configuration of commemoration today gestures toward something radical, what literary scholar Dagmawi Woubshet (2015, 12) mentions in his notion of "disprized mourning." In a "political and cultural context that devalued the AIDS dead," he argues, grief becomes a "radical basis of group ties and survival," part of "an immediate political act to enfranchise the dead and stymie this catastrophe [of AIDS]," and "a fundamental ethical act to inhume the dead and consign them to posterity." In Swaziland, though, work such as putting up tombstones in new public cemeteries and holding onto keepsakes of the dead make up a sentimental cultural force that prevents the dead from being "disprized" or undervalued. They are commemorated in ways that both dignify and locate them as part the sociopolitical landscape forever changed by the epidemic.

"There Is No Hill without a Grave"

Popular tourist guidebooks to southern Africa sometimes note that hikers should be careful in their treks across mountains because they are likely to step across ordinary people's graves without knowing it. The siSwati proverb "There is no hill without a grave," *ayikho intsaba ingenaliliba*, speaks to a deep history of burial, sociality, and landscape in southern Africa. Graves long took shape as cairns (*tivivane*), discreetly stacked piles of stones that populate many groves and fields and some roadsides. Roadside cairns may not mark an actual burial site but rather sites of car accident deaths such that of LaGija's sister-in-law. These sites can also be commemorated with small crosses. Cairns are still auspicious forms that travelers are encouraged to build up by placing a stone when passing by, materializing a shared collective journey, *indlela*, that all humans follow from birth to death and beyond. The more adventurous hikers going off the path come across what discerning archaeologists and local denizens know to be cairns that quietly mark actual graves—*ematfuna, emadliza*, or *emaliba*—sites to be treated with utmost respect.

Burial cairns were usually constructed in the immediate aftermath of the burial by men who helped to dig the grave and refill it. Stones were gathered from nearby or found in the ground while digging the grave. Cairns qualified the deceased in a specific, characteristic way other than marking the presence of the deceased in a yard or hillside. The biography or identity of the deceased echoed in the oral histories of families and local communities or in the precise location of the grave itself. Different interment sites within homesteads reflected values of Swazi Culture regarding the deceased's age and gender. Older, socially senior married men tended to be buried near or inside the cattle pen, while wives might be buried nearer to their respective dwelling within the homestead and children near their mothers. This symbolism is not of course determinative, nor does it play out in every homestead yard. Some graves are marked with more stones, some with fewer, depending on the resources available, the efforts of those who built the cairn at the funeral itself, and subsequent efforts to situate or commemorate particular dead (see fig. 6.1).[3]

The dead and the living have long domesticated one another in the landscape architecture of the homestead. The living gave room for the dead to dwell so that they would not be forgotten and would be benevolent ancestors in keeping the

Fig. 6.1 Cairn grave inside a homestead yard near Madulini, 2011. Photograph by author.

living safely on the right path. Like the *umchinso* and *kugeza emanti* rites discussed in chapters 4 and 5 show, graves and other constructions for the dead are important sites of sociocultural reproduction. Graves in or near the cattle pen are reminders of material transactions such as bridewealth that bind families across generations and wholly incorporate people across the life course. Some cattle occupying these pens are the received gifts of such transactions and are consecrated by elders in verbal rites and anointings for the deceased. Cattle are kept and slaughtered in the pen for these ceremonies, and the blood is spilled where the dead lie, satiating both their hunger for blood's nourishing qualities and the aspired sociability between in-laws conducting this and anticipated future exchanges.

Along with the cattle pen as a customary dwelling for the dead were *rondavel* houses such as Nik's at Madulini: round-shaped with conical roofs emulating indigenous architectural forms of thatched beehive-shaped dwellings. A round house could also be known as *kagogo*, meaning "grandmother's house," and had been a crucial heritage site for families. This house was where memorabilia of the deceased was often preserved, along with other objects such as clay beer pots and grass mats associated with Swazi Culture. Kuper ([1947] 1980, 183) writes that these were stored on a short altar called *umsamo*—interestingly, the same word used for the National Museum—in the rear of the house. One's *kagogo* served then as a shrine of sorts, a place to recollect the dead and collect their objects that, in total, materialized cultural values. *Kagogo* was and is still used at critical junctures in people's lives, where families communed with the shades over matters of fertility, marriage, illness, and mobility. Before going on long journeys or returning from them, for example, elders asked the shades to protect travelers, venerating them with food the traveler carried (*umphako*), home-brewed beer (*umcombotsi*), and other victuals. Newborn children of families' sons, as well as the dead as the newest members of the spiritual patriline, were ceremoniously introduced to elders there.

While much of what I learned about customary cairns and these constructions for dead was said to be important parts of Swazi Culture, most people told me they were of less practical concern or mostly the concern of those living in "rural areas." Such remarks shored up critical separations between what were implied to be educated, Christian ways of doing things and that which had long been construed in local church and mission education as the work of paganism. While these sites of customary rites of remembrance for the dead (*kuphahla*) existed, it was telling that most people I spoke to mentioned that *kuphahla* was the least practiced ritual of Swazi Culture today. The round houses of families I knew, such as the one at Vuyo and Nokwenza's, had little ceremonial charge and were otherwise used as storage spaces or extra bedrooms for visitors like Nik.

Interestingly, the *kagogo* archetype had been translated into a form of HIV/AIDS programming but with indirect reference to the dead. For UNAIDS (2006), *kagogo* featured prominently as part of their "best practice collection" of policies, called a "revival of old traditions [that] brings hope" to communities burdened by parent and guardian mortality. In 2003, several government ministries, NERCHA, and a British NGO, Save the Children, implemented a nationwide construction drive to build "*kagogo* social centres," mostly in rural communities, after a group of women in Hhohho organized a call for state assistance when their impromptu volunteer work of caring for and feeding orphaned children became too immense. Usually built near a chief's compound (*umphakatsi*), these centers were small, usually square-shaped structures equipped with electricity and water, and cost around US$10,000 to build. Socially and politically, they functioned to shore up local leaders' accountability and response to HIV/AIDS and thus "empower the community." Practically, they functioned as storage facilities for emergency food donations and office or meeting points for public health, humanitarian, and community-based entities conducting a variety of work.

At Madulini, for example, the World Food Programme, Doctors Without Borders, UNAIDS, and academic researchers all used the *kagogo* center as a point for data collection and service provision (see fig. 6.2). The *libandlancane* held its weekly community court sessions there and also stored local birth and death records in one of the two locked rooms. The term "*kagogo*" was fitting, as it was often older women and grandmothers who occupied their time there,

Fig. 6.2 Children and women queue for food after a public health and social welfare event at the community *kagogo* center, Madulini, 2011. Photograph by author.

preparing to visit the infirm or dying as members of SHBC or organizing events for orphaned and vulnerable children. These state and global health entities' versions of Swazi Culture in the form of *kagogo* were domestically familiar, but the *kagogo* as a house for the dead got a new sort of life as an institutional form of intervention for survivors. The dead emerged not as venerated or individually known people, and there were no commemorative public plaques or markers for them in these centers. There, the dead were not present as benevolent overseers but instead as data points, as in death certificates and clinical cards documenting orphans' birth parents. They were rather a public echo, resounding the collective historical tragedy of disease and driving national construction projects for social welfare. Mourned without ceremony, the dead were rather put to work as part of the infrastructure of state and global public health and development.

Like the embedded silence of new *kagogo* centers, customary cairns and the dead therein faded without ongoing cultural practices of oral historical transmission to animate them. When the living who told stories of the dead moved away, forgot, or died, biographies of the dead did not get repeated. The grave itself was eventually covered through seasonal cycles of overgrowth. The pile depressed further into the earth. Fewer and fewer of the living were reminded of the identity of the dead when oral histories and verbal rites of remembrance, both the prerogative of elders rather than youth, were not recited.

One young mother I knew named Khetsi became the main tenant and caretaker of her grandmother's home on the edge of a chiefdom on Swazi Nation

Land and the municipal land of Manzini's City Council. Her uncles, who were her father's brothers and would have otherwise taken over the property, had all died between the 1990s and 2000s. Khetsi's grandmother (who were these men's mother) passed on in 2008, leaving the young adult grandchildren as the remaining generation. In the yard under a tree were eight graves made of piled stones. Four newer graves were of contemporaries: Khetsi's cousins—some of whom she guessed died of AIDS—and some of their small children. The identities of the older graves, barely visible after being papered with years of fallen leaves, she did not know.

Our conversation about who she could identify or not perhaps incited Khetsi to eventually tell me she wanted to tidy up the graves by removing the leaves and household detritus of wrappers and other things stuck there after blowing through the urban yard. To her, despite their biographical mystery, the cairns' age and permanence amounted to a claim to belong there. If she could at least show respect for these unknown dead by cleaning the cairns, her work would remind her neighbors and local councilors that their descendants remained and occupied the house in their absence.

In these ways, the *kagogo* and cairn as forms of Swazi Culture seemed to no longer work to commemorate the dead, or at least did not accomplish it with the same strength as they might have in the past. How then could the dead be remembered otherwise? How could their (former) lives be valued? For Magdalene's grandmother, and Magdalene herself, something more was needed besides the grandmother's original cairn at her rural marital homestead. For more and more families now living on municipal land in urban areas, where in-yard burial was not an option, someplace else was needed. Municipal and state leaders might provide this alternative place—a public cemetery—but still had to account for the remembrance of many unrelated dead in one place. Solicitously, the epidemic's respondent mortuary market answered these calls and in turn changed the possible forms of commemoration.

Tombstones: Object Permanence

In many rural communities, along with general stores and roadside stands organized by development agencies for women to sell fruit, vegetables, or firewood, one might now find a funeral parlor dealing in coffins and contacts for mortuaries. In towns, funeral parlor offerings were more expansive and included the radical newer form of memory making: the tombstone. Tombstones were not totally unheard of, and any visit to an urban cemetery would show that some people had been buried with these more biographical markers for a long time. Still, the spate of mass death at the turn of the millennium and the expanded set of commercial mortuary retailers led many people to tell me that tombstones were now distinctively popular in contrast to customary grave markers.

Over cups of tea and a plate of lemony biscuits, an administrator at an insurance company described how tombstones represented a popular innovation in commemoration practices: "The tombstones things are new, too," she began:

> Before, we just put the rocks on top of the grave and then put the sand there to keep it all in place. I think they are getting more used to the tombstones now because you can get them in the towns. For the cemeteries in town they use the tombstones more. You know, there are some graves there without the tombstones, maybe they will get them later, but maybe they will just leave them because they know that is what they do [in] our culture. In the past, your friends and colleagues will all just place a stone on there, you know, ones they find lying around the place where you are buried. You know, today, I think all this funeral business makes big money, and it is a business for many people. When you take away all the frills and whistles, it is just a funeral.

Tombstones were themselves configurations of several elements. They included a headstone with biographical details of the deceased, a base to hold it, a rectangular stone perimeter called a ledger, and a concrete filling or a scattering of small, decorative, sometimes colored stones within the ledger. In this way, the ledger essentially contained a different type of cairn within a perfect geometric form. Headstones were typically granite or polished fieldstone. As large manufactured blocks, some shops also doubled the stones' potential use by selling the material as kitchen countertops for home construction or renovation. Most Swazi companies imported already-cut blocks for resale from larger South African companies such as Tombco and had engraving done there, as well.

Putting up a tombstone was a pricy, lengthy process. At one shop, a simple headstone engraved with a name, birth date, and death date ran E1800 (US$169), not including the delivery and set-up costs by shop employees. Usually the customer provided the building materials if the employees erected the stone, which consisted of upward of six wheelbarrows of cement and five twenty-liter buckets of water. Like other shops' options, prices rose according to size and styled cut and color of the headstone. The addition of other elements such as ledgers could run up the cost to anywhere from E7000 to E10000 (US$656–US$937). Most salespeople I spoke with in their shops noted that engraving the name and dates details were free. Some customers chose to include the clan praise name (*sinanatelo*) of the deceased and stock phrases such as "*lala ngoxolo*" ("rest in peace") that they themselves chose or else chose from a selection offered in shop catalogs.

Headstones and bases were offered for purchase on credit or as add-ons on insurance policies through brokers and funeral parlors. Metropolitan Insurance, for example, offered a "tombstone benefit" policy add-on that would eventually pay out E5000 (US$469) to use for a tombstone sourced through another local shop. Layaway or credit plans worked well too, given that most families I knew and salespeople I spoke with said that tombstones were expensive and would not go up at a grave until long after the burial or initial purchase. Purchasing graves and bases to produce dignity for the deceased was similar to Deborah James's (2015, 102) description of South African life-cycle rites. There, purchasing furniture on credit marked momentous transitions such as marriage in a consumer culture-driven life course that also manifested modernist values of sophistication.

Families and customers purchased tombstones for the obvious reason of remembering the dead (*kukhumbula*), and the temporality of remembrance in tombstone consumption took on social and ecological forms. In the first sense, because the dead affected a wide web of social relations, decisions and down payments on tombstones were often made at family functions. People often gathered at rural homes at Christmas and made good on loans, debts, exchanges, and collective projects. As Khetsi did, families felt increased pressure from chiefly authorities to show belonging in rural areas by plowing fields and keeping up graves when most people now otherwise worked in town. One tombstone salesman in Manzini told me he recently had a family purchase ten tombstones at once to mark the previously unmarked cairns at their rural homestead yard.

As with Magdalene, the compulsion to buy a tombstone came from calls of the dead in subjective visions or dreams of the living and were usually between more intimate kinship relations. The dead were not usually unknown, and there was a multiply social, spiritual, and physical risk in ignoring the call. A saleswoman at another tombstone shop in Matsapha explained how "hauntings" by some recent and some long-term dead led many customers to her store:

> I had one tell me that her grandmother, who was dead 15 years, appeared in her mind and in her dreams and began requesting a tombstone. Another one told me that the deceased told her in her dreams that he had been bewitched because someone had taken the dirt from the grave. This was a reason they wanted to buy the ledger to cover the grave in cement. The dead can send the living any number of messages that speak to family problems that now affect the dead. Maybe someone took their money or someone gave it to lawyers to sort some business of the inheritance, or maybe their house was rented out or sold in a bad manner. The dead will call on them to sort the situation by asking for a tombstone.

In her account, and similar perhaps to Magdalene's grandmother, the dead sought some object of permanence, a material testament in place that would mark them long after the deaths of others. In the example given by the saleswoman, improper redistribution of the inheritance or memorabilia by kin and close social relations led the dead to solidify what was otherwise a fragmentation of their material presence in the world. This took form in their initial grave, their house, and other objects that continued to embody their existence among the living. This possibility of fragmentation or destruction of material wholeness was, for the dead, an unethical postmortem process: the theft of dirt from the grave was like the extraction of a body's parts while it lay at the mortuary or like the social predation in buying life insurance policies to produce value from another's loss. Given that the dead could withhold protection if they felt disrespected, the living mitigated this risk by setting up tombstones to show that their memories were tangibly constant.

Salespeople I spoke with also pointed out the struggle of Christian customers to reconcile their religious ideations of the dead in their respective church communities with the hauntings that drove them to the store in the first place. The saleswoman in Matsapha described how a male customer came in discreetly inquiring about a tombstone. He told her he had always been a devout and strict Christian, but a few months after his brother's death, the brother began to visit him daily in his dreams. The experience shook him to the foundations of his faith and led him to commemorate the brother in buying a tombstone. Another saleswoman at a tombstone shop in Manzini said simply that people must do this work because of Swazi Culture, despite their reservations about cost and religious orientation. Still, given the historic shift in the popular religious landscape toward neo-Pentecostal Christianity and its stipulations about discerning materiality, it makes sense that some consumers would be suspicious.

Tombstones were not put up without ceremony. In fact, tombstones and their long-term production in credit or insurance policy payments has led to the creation of a new type of *umsebenti* ritual: the unveiling party. Historically, after one to three years, the family would reconvene at the grave to conduct the *umchinso* or *kugeza emanti* rite. Today, people told me, unveiling parties incorporate or take the place of these secondary-phase mortuary rites. LaGija's sister Buyiswa brought home an invitation to such a party after her Tuesday seminar at the university, laughing at its strangeness. With the unveiling party to be held on a Saturday afternoon, the family of the deceased planned to put up a small tent at the grave in the public cemetery (see fig. 6.3). There would be a short service before the unveiling itself, which involved pulling off a sheet, tarp, or other covering wrapped around the new tombstone after it was set up. Lunch would conclude the event.

A saleswoman at a tombstone shop in Manzini described how unveiling parties were popular among some Christians, who called the event *inkhonzo*, the same term for a church worship service. In a way, she said, doing so might temper concerns about seeing the whole affair as too akin to ancestral veneration. As with *kugeza emanti*, the unveiling party occurred one to three years after the death in conjunction with the completion of payment on the tombstone and a commensal event that enabled the living to move on with life and establish some permanence of place for the dead. Unveiling could also connote the unveiling of widows, who ceremoniously removed their mourning gowns at or after the secondary phase rites.

Fig. 6.3 High-end ledger and tombstone waiting to be unveiled, Manzini, 2014.
Photograph by author.

Finally, local ecology shapes the timing of commemoration by tombstones, with August, winter's end, being the most productive month of the year. By May, most of the maize has been harvested, leaving expansive fields of yellowed, withered stalks for cattle to graze on. Many people will burn the remaining dried grasses, setting the hills alight in dramatic nighttime shows of smoking orange, red, and yellow waves so as to encourage new grass shoots to grow up in the coming spring. With vegetation cleared, a good spot can be found around the grave for placing the concrete structure. Without heavy rainfall through the winter, the ground hardens. Once it begins to soften with the spring rains, retailers and families find it best to then settle the tombstone in the ground in what some call "to open the grave," *kuvula litfuna.* The same saying is used to describe some families' practice of going to graves around Easter or Passover holidays to clear debris and overgrowth. Over the course of August and September, glossy new monoliths rise up across the country, citing the return of the dead.

In contrast to cairns, tombstones, as part of contemporary funeral culture, had a value in their permanence that the dead desired to be remembered by. The dead wanted sleek lines, perfected geometry, incise lettering, and a durable structure that withstood seasonal weathering and the mortal life course of their survivors. Even when there was no one related left to mourn, the dead could still be known by name with a personalized tombstone. The call of the dead to remember now entailed more work for the living, in construction, credit or investment, party organization, and social maneuvering to either avoid or encompass Christian sensibilities—and this was just to get a special stone set in place. Once the tombstone finally went up, though, the dead did not simply stay put. They continued to move, speak, and animate public commemoration in the stuff they left behind and the ways the living put them to work beyond the grave.

Memorabilia: Wearing Memories

Tombstones were newer and largely immobile forms of commemoration, but contemporary mourning also involved more portable and diffuse displays of memory that made the dead even more visible as part of everyday life. Memorabilia such as photographs and personal ephemera of the deceased—especially clothing, both regular (*timphahla* or *tingubo*) and customary (*imvunulo*)—were profound material traces of lives that circulated with the living who carried them. They enabled the living to materialize their relationship with the dead, albeit a relationship that was now transformed. Like cairns and other constructions for the dead, memorabilia played on enduring customary practices but permitted the bereaved to creatively transcend some stipulations that would prohibit working through their grief.

People who mourned according to Swazi Culture were easily noticeable all across the kingdom, and by and large these were women. As in many societies around the world, death in Swaziland involved the social transformation of women and widows.[4] Precolonial, traditionalist, and non-Christian mourning attire was produced from the natural environs in elaborate material constructions (Kuper [1947] 1980). For an ordinary man's death, his wives, sisters, and mothers shaved their hair at a river and made rudimentary caps (*emahlokohloko*), which they weaved from *tingqoboza* grasses. The women also turned their cattle-skin skirts inside out. They remained in the main widow's house for the first month, and in that time wove more refined caps (*tincwati*) made from the grasses used to construct houses.[5] Women in mourning also wove long, yellowed grass ropes (*tintsambo* or *tincotfo*) to wear on their shoulders or neck and waist. Men simply shaved their heads in mourning a male relative. In the case of the death of a married woman, the woman's father removed his head ring (*umbodze*) and cut his hair.[6] A husband did the same and took on a single grass rope around the waist called *ligodza*. Men faced fewer prescriptions of seclusion and movement than women and wore fewer items to signify their mourning.

Later, at the *umchinso* or *kugeza emanti* rite, women reversed their skirts, and most mourners threw away their ropes or caps. The personal belongings of the deceased were also "washed" at this time (Kasenene 1993). Despite the return of the dead and their emplacement in the grave, some women, usually mothers and wives, continued to wear the ropes and caps for up to three winters or three years, until their in-laws deemed it appropriate to remove them. Zakhe Hlanze, a researcher at a women's rights organization, told me that in her mother's time, from the 1940s to the 1970s, mourning for widows was prescribed to be three winters long per Swazi Culture. "If your husband died at the end of August"—the end of winter—"well, you'll just have to wait a little longer," to a nearly fourth year. Hilda Kuper (n.d.) wrote that the women were thanked for their emotional labor—"You have carried well your mourning ropes," she noted one informant telling her.

As in the case of Nansi's relative Nontsiky, in-laws were supposed to organize a ceremony for when the widow removed the gowns. Tiny, a widow I knew who worked at an old-age home, explained that her own respective ceremony was also a time for in-laws to encourage her and other widows to take one of her deceased husband's brothers as a new husband, a form of levirate marriage (*kungenwa*) in Swazi Culture.[7] Luckily, Tiny told me, she had a son by her deceased husband and could avoid this arrangement by stating that her son, once grown, would eventually be her social support and thus did not need this paternalistic care.

Today, widows are still compelled by their in-laws to wear mourning attire: long black pinafores or jumper dresses with long sleeves, black shoes and stockings, and black caps. Mothers and some sisters and daughters of deceased men will put on similarly severe dress. The all-black ensemble is a product of the influence of colonial-era missionaries. Widows are currently being empowered to throw off these material and social stipulations of what is called an "antiquated and convoluted system" by global human and women's rights entities.[8] Some neo-Pentecostal and evangelical Christian churches that run against traditionalist materiality also level criticisms of mourning. Former traditionalists such as the Reverend Grace Masilela and other pastors have campaigned against mourning gowns.[9] One inter-church organization even commissioned theater troupes to travel to rural communities to act out scenes of widows refusing to wear gowns in the face of their in-laws, citing the 2005 constitutional reforms and broader women's and human rights discourses.

In these ideations, mourning did not need to focus on materiality, but rather on one's emotional and independent will or faith. A common theme in sermons and testimonies at neo-Pentecostal-inspired worship services I attended was that objects left behind by the deceased, as with the body itself, were dangerous vehicles for dark powers. They could overtake the bereaved, who were already considered to be "sick" in their emotional state. In transcribing a sermon from a visiting pastor at the Reformed Church in Madulini, Nokwenza explained to me that certain objects such as "clothes, necklaces, earrings, and especially pastors' suits," when flashy and unethically coveted, were means for demons to latch onto humans. As with neo-Pentecostal attempts to discern the materiality and efficacy of different substances in different churches, attempts to ethically mourn were threatened by objects of the familiar world.

Yet these prescriptions rallying against the material culture of mourning did not undo its enduring power for the bereaved. If Swazi Culture was too traditionalist or restrictive with regard to gendered mourning attire, more subjective, personal practices came to the fore in funeral culture that enabled everyday productions of memory.[10] Take, for example, my friend Nozipho. The daughter of a lawyer, she was encouraged to try technical school but skirted her guardians' wishes in order to live a wilder lifestyle. I first met her in 2008 while visiting her urban Manzini neighborhood and usually found her discussing the aggravations and pleasures of intimate relationships with friends over *dagga* (marijuana) cigarettes and bottles of beer. She lived in a small, fine house, a pink three-room structure that stood out from her neighbors' impromptu stick-and-mud or concrete rental units. Nozipho got the house through a suitor who was more than forty-five years her senior, a Dutch man she met at a party for expatriate airplane enthusiasts. The man had since provided her with both affection and goods. The man was also reportedly HIV positive. Khetsi, also one of Nozipho's friends, told me this as we went around the neighborhood conducting surveys, saying wryly, "We don't know if she is HIV positive, too."

While maintaining her relationship with the Dutch man, Nozipho was also involved with a boyfriend named Sugar. Like Nozipho, Sugar liked to party, and the two got along famously. The two were involved off and on for more than five years. Sugar died suddenly in September 2010. "He passed from BP (high blood pressure). He got sick, and after four days, he went just like that," she explained. Sugar's mother put an obituary in the *Times of Swaziland* and had the means for a funeral through a life insurance policy. I did not see Nozipho again until a month after the funeral. She later told me she stayed in her house to "think about other things," but also warned me that being alone with one's thoughts and doing nothing else is a dangerous action that lands people in the state psychiatric hospital. After I picked her up in town and rode to her flat to visit for the afternoon, I asked her how she was getting along. "Good," she said, "very good!" I asked her whether or not she had kept any of Sugar's things, using the word *timphahla*, which connotes a broader range of household items, including clothing. "Here!" she laughed. Yanking up her zippered fleece jacket and a white T-shirt with one hand, she exposed a baggy black shirt with the other. It was noticeably larger than her small frame. I laughed along with her as she told me it was Sugar's. "It reminds me of him," she explained. "I like to wear this shirt when I go to sleep in bed at night. Maybe I will dream about him."

Nozipho reiterated what Magdalene and others in Swaziland and cross-culturally know: that dreams are portals to contact the deceased.[11] Formerly, carved wooden headrests (*ticamelo*) both kept the head elevated to protect indigenous hairstyles and provided a portal for ancestral contact. More contemporary forms now enable this contact. Because Nozipho and Sugar used to sleep together, the T-shirt evinced more sensual memories. She asked his family for the shirt, and they obliged to give it to her after the funeral, along with a fine aviator jacket. This was somewhat extraordinary, as Nozipho was not related to Sugar and less likely to receive any of his stuff. Unmarried lovers, even if they are mothers of the deceased's children, are often excluded by the deceased's kin from participating in the more public and formulaic actions at a funeral, if not made the butt of jokes and criticism (Dlamini 2006). Yet her long-term commitment to him of five years was enough to persuade his mother to release a few pieces, enabling Nozipho to memorialize her boyfriend in this "reminder," *sikhumbuto*, and constitute enduring intimate exchanges across realms.

As elsewhere in Africa, some young people in Swaziland often forge multiple relationships with others across class, racial, and transnational differences for the multiple benefits of consumption, material exchange, and desire for romance or personal affection.[12] Sometimes this is in secret or in collusion with each respective individual. Jennifer Cole (2009), for example, shows how young women in Madagascar seek out older foreign men to fulfill material needs and wants, and a younger local man, a *joambilo*, who fulfills more passionate and romantic longings. Nozipho's relationships are similar in that she has a lucrative yet potentially dangerous relationship with the Dutch man to secure material well-being while she was also seeking Sugar for a youthful sexual relationship. LaGija's college-age sons described to me the new importance of material gift-giving as part of this romance, using the term "tender care" or "TC."[13] For Nozipho too, the use of clothing was a form of self-expression, indicating her personal and emotional aspirations and her social position as a youth participating in commercial-material exchange relationships that also shaped the local field of HIV transmission.[14]

Unlike the black pinafores of widows, T-shirts and other mundane clothing items enabled the bereaved to remember the dead outside of the gendered social relations of Swazi Culture—they could do it on their own creative terms. Clothing and other memorabilia carried significant weight as resources for psychosocial transition, permitting the living to locate themselves in and piece together another world shattered by death. For some I met who had lost someone close to them, these mundane objects were instrumental for mourning. Such objects were described as having psychological value in enabling "closure," "healing," and movement through the bereavement "process" (Golomski 2015c). Popular neo-Pentecostal sensibilities suggested that this materiality could be problematic unless it was prayerfully discerned, yet other Christian interpretations interestingly blended with humanitarian responses to HIV/AIDS regionally.

In South Africa, for example, theologian Philippe Denis describes families' production of "memory boxes," small boxes filled by survivors or orphans with memorabilia of the deceased. These include small clothing items, jewelry, and personal affects such as cups, identification cards, and photographs. For Denis and others, the production of these boxes and the narratives that surround them can facilitate status disclosure and importantly assuage the shock of families experiencing death from HIV/AIDS.[15] Some argue that this method is congruent with customary forms of Nguni cultural commemoration (Ntsimane 2005), perhaps akin to the *umsamo* altar in indigenous homes. Some organizations working in Swaziland have promoted this method in working with children. These include Lulisandla Kumntwana as part of the South African-based Serving in Mission, the New Hope Centre, the Bantwana Initiative for Orphaned and Vulnerable Children, and Baphalali Swaziland Red Cross Society's project at Sigombeni. Such projects show local recognition for the power of using the materiality of the dead for mourning.

What is the overall relationship then between ordinary clothing and objects as memorabilia and stereotyped mourning attire? People have long been classified in Swazi Culture in forms of gendered traditionalist clothing (*imvunulo*), according to Hilda Kuper (1973a, 365), who states that its importance lies in "a means of relating individuals to one another." Within this social world, however, are more intimate spaces for personally creative forms of memory and cultural production. I think she alludes to this when she depicts elsewhere how people have also long been keen to make themselves "shine," *kukhanyisa*, in clothing by keeping up personal appearances and to generally look and act nice.[16]

The same affect, I think, goes into the impetus to look nice for mobile phone selfies posted to Facebook and Instagram. Some fashionably do so before and after funerals, too. To make oneself shine in clothing—of the deceased or otherwise—and other goods is not done solely out of vanity, though. It is to feel dignified, have self-worth, and establish commemorative relationships in a social world that includes both the living and the dead. The personal use of memorabilia, then, is of spiritual, symbolic, and practical value for the bereaved. It is empowering for those who feel burdened by Swazi Culture's stipulations of mourning and have a greater affinity with contemporary religious or humanitarian entities promoting the right to do something else with one's grief.

Public Cemeteries as Radical Mourning

Newer forms of commemoration derive part of their value from being situated in place. Cairns and burials at home have customary significance tied to Swazi Culture. The new major mode of interment in the kingdom takes place in public cemeteries, however, which confounds royalist-centered cultural productions of death. Public cemeteries make up a material configuration of what I call "radical mourning." Again echoing Dagmawi Woubshet (2015), the immensity of HIV/AIDS-associated losses in Swaziland drives new kinds of sociability, where death becomes, in his words, "a radical basis of group ties and survival" and impels the living to consign the dead in an ethical way. Turning with this approach to anthropology, Michael Lambek (2013) argues that people's ethical imperatives become "objectified" in ritual action. In other words, people creatively express and produce what they know and feel as dignity. Social concerns for the dead become tangible or, quite literally in the form of a tombstone ledger, concrete in the work of commemoration.

What makes this radical has to do with the forms public cemeteries take. On the landscape, cemeteries are massive, visible, and utterly public. The tombstones therein are mass-marketed, and they are productions that are explicitly human-focused. Public cemeteries contrast strikingly with what is done for the royal dead, the kingdom's political and cultural leaders, as arbiters of Swazi Culture. Dlamini royalists, it is well known, have long buried their dead in hidden caves in mountain ranges such as Mdzimba, an escarpment most identifiable as running parallel to the national highway descending from Mbabane to the Ezulwini Valley. Rumors abound that armed security forces still patrol and guard the mountain graves. This secrecy and envelopment of the royal dead in the landscape has a long history (Kuper [1947] 1980). In 1916, for example, Queen Labotsibeni turned away a scientific expedition from the South African Transvaal Museum wishing to study indigenous bats and birds at the Horo mountain range. This was meant to keep non-royalists and strangers from going near what were ancient graves of royal children and wives from the reign of Mswati I, with Labotsibeni saying, "It is my earnest desire that all the burial caves should be well protected."[17]

The commemoration of royalists in this way is monumental: being buried in grandiose yet removed form, where all resident citizens of the Hhohho region and passersby face the graves but do not (care to) see them. Indeed, besides the national monument to King Sobhuza II in Lobamba, royalists hide their dead in plain sight. The implements of royal burial are also unlike what the majority of Swazi do to consign the dead. The interments of royalists are kept highly secret and are undertaken by a group of ritual specialists known as *bantfu bentsaba*, "people of the mountain." One princess told insider anthropologist Gabby Dlamini (2012, 35), "As much as it is a royal funeral it is not all glitz and glam with luxury everywhere, in fact quite the opposite. It is back to basics, all natural, even the instruments used, grass mats, no smart dress."

While ordinary people's funerals also include elements such as grass mats, the commercial mortuary market sells "modern" and "dignified" consumer options that complicate what would patently be described as Swazi Culture. Likewise, the work put in by *bantfu bentsaba*, Gabby Dlamini argues, exceeds its value as mere commodity because of the symbolic power granted to these commoners in handling the royal dead. For a short while, they become equivalent with royalists in what is otherwise an obviously socially hierarchical relationship. The mountain people do not choose this work by their own volition. Historically, it is assigned to them because they are members of certain clans, and it is a task they would not readily avoid.

In contrast to the secretive traditionalist burials of royals in mountains, ordinary Swazi burials take place in public at sites of radical visibility that cannot be ignored. They are public places where unrelated people are collectively buried, the antithesis of a homestead where patrilineal family is placed together. Urban and public cemeteries developed as part of the landscape architecture of late nineteenth- and early twentieth-century Afrikaner and British settler colonialism.[18] Cemeteries were features of growing colonial towns such as Mbabane, Bremersdorp (Manzini), Goedgegun (Nhlangano) and Stegi (Siteki) and were segregated between Europeans and "natives."

Public cemeteries also set the stage for the uptake of personalized tombstones in that colonists identified graves by markers called pegs. These were temporary markers of wooden stakes affixed to the heads of graves and on which names could be inscribed, anticipating more permanent markers made of stone. These uniform markers were purchased for the municipality through the colonial government buyer in Johannesburg and placed at graves as part of the burial fee. Wandering cattle, goats, and other animals sometimes toppled the pegs, leading to the concern about who would do the work of managing the cemetery in keeping them out and cutting the grass. For this practical and important work, the colonial office used a motley crew of labor, from prisoners to others similarly deemed peripheral in colonial society.[19]

The national landscape changed dramatically in the twentieth century in colonial land partitions and development projects. Before and after independence, municipalities increasingly faced the problem of how to best house the dead in rural and urbanizing areas. Public accommodations for the dead inevitably rubbed up against living neighbors, and with HIV/AIDS driving greater numbers of deaths, urban cemeteries developed in the mid-twentieth century have quickly reached maximum capacity. New cemeteries and morgues are being developed despite overall decreasing space within zoned municipal boundaries.

One man whose home was adjacent to a new morgue commissioned by the Siteki Town Council complained, "Our children will be able to see coffins being transported [there] and that is not acceptable" (Zulu 2009b). In 2015, the Nhlangano Town Council included funds to expand their existing cemetery as part of the capital budget. In 2013, the City Council of Manzini purchased a plot of farmland within the city to develop a new cemetery and hired security guards to patrol the municipal landfill to prevent people from dumping trash in a nearby existing cemetery. In Manzini, the Ngwane Park cemetery was opened after the Golf Course cemetery became full. In Mbabane, the Mangwaneni cemetery was closed as it reached maximum capacity, with burials permitted only to families who had bought plots in the 1990s and early 2000s.[20] "Lately, between three and five people are buried at Ngwane Park cemetery every week," said Manzini City Council public relations officer Mathokoza Thwala. "However, we do not want to be caught with our pants down, hence, as a proactive initiative, we are already scouting for alternative pieces of land wherein the people of Manzini will bury their loved ones" (Nkambule 2014a). Urban cemeteries are sometimes sites of criminal activity, with mourners being robbed by desperate criminals.[21]

Urban overcrowding is doubly problematic because urban residents are encouraged to bury relatives at rural homes while at the same time rural chiefdoms are forbidding burial in private homestead yards. There are some rural community cemeteries, often the byproduct of development projects where the state claims the right to Swazi Nation Land use. In one case, senior members of the Hlane royal residence forbade area residents to continue home burials soon after it began plans to expand a sugar cane cooperative. One family, the Hlophes, defied such orders, citing past burials on long-tenured land. In the middle of a night vigil for a young woman relative, police were deployed to stop the event, forcefully leading the family to dig instead at a new cemetery.[22]

Another major project involving exhumation was the building of the kingdom's new King Mswati III International Airport at Sikhuphe. Eventually, 186 bodies were removed from the area in a mass exhumation so development could proceed. Said one woman, Siphelele Ndzimandze, who saw her twin sister disinterred, "The reburial is more painful than the ordinary funeral" in that "you dig the grave to expose only a few dry bones" (Dlamini 2010). Indeed, most of the witnesses at the exhumations identified their relatives by the clothing and blankets interred in the grave during the original funeral. That royalists try to reclaim land by disinterring burials of long-time residents, as chapter 4 shows for chief Mzikayise Ntshangase, is cause for many ordinary citizens' concern.[23]

Casual passersby of public urban cemeteries might think they are badly littered, perhaps lending to the sensibility that they are also unsafe. From the roadside, plastic bags and tarps might billow up like sheeted ghosts, hooked on something invisible from afar and rendering a flag-like stationary dance. Pops of brightly colored plastic, in the petals of artificial flowers, wrappers, and bottles. Signs and crosses, metal and wood. These are not trash, but idiosyncratic forms of memory marking graves, purchased and cobbled together from housewares, wholesalers, and smaller vendors. They speak to ordinary people's subjective tastes, social relations, and the material lives as part of a regionally uniform consumer culture. Some graves are marked by soap packages and empty aerosol cans of deodorant. One friend of mine interpreted these objects as perhaps the favorite or regularly used scents of the deceased person, fondly and sensually remembered by the one who placed them there. Other objects such as drinking cups, empty bottles of soda and sparkling water, and bits of clothing left behind by the deceased are also left as material forms through which the living can enact embodied memories at the grave.

Most graves are adorned with artificial flowers, which are considered as both tasteful and, importantly, durable, although they are not a conventional form of condolence like food. Roses, daisies, and chrysanthemums of different colors are popular varieties and are arranged in smaller bouquets or sprays and sold mostly by funeral parlors. Sometimes complementary, sometimes contingent on a funeral policy, parlors might provide the only set of flowers. It is clear who contributed the flowers because they come with small cards that are ceremoniously read aloud at the morning burial service. Besides the general condolences, siblings, in-laws, church organizations, and coworkers all tend to pitch in their own and get acknowledged. Artificial flowers are usually laid on the coffin and then kept to decorate the gravesite rather than being buried. Later, despite losing their dyed color from the sun or being shredded by other elements of the changing seasons, flowers mark the consumer's ethical imperative of funerary dignity.

However, as Dumisa Dlamini (2006) stated in his op-ed about funeral culture that opened this story, people are often wary about these flowers and other accoutrements that mark this new landscape of death. The commercial detritus of public cemeteries is radical in that it is the form through which a commemorative ethics of dignity is materialized. Yet it utterly transforms the landscape into unnatural cities of the dead, unlike the way royalists would consign their own. For ordinary citizens, the dwellings for the dead are geometrically perfect homes of tombstones contrasting to the otherwise scraggly, undulating terrain of the kingdom's mountains. This consumptive materiality infills the landscape in municipally zoned and ever-expanding matrices and compels the living and those in power to know the HIV/AIDS dead as a more permanently situated public. Their personalized tombstones, flowers, and memorabilia shore up their biographies.

Finally, public cemeteries are radical reminders that popular commemoration takes such a distinctly nontraditional form. It is something uncannily similar to yet other than Swazi Culture. As with Magdalene's case, Hylton White (2010, 515) describes how the dead call on some families in KwaZulu-Natal, South Africa, to build spaces for them to dwell at rural homesteads. White notes that the predominant form of these buildings echoed customary or ethnoculturally Zulu styles such as the thatched, rounded *iqhugwane*. Once constructed, though, they remained vacant, as the living chose to build and live in metal-roofed, rectangular flats. White notes that this sentimental "scorn" for the customary style is produced in the collapse of a geographic and racial difference that apartheid policies aimed to construct. This process also cut apart Swazi communities, as Shireen Ally shows.[24] The state-driven historical separation of the indigenous majority into race- and culture-specific "homelands" or "Bantustans" was increasingly undone in late- and post-apartheid peri-urban housing and transportation developments. In this postcolonial contraction and production, for White, rural homesteads and houses were revalued as sites where labor migrants could return to singular cultural identity.

It seems that in the wake of AIDS, the dead in the kingdom do not make claims to dwell in such forms of Swazi Culture. They demand glossy, sleek, straight-edged tombstones and personal biography. Their demands for housing in the afterlife reflect the differences in historical geopolitics between Swaziland and South Africa, despite affinities between Zulu and Swazi Culture. The dead in Swaziland want modern, dignified deaths. Swaziland gained independence in 1968, and racism tempered the landscape there throughout the twentieth century.[25] Yet it was not as codified to such extremes as it had been in South Africa. Distinguishing oneself and the dead in commemoration then takes different trajectories in different political and cultural fields: in South Africa, a multicultural and multiracial democracy whose post-apartheid politics can lead citizens to materialize their lives and deaths in evermore ethnonational forms;[26] in Swaziland, the secretive necroculture of the monarchy pales in comparison with widespread commercial commemoration. The public marks itself as distinct from royalty, saying the names of the dead and giving a range of historical death dates that evidence the age of HIV/AIDS. It reveals the power dynamics of postcolonial cultural production, one rooted in a narrow vision of Swazi Culture carving away land from ordinary citizens.

Conclusion

Unlike unmarked cairns of the past or royal graves of the present hidden in plain sight, the contemporary ordinary dead will not be forgotten. They are embedded in the landscape—they cannot be forgotten. Their tombstones creep beyond where state and municipal authorities wish to hold them, and authorial-commercial alternatives to burn are popularly extinguished. As material and documentary traces, the dead and their public graves say something *now*, historically, and *back to* oppressive forms of power in ritual configurations of texts, images, and artifacts (Auslander 2005). At this point in history, they are testimonies to the immensity of loss from HIV/AIDS and to the ways the state's funereal iterations of Swazi Culture do not match or accommodate popular practices of commemoration.

Notes

1. See also Fassin 2007; Golomski 2015b, 2015c; and Lukhele 2016.

2. See Susser 2009; McNeill 2011; Mbali 2013; Thomas 2014; and Woubshet 2015.

3. On burial according to age, rank, and gender, see A. Kuper 1980 and H. Kuper [1947] 1980. Importantly, seasoned in the art of verbal performance, elder men asked the deceased to come back to the homestead. Despite burying the body in the yard, the whereabouts of the spirit or soul were more ambiguous in the wake of death.

4. For other African examples, see Christiansen 2009; Dilger and Luig 2010; Geissler and Prince 2010; and Klaits 2010.

5. The form and adornment of women's mourning caps were contingent on the presence of living sons: a hole was woven out of the cap if the woman had a son and made without a hole if she was without; sons who had not reached puberty were not permitted to enter the woman's hut if she had not yet put on the refined cap. See Kuper 1980 (1947) and Beemer 1941.

6. Head rings were made from clay, brass, or wax produced by grubs (Junod [1912] 1966, 129–30).

7. Arranged or levirate marriage as "widow inheritance" has been made a cultural matter amid HIV/AIDS in several African countries. See UNDP and CANGO 2007; Christiansen 2009; Dilger and Luig 2010; and Geissler and Prince 2010.

8. See Ezer et al. 2007, 809; and Physicians for Human Rights 2007.

9. See Z. Sukati 2009 and Mngomezulu 2010.

10. I expand on this point and draw examples here from a longer article on the topic (Golomski 2015c).

11. See Hollan and Wellenkamp 1996; and Mittermaier 2011.

12. See Cole 2009; Hunter 2010; Mojola 2014; Wyrod 2016; and Meiu 2016.

13. The first Hallmark-type shop in Swaziland had its grand opening in 2010, selling trinkets, cards, and other objects to symbolize a consumable and exchangeable tender care. Local broadcasts of South African and global television programs represent newer material formations of romantic and gay and lesbian love. These visual representations ritualize kinds of affective and political freedom from familial custom and the state (Mupotsa 2015).

14. See Mojola 2014; Fielding-Miller et al. 2015; and Rhine 2016.

15. See Denis and Makiwane 2003; Denis 2005; and Thomas 2014.

16. See Beemer 1941; Kuper 1965, (1947) 1980. Beemer's (1941) essay, for example, is accompanied by several photographs of men admiring themselves with hand-carved mirrors at a river and carefully pressing their loincloths (*emajobho*) at a homestead.

17. See File RCS 526/1916 "Royal Graves" at the National Archives in Lobamba, Swaziland.

18. I explore this history in a related article (Golomski 2015b). Information on colonial cemeteries can be found at the National Archives in Lobamba, Swaziland: Cemeteries: General File no. 449; RCS 486/25, Bremersdorp Cemetery; RCS 209/19: Mbabane Cemetery; and RCS 661/37 Goedgegun Cemetery.

19. In 1925, for example, Miss S. S. Vermaak, a single mother, expressed interest in doing this work for a cemetery of 115 graves in a letter to Assistant Commissioner Basil Warner: "I am living just next to the graveyard I will take care of it and keep it clean and keep it in a good order then the Government can pay me a small salary every month as Mr. Warner it is a shame to see the graveyard like this even the cattle is grazing in it to and I will be sure to keep it in very good order clean it and keep it so as to be worth looking at that will keep me

with my 2 kiddies to keep them to because the wire fence is down to and I will have to fix that up to" [*sic*]. A corroborating letter to Warner from the prominent farmer Sidney Williams supported Vermaak's request and a monthly salary of 1 pound, saying that because of the "scarcity of prison labor," the cemetery had had no maintenance and that grassy overgrowth led to damage by wildfire. Warner aimed to close the matter a few months later, noting that she was "constantly applying for assistance to the government," and while already receiving from them a sewing machine and private bursary for her "illegitimate child," she was "not really entitled to have a special job made for her." The Resident Commissioner, George Honey, disagreed, and Vermaak was supported for managing the cemetery. See: Cemeteries: General File no. 449, National Archives in Lobamba.

20. See Mabuza 2005 and Nkambule 2014a.
21. See *Times of Swaziland* 2007 and Dlamini 2009.
22. See Mathunjwa 2010; Dlamini 2010; Shaw 2011; and Nkambule 2014b.
23. See *Times of Swaziland* 2011; Thwala 2013; and Matsebula 2014.
24. See Ally 2011a, 2011b; and Ginindza 2012.
25. See Crush 1987, 1996; Simelane 1991; and Dlamini 2007.
26. See White 2010, 2012; and Hickel 2014.

Conclusion: The Afterlives of Work

The origin myth of Swazi Culture tells that humanity emerged from a bank of reeds and was made, like all other elements of the world, by a great ancestral force, *Mvelinchanti*. When finished making the world, *Mvelinchanti* called on one of his creatures to go out and tell the first people about the nature of life. The first was the chameleon (*unwabo*), who was tasked to tell the first people that they would live forever. The chameleon went out, but along the way he came across a bushy patch of berries. The chameleon feasted and fell into a deep sleep off the side of the path. *Mvelinchanti* saw the chameleon sleeping and called upon the stone lizard (*intulo*) to be the new messenger. The message, however, and the fate of humanity had changed: people would inevitably die. The stone lizard went out and passed the chameleon to deliver the message, and the first people came to know mortality. Meanwhile, the chameleon awoke from slumber and rejoined the path. The chameleon arrived and delivered the original message. The people were angered. Having heard about their eventual fate, they were now promised eternity. The people picked up rocks and stoned the chameleon to death.

In the myth, the creatures' burden is acting on knowledge of fate. Shirking the burden had mortal consequences, and for humanity, accepting fate was agonizing. In some popular interpretations of the myth, the stone lizard is despised for bringing humans their mortality, whereas others criticize the chameleon for failing to deliver immortality. Others cite the harsh killing of the chameleon and emphasis on the chameleon's laziness as colonial interpretive impositions. In their historical rereading, Christian missionaries aimed to instill a particular work ethic in local communities that would have serious repercussions if not enacted. Most interpretations do not focus on the Creator at all, the original commandment a seeming given if not beyond critique. In this myth of life and death in Swazi Culture, immortality and the desire for it cannot be entertained. Life's finality and impossibility for alternative paths seem given as part of the human condition.

This perception of finitude no longer seems to hold ground. Moving from primordial origins into the new millennium, new forms of dissent and cultural reinterpretations surrounding death have come to the fore in Swaziland. Today, people aspire for something beyond death, despite its omnipresence. These aspirations were traced in this book: a healthier, longer life with pharmaceutical medication; a heavenly afterlife; a financially secure and food-secure livelihood for one's family; and more permanent forms of commemoration. The story of cultural dissent and change retold here was one animated by HIV/AIDS, and like other disease epidemics in human history, HIV/AIDS powerfully shook apart forms of living and dying that had been taken for granted. Anthropologically, this story shows how shocks raise people's consciousness about the value of culture they produce on a day-to-day basis and what kinds of culture differently emerges in comparative epidemiological, political-economic, and historical contexts.

In conclusion, I reconsider how matters of health and well-being drove cultural production, or "work," in ways it is described in this book and how work was an agent of cultural change in ordinary people's everyday lives and in their communities. Critical events such as loss and death abruptly reveal how widely interdependent and connected we are to others. Our responses and remedies to loss cast sustained light on these connections and the long-term work to repair or strengthen them. This is what I mean by the after-lives of work: that our engagement with critical events or crises often resonates beyond a discrete act or moment in history. Acts of restoration and healing after death implicate much more than a single death and make up a broader, ongoing production of life that is cultural, generative, and shows us what we value.

This was made clear to me at the funeral of my friend Yenzo in October 2010 at Bethany near Matsapha.[1] In the tent that night, an all-male Wesleyan church choir percussively smacked tiny pillows to keep the musical tempo. The wind-struck vinyl of the tent bore an unsteady rhythm of sharp snaps that accompanied the ebbs and flows of our songs. Around midnight, one of Yenzo's paternal aunts shuffled to the microphone to speak, a crackling speaker and chords of an electric keyboard enriching her words:

> *Kufa kuyahanjwa kwekuthi indlela ivutsiwe. Kufuna kuthi lomsebenti ugige lomtfwalo wakho. Wena, usahamba la, kulomhlaba. Lomtfwalo wakho kwekugiga ngalo kuthi lomsebenti athi chumane sekaNkulunkulu wakho. Usaphila.*
>
> Death traverses so that our path in life is well worn. This means that this work is woven to you as your burden. You too will pass from this world. This work is woven to you, but it is also from which God springs forth. Doing it, you will live.

Yenzo's aunt was consoling as well as instructive. As in the origin myth, she told us in customary and religious terms how facing death is part of the human condition. It takes work, which is part of our being and is "woven" to us by forces that are greater than us. The word she used to describe this, *kugiga*, refers to the weaving of grass mats, which the living receive at life cycle rites and are interred with in death. Forced to take pause in such moments of loss, we reorient ourselves and take account of where we have been. We rethink how we might prepare for where we are now headed, given that personal circumstances or much of the broader milieu we live in has changed, because of disease, for example. Standard iterations of culture we find—in this case, Swazi Culture—may not provide all the resources we feel we need to get the job done.

The aspirations and obstacles of people I depicted in this book are representative of ordinary livelihoods in one southeast African kingdom, yet they likely reflect more fundamental human imperatives to live well and strive for something like dignity. Amid HIV/AIDS, much of what people did was also directly and indirectly bound up with death, dying, and funerals. Life thus twinned with death, and both could be dignified through hard work, which entailed material, social, and existential aspects. Each of these could be seen in the stories of my friends and informants, and I aimed to tell several, being mindful of Nolwazi Mkhwanazi's (2016) call to diversify our understanding of medical anthropological phenomena in Africa beyond a single story.

In the introduction you met LaGija, a middle-aged mother, educator, and globally minded feminist. Having grown up traditionalist—her father was a customary herbalist and her family were members of an AIC before developing their own ministry church—her daily undertakings were productive of the kind of modern and contemporary life she wanted to live. In one respect, she kept her household well prepared, or sorted (*kulunga kahle*), in her professional career. This endeared her to her children and sister who lived with her, as she was a provider and a loving person who cared for their well-being. I felt this too, in the religious ritual lengths she went to concerning my own health, as described in chapter 2. The fact that she kindly hosted an anthropologist, a stranger, in her home was a testament to her willingness to engage with novel people, ideas, and situations that rendered life extraordinary.

In another respect, LaGija continually affirmed herself to be an ethical and heart-felt Christian living by the standards of Jesus in times of great suffering. Her work was evident in her worshipping and preaching at different ministry churches, prayer healing for others, consuming religious media, and consulting prophets such as Blessing. Through her faith she could show others and herself how one could make a difference or change aspects of life in this world and engender a life beyond this world. With respect to her in-laws like Roxanne and Magdalene, LaGija's negotiated contributions to and withdrawals from funerary functions—such as serving tea and scones at a night vigil or paying for a tombstone—held in abeyance darker qualities she associated with death in Swazi Culture.

In chapter 1, you met Nik, whose work was about surviving near-mortal injury and AIDS as much as it was about wage labor. His story of overcoming social obstacles in his extended family, accessing treatment, and advancing his career embodies the achievement of a dignified life when illness would otherwise slowly destroy it. The ways the disease disrupted his body and his ability to interact ethically with others were laid bare in his time at Madulini. There, for example, household dinnertime dramas with his aunt Nokwenza were material examples of an impending, slow social death. Thankfully, other relatives supported and strengthened him to begin reckoning a new, longer life by testing and treatment.

Nik got better through complementary, critical forms of care: pharmaceutical medication, food resources, and good-hearted people. These ably illuminate the wider field of social and biomedical interventions that culturally informed his personal journey and his ability to work on himself. Through these, Nik learned how to let others care for and talk with him about HIV and ARVs. He learned from his clinicians how to discern the effects that medication had on his mind and body and how to find or make the time to take medication as part of his daily routine. His restoration to social and physical wholeness was life changing. His story is representative of generations of people who have been aided by the cadre of activists, researchers, policymakers, and volunteer and paid health workers who have been treating and preventing HIV/AIDS globally for more than three decades.

Stepping outside of the hospital or clinic, Nik's story shows how HIV/AIDS treatment became part of everyday life in places of home and work, the latter being of major importance to his and many other people's sense of dignity. Work as wage labor allows people in this cultural and historic context to feel like they have value in a socioeconomic sense. As a man and father, he could provide for his daughter and her mother and repay those who helped him, such as "small mother" Nomvula. His openness to dialogue with others about the disease was an outcome of learning to live with HIV from both health-related education at his workplace and post-test counseling sessions. Getting back to work helped him better deal, both literally, with playing cards, and figuratively, with a variety of cosmopolitan customers at the casino and with life in general as it presented new, hopefully lucrative opportunities. Getting back to work made him feel human again.

Returning to Madulini, the married couple and parents Nokwenza and Vuyo Matimba featured throughout the book sought to make a dignified life for their young family. Nokwenza, as a mother, wife, and daughter-in-law, manifested her stakes in her family's livelihood by keeping their gardens, fields, and animals alive and productive so as to keep everyone well fed. In learning about and participating in local global health and development-related initiatives such as World Vision, she extended her carework into the community. Altogether, through her daily tasks as *makoti*, she would engender a sense of well-being (*kukhona kahle*). Household disruptions had to be dealt with, as in Nik's complicated presence. Because the effects of disease were also complicated, creating uncertainty and secrecy, her path to craft a good life ended up cutting across the path of another.

Still, Nokwenza's efforts largely benefited the lives of others, and most importantly for her, her daughters' lives. As the "flowers of the nation," *timbali*, they are the newest and youngest generation of Swazis, those who global health entities and the state desire to be an HIV/AIDS-free generation. Providing for their education in both regular school and Sunday school, Nokwenza also enrolled them in the World Vision programs she worked for. Sponsorship and intermittent gifts of clothing, books, and toys donated from abroad might keep them preoccupied and interested and showcase to others how well she could provide for her children. As of 2017, Nokwenza had ascended the organization's ranks and often gets to travel to participate in workshops on HIV/AIDS education and developing women's income-generating projects in Madulini. Happily, through these efforts she frees herself from housework and gets some time away from her children, something many parents around the world likely value once in a while.

Nokwenza's hard work was obvious at funerals, too. When I attended them with her, she carried a smiling, quiet demeanor that the bereaved appreciated and got her hands dirty cooking food and washing dishes. For her in-laws, her ritual labors exemplified her good-heartedness; it showed them that she loved them. However, as with LaGija and the women described in chapters 4 and 5, gendered forms of Swazi Culture surrounding death did take a toll on Nokwenza's sense of dignity as a woman. A last ethnographic note on this toll recalls the larger ambiguities traced in this book that new forms of funerary cultural production engender.

In the Matimba family's yard, above the small fields of maize and sweet potatoes, lie Vuyo's parents and brother. The family's dead all lay there together: *kubakhona bonke*. The parents died in the early 1990s in old age and were joined in their resting place by Vuyo's only brother, Muzi, after he passed from undisclosed illness in 2010. In 2012, the little graveyard became home to four. Knowing the Matimbas for several years at this point, I was surprised to have never heard of this new occupant. It was Vuyo's own son, Bongani.

Bongani was nineteen when he died, making him about four years older than Vuyo and Nokwenza's eldest daughter. Vuyo and Nokwenza had known each other since they were both secondary-school students and were already romantically involved when they decided to begin a marriage. They undertook *kuteka* rites of betrothal. Said Nokwenza of the rites, "I cried like I was supposed to *esibayeni* [in the cattle pen], and his sisters then brought me into the house. We were married then." Sometime during the year of this marital rite, Vuyo met Bongani's mother around Matsapha, where he worked.

Bongani never lived with Vuyo—that is, until he died. He had stayed with his mother in Matsapha after he was born. Under pressure from his sisters, Vuyo organized some of his uncles to discreetly visit Bongani's mother's family with him to pay respects and acknowledge paternity. Vuyo then moved with his new wife, Nokwenza, back to Madulini. The house had been unoccupied since his parents died. Grasses were overgrown, fields untilled, and the chiefly council questioned whether the family still saw itself as part of the community. Over the years, the young couple, especially Nokwenza, cleaned up the Matimba yard, began farming, and in mortuary form, accreted a social history of their belonging by putting up tombstones to mark grave cairns.

From what Vuyo was told, Bongani's death was sudden and circumspectly due to "blood sugar problems." Although he had never visited nor lived at Madulini, Bongani was buried according to Swazi Culture and with a small funeral; despite estranged family histories, wives should be buried at their husband's people's homes, and critically, children belonging to the husband should be, too. Although some prayers were said and bread and tea were served on the Saturday evening gathering, Nokwenza told me without much expression that it "wasn't really like a night vigil. It was just small." She stayed away from most of the happenings, chatting with her own relatives on her phone and with a few neighbors who attended. Bongani was buried the next morning, next to his father's people. Compared to his other relatives' tombstones in the yard, Bongani's grave is less remarkable: an earthen mound topped with a few stones and ringed by cinder blocks. There is no sign bearing his name.

Here was a son that was not Nokwenza's own, and now his grave would lie every day in plain view, an unmarked yet visible grave commemorating a life as well as an infidelity. Vuyo apologized for his indiscretion. The couple would later make amends, and the setting of their home would be altered by the tenets of kinship and burial per Swazi Culture. Unlike Dumisa Dlamini's (2006) introductory depiction of elaborate funerals with roses and condolence messages causing a dramatic scene, Bongani's funeral was not so materially substantial. His mother had no insurance policy, and Vuyo did not list him as a dependent on his own. In the aftermath of the death, and given the changed cultural circumstances in Swaziland, what might likely be burdensome to the Matimbas was facing a grave that was indeed very simple. These circumstances may likely lead the family to wonder whether or not this grave qualifies as something dignified.

Such life stories show us how people's everyday practices surrounding death, dying, and funerals were a form of cultural production. They did not always directly involve aesthetics, media, or what standard approaches to cultural production might focus on. They did not always involve what people consciously called "Swazi Culture." In fact, what they had to do to deal with death was sometimes the antithesis. Burning bodies in cremation, feeding many visitors as a mourning family, and having a tombstone-unveiling ceremony were all often talked about as being thoroughly unSwazi, yet many in the kingdom carefully undertook these forms of work, seeing them as imperative to prepare for and ultimately produce a good death.

Funeral Culture shows how HIV/AIDS and its many respondents incited popular consciousness about life and death in Swaziland that also effected cultural changes in the ways people saw themselves, their communities, and the kingdom at large. As with other countries worldwide, HIV/AIDS further integrated Swaziland into global flows of health care, humanitarian aid, religious faith, and finance. While not disregarding the ambiguous promises and pitfalls of globalization, these connections drove new forms of work to craft healthier, religiously fulfilled, and economically secure lives. The first half of the book showed how these practices unfolded and sometimes disrupted otherwise normative ways of getting by. The afterlives of this work were manifest in the production of a funeral. Death was what people had been preparing for with new charge. The second half of the book showed how funeral rites of burial, feeding, commemoration, and the possibility of heavenly resurrection were all contingent on foregoing efforts. Though savvy, new commercial mortuary goods and forms of interment were also uncanny. These included cremation, successful resistance to patrilocal burial, catered funeral feasts, and glossy, personalized tombstones. As death became a familiar problem due to HIV/AIDS, the commodified means to conduct funerals and remember the dead became increasingly and culturally unfamiliar.

On this last point, *Funeral Culture* shows how the cultural work of ordinary citizens, as part of a changing and globally connected world, can powerfully disrupt cultural essentialisms and political claims about cultural authenticity and morality. This point is crucial given that such essentialisms and claims are often foundational for the operation of political and biomedical sovereignty, or how configurations of power shape the way people may differently live and die.[2] The ways people value or champion new kinds of popular cultural work portends the remaking of identities and sociopolitical life.

The successful response to HIV/AIDS is a case in point. Ordinary citizens and health care practitioners in Swaziland and their global collaborators have again made headlines surrounding the epidemic. This time, the news is not about death; it is something to resoundingly celebrate. Widespread treatment and prevention initiatives coupled with behavioral changes on the ground helps explain recent findings that new HIV infections in the kingdom have been cut by 44 percent. UNAIDS's recent global treatment target is called 90-90-90, whereby 90 percent of people living with HIV in a given country should know their status, be on ART, and be virally suppressed by 2020. As of 2017, Swaziland has nearly met all of these goals.[3] Indeed, Swaziland may be on track to show the world how to best engage the epidemic on sub-Saharan African terms.

Documenting people's successes and practical engagements with the disease, here in ethnography, clarifies the kinds of livelihoods people *want* to make, even when the conditions of their milieu make this difficult to achieve. This kind of documentation and interpretation is challenging, however. It requires an approach that bears witness to suffering and to sometimes extreme conditions of inequality, violence, and power. The successes of HIV treatment and prevention do not erase the cultural history of AIDS deaths. The latter motivates the former, and both may require us to invoke or locate more capacious concepts of work in "endogenous intellectual and sociocultural ideals" (Olukoshi and Nyamnjoh 2011, 1).[4] The stakes involved in this documentation are more extensive than public health matters. They are about contributions to a postcolonial production of knowledge involving "kinky" kinds of engagements between researchers and audiences insofar as "culture" gets unmoored from the way it is understood or presumed to work for people.[5] There is also inherent political power in this dynamic as reified cultural forms are questioned and new forms become means for liberation.

Work is a political-economic matter as much as I showed it was an existential and health-related one, too. Work in varied material, social, and existential forms makes up what people aspire for as a good or dignified life. In this case, as seen comparatively, ideations of work and illness can generatively combine under particular historic and epidemiological circumstances. Critical consciousness about the value of life and death under these circumstances has the potential to drive significant cultural changes and open alternative paths to get along with others, get well, and get by. Many people in one small yet globally connected place in Africa show us this very fact in this book.

Notes

1. The South African General Mission founded Bethany in 1891 as a mission station.

2. See Nguyen 2010; Marsland and Prince 2012; Mbembe 2003; and Mbembe (2001) 2015. Thinking about disruptions to sovereignty in Swaziland, one could use Mbembe's ([2001] 2015, xiv) terms and undertake a "political and aesthetic critique of the Father ... that would enable us to write an alternative history of the present." Here, interrogating a symbolic "Father" figure can multiply reference a Creator or other god, kingship, or patriarchal power.

3. See Justman et al. 2016; Cohen 2017; ICAP 2017; Fielding-Miller 2017; and Vernooij et al. 2016.

4. See Fajans 1997; Jackson 2011; Weeks 2011; Makhulu, Buggenhagen, and Jackson 2013; Bear 2013; and Ferguson 2015. Recently, anthropologists have been explaining how culturally situated forms of action as work are reproductive for particular forms of life amid precarious conditions, and this goes beyond sub-Saharan African societies. In discussing industrial shipbuilding in India, Bear (2013, 156) shows how workers' daily consecrations and rites in the workplace involve "polyvalent comprehension of productive powers" that actionably crosscut social, ethical, and spiritual lines. This goes beyond the conventional critical approaches to work and labor of theorists such as Karl Marx and Hannah Arendt, who conscript notions of work to the domain of secular naturalism. This may obscure cultural accounts of local, alternate forms of fertility, productivity, and life that emanate from ordinary human action or other sources. By focusing on action's historical valuation and embodiment in cultural milieus, we explode apolitical and reductively economized ideas of what work is and can do. In Russia, for example, Zigon (2010, 206) showed how one Christian treatment facility consigned ill and addicted people living with HIV to "labor therapy" programs. These programs trained people in manual labor—having them build furniture and

grow food—so they could find work once they recovered and left the facility for life as part of "capitalist labor culture" of post–Soviet Russia. With respect to their religiously therapeutic surroundings, their daily work and interactions with treatment specialists cultivated in them moral notions of responsibility and love for others. Parsons (2014) questioned why mortality rates for an older generation of Russian men increased so dramatically after the fall of the Soviet regime in early 1990s. There, she showed the communist system that had guaranteed socioeconomic support ultimately collapsed, leading many men to feel culturally "unneeded" and die earlier due to alcoholism, injury, and violence.

5. In writing about culture in postcolonial Swaziland, where culture is politically volatile, I borrow some terms from anthropologist Danilyn Rutherford (2012, 465). She notes that ethnography is a "kinky" method, both empirically and ethically. An honest writer can acknowledge the fact that one's research on something like "culture" might "never [get] to the bottom of things" fully. This does not mean that cultural analysis is impossible or cannot explain authoritatively how the world works. Anthropologists do such analyses successfully every day in universities and schools, museums and libraries, businesses, and government entities, and NGO and activist organizations. To be kinky here is to ask how relations between foreign researchers and local audiences spring out and toggle back in the historic making of knowledge about people living amid inequality and duress. Anthropologist of Swaziland Hilda Kuper faced this fact as political power shifted in Swaziland with King Mswati III's succession, acknowledging that her fifty years of research with Dlamini royalists was deemed peripheral by the new regime which has its own nationalist scripts of Swazi Culture to author and implement (Kuper 1987, 1984).

Appendix

I. siSwati-American English Glossary

babe	father
banakekeli	caregivers, careworkers
bantfu bentsaba	people of the mountain—ritual specialists who conduct royal burials
Buganu	national ceremony in February for married women's celebration of the harvest and brewing of *marula* fruit (*Sclerocarya birrea*)
butsakatsi	malevolence, evil, witchcraft
emadloti	ancestors, ancestral shades
emahewu	fermented maize meal beverage
emalobolo	bridewealth payments
emaphilisi	pills, name for biomedical and pharmaceutical medications such as ARVs
emasiko	customs, customary rites
ematfuna	graves
gogo	grandmother
imihambo	customary practices or ways of life
imoshali	mortuary, morgue
imphilo	life, health, well-being
imvunulo	customary or traditionalist clothing
iNcwala	national ceremony in December to celebrate kingship, harvesting, and seasonal cycle
indlela	path, journey, or way, used sometimes to refer to the life course
inhlitiyo	heart
kagogo	round-shaped house in customary architectural style associated with grandmothers and ancestral shades, and the name given to new community centers built through state and global public health and development initiatives
kubakhona bonke	to be among others, to be well attended
kufaka esiswini	to put (a child) in a belly, surrogacy
kugeza emanti	to wash with water, a family rite to symbolically purify mourners

kukhona kahle	to be well
kukhuleka ekhaya	to raise up or "grow" a home
kulunga kahle	to be well prepared, to be well organized
kunatsa	to drink
kuphahla	family rite of ancestral remembrance and veneration
kuphilisa	to enliven, to make healthier or better
kuteka	marital rite of betrothal
kuzila	to mourn
libandlancane	chief's council
lobola	exchange bridewealth
lutsandvo	love
make	mother
makoti	bride, daughter-in-law
mutsi	herbal and/or customary medicine
samp	hominy, moderately ground maize kernels
sikhumbuto	reminder, memorabilia
sinanatelo	multi-verse, poetic clan praise name recited after one's surname
sinyama	death pollution, darkness
siSwati	Swazi language
sitfunti	dignity, shadow, prestige, influence, respectability
skoni	sister-in-law
tangoma	diviners who diagnosis affliction and communicate with ancestors
tigedla	healing specialists who mix herbal and/or customary medicines
timphahla	clothing items
tinkhukhu	free-range chickens
tinkhundla	governing system of state-appointed royalist administrators overseeing fifty-five districts comprising Swaziland's 385 chiefdoms, originated in 1978
tinyanga	healing specialists who (dis-)empower others in herbal and/or customary medicines
umchinso	family ritual to cease mourning
umcombotsi	home-brewed maize meal beer
Umcwasho	national chastity rites, performed 1935–36, 1945–46, 1969–71, 1982, 2001–05
umhlambiso	dowry
Umhlanga	reed, national Reed Dance ceremony in August for girls' age grades
umlindzelo	night vigil
umngcwabo	burial

umphakatsi	chief's compound, community, enclosure
umphako	packed food to be taken and eaten on a journey
umsamo	altar or shelf for ancestral objects in a customary house, museum
umsebenti	work, labor, funeral, life-cycle rite, function, or event
umtfwalo	burden

II. List of Abbreviations

AICs	African initiated and independent Christian churches
ART	antiretroviral therapy
ARVs	antiretroviral medications
AIDS	acquired immunodeficiency syndrome
CANGO	Coordinating Assembly of NGOs
FRSA	Financial Regulatory Services Authority
HIV	human immunodeficiency virus
OVC	orphaned and vulnerable children or child
PEPFAR	President's Emergency Plan for AIDS Relief
PMTCT	prevention of mother-to-child transmission
PReP	preexposure prophylaxis
MMC	medical male circumcision
NAPSAWU	National Public Services & Allied Workers Union
NCP	neighborhood care point
NDS	National Development Strategy
NERCHA	National Emergency Response Council on HIV/AIDS
PEPFAR	President's Emergency Plan for AIDS Relief
RIRF	Registrar of Insurance and Retirement Funds
SASO	Swaziland AIDS Support Organisation
SASCCO	Swaziland Association of Savings and Credit Cooperatives
SHBC	Shiselweni Reformed Church Home-Based Care
SNAP	Swaziland National AIDS Programme
SNAT	Swaziland National Association of Teachers
SRIC	Swaziland Royal Insurance Company
SWABCHA	Swaziland Business Coalition on Health and AIDS
SWANNEPHA	Swaziland National Network of People Living with HIV/AIDS
TasP	treatment as prevention
UNAIDS	United Nations Programme on HIV/AIDS
UNISWA	University of Swaziland
WHO	World Health Organization

Bibliography

Akin, David. 2013. *Colonialism, Maasina Rule, and the Origins of Malaitan Kastom.* Honolulu: University of Hawai'i Press.

Ally, Shireen. 2011a. "'If You Are Hungry, and a Man Promises You Mealies, Will You Not Follow Him?' South African Swazi Ethnic Nationalism, 1931–1986." *South African Historical Journal* 63, no. 3: 414–430.

———. 2011b. "Peaceful Memories: Remembering and Forgetting Political Violence in KaNgwane, South Africa." *Africa* 81, no. 3: 351–372.

Amusan, Oluwole. 2009. "Herbal Medicine in Swaziland: An Overview." *African Natural Plant Products: New Discoveries and Challenges in Chemistry and Quality,* edited by H. Rodolfo Juliani, James E. Simon, and Chi-Tang Ho, 31–49. Washington, D.C.: American Chemical Society.

Apter, Andrew. 1983. "In Dispraise of the King: Rituals 'Against' Rebellion in South-east Africa." *Man* 18, no. 3: 521–534.

Ashforth, Adam. 2010. "Spiritual Insecurity and AIDS in South Africa." In *Morality, Hope and Grief: Anthropologies of AIDS in Africa,* edited by Hansjörg Dilger and Ute Luig, 43–60. London: Berghahn.

Associated Press. 2015. "Dozens Killed in Swaziland Truck Crash." *The Guardian* August 29.

Astuti, Rita. 1988. "Ritual, History and the Swazi Ncwala." *Africa: Rivista Trimestrale di Studie e Documentazione dell'Istituto Italiano per l'Africa e l'Oriente* 43: 603–618.

Atkins, Keletso E. 1993. *The Moon is Dead! Gives Us Our Money! The Cultural Origins of an African Work Ethic, Natal, South Africa, 1843–1900.* Portsmouth, N. H.: Heinemann.

Auslander, Mark. 2005. "Saying Something Now: Documentary Work and the Voices of the Dead." *Michigan Quarterly Review* 44, no. 4: 685–703.

Bähre, Erik. 2007. *Money and Violence: Financial Self-Help Groups in a South African Township.* Leiden: Brill.

———. 2011. "Liberation and Redistribution: Social Grants, Commercial Insurance and Religious Riches in South Africa." *Comparative Studies in Society and History* 53, no. 2: 371–392.

———. 2012. "The Janus Face of Insurance in South Africa: From Costs to Risks, from Networks to Bureaucracies." *Africa* 82, no. 1: 150–168.

Bähre, Erik, and Daivi Rodima-Taylor, eds. 2014. "Mutual Help in an Era of Uncertainty." Theme issue *Africa* 84, no. 4.

Baril, Jean-Guy, Patrice Junod, Roger LeBlanch, Harold Dion, Rachel Therrien, François Laplante, Julian Falutz, Pierre Côté, Marie-Nicole Hébert, Richard Lalonde, Normand Lapointe, Dominic Lévesque, Lyse Pinault, Danielle Rouleau, Cécile Tremblay, Benoît Trottier, Sylvie Trottier, Chris Tsoukas, and Karl Weiss. 2005. "HIV-Associated Lipodystrophy Syndrome: A Review of Clinical Aspects." *Canadian Journal of Infectious Diseases and Medical Microbiology* 16, no. 4 (July–August): 233–243.

Barnett, Tony, and Alan Whiteside. (2002) 2006. *AIDS in the Twenty-First Century: Disease and Globalization.* New York: Palgrave-Macmillan.

Barz, Gregory, and Judah Cohen, eds. 2011. *The Culture of AIDS in Africa: Hope and Healing through Music and the Arts.* Oxford: Oxford University Press.

Bataille, Georges. (1949) 1991. *The Accursed Share: Volume 1: Consumption.* New York: Zone Books.

Bear, Laura. 2013. "'This Body Is Our Body': Vishwakarma Puja, the Social Debts of Kinship, and Theologies of Materiality in a Neoliberal Shipyard." In *Vital Relations: Modernity and the Persistent Life of Kinship*, edited by Susan McKinnon and Fenella Cannell, 155–177. Santa Fe: School of Advanced Research Press.

Beck, Ulrich. 2009. *World at Risk.* Cambridge: Polity Press.

Becker, Felicitas. 2014. "Fashioning Selves and Fashioning Styles: Negotiating the Personal and the Rhetorical in the Experiences of African Recipients of ARV Treatment." In *Religion and AIDS Treatment in Africa: Saving Souls, Prolonging Lives*, edited by Rijk van Dijk, Hansjörg Dilger, Marian Burchardt, and Thera Rasing, e35–e53. ProQuest Ebook Central. Farnham: Taylor and Francis.

Becker, Felicitas, and P. Wenzel Geissler. 2009. "Introduction: Searching for Pathways in a Landscape of Death: Religion and AIDS in Africa" In *AIDS and Religious Practice in Africa*, edited by Felicitas Becker and P. Wenzel Geissler, 1–28. Leiden: Brill.

Beckmann, Nadine. 2009. "AIDS and the Power of God: Narratives of Decline and Coping Strategies in Zanzibar." In *AIDS and Religious Practice in Africa*, edited by Felicitas Becker and P. Wenzel Geissler, 119–154. Leiden: Brill.

Beemer, Hilda. 1937. "The Development of the Military Organization in Swaziland." *Africa* 10, no. 1: 55–74.

———. 1941. "The Swazi." In *The Bantu Tribes of South Africa: Reproductions of Photographic Studies, Volume III, Section IV: The Swazi*, edited by Alfred M. Duggan-Cronin, 9–32. Cambridge and Kimberley: Deighton, Bull & Company and the Alexander McGregor Memorial Museum.

Beidelman, Thomas O. 1966. "Swazi Royal Ritual." *Africa* 36, no. 4: 373–405.

Berglund, Axel-Ivar. 1976. *Zulu Thought-Patterns and Symbolism.* Bloomington: Indiana University Press.

Benton, Adia. 2015. *HIV Exceptionalism: Development through Disease in Sierra Leone.* Minneapolis: University of Minnesota Press.

Benton, Adia, Thurka Sangaramoorthy, and Ippolytos Kalofonos. 2017. "Temporality and Positive Living in the Age of HIV/AIDS: A Multisited Ethnography" *Current Anthropology* 58, no. 4: 454–476.

Bernault, Florence. 2006. "Body, Power and Sacrifice in Equatorial Africa." *Journal of African History* 47, no. 2: 207–239.

Bicego, George, Rejoice Nkambule, Ingrid Peterson, Jason Reed, Deborah Donnell, Henry Ginindza, Yen T. Duong, Hetal Patel, Naomi Bock, Neena Philip, Cherry Mao, and Jessica Justman. 2013. "Recent Patterns in Population-Based HIV Prevalence in Swaziland." *PLoS One* 8 (October 15): e77101.

Biehl, João. 2007. *Will to Live: AIDS Therapies and the Politics of Survival.* Princeton: Princeton University Press.

Black, Steven P. 2015. "The Morality of Performance: HIV Disclosure in Speech and Song in South Africa." *Ethos* 43, no. 3: 247–266.

Bonner, Philip. 1983. *Kings, Commoners and Concessionaires: The Evolution and Dissolution of the Nineteenth-Century Swazi State.* New York: Cambridge University Press.

Booth, Karen. 2004. *Local Women, Global Science: Fighting AIDS in Kenya.* Bloomington: Indiana University Press.

Borofsky, Robert, Fredrik Barth, Richard Shweder, Lars Rodseth, and Nomi Maya
Stolzenburg. 2001. "WHEN: A Conversation about Culture." *American Anthropologist*
103, no. 2: 432–446.

Bremersdorp Urban Area Advisory Committee. 1943. "Meeting Minutes, October 12." File
449 Cemeteries: General File. Lobamba: Swaziland National Archives.

Burchardt, Marian. 2015. *Faith in the Time of AIDS: Religion, Biopolitics and Modernity in
South Africa*. Basingstoke: Palgrave-Macmillan.

Cabrita, Joel. 2018. *The People's Zion: Southern Africa, the United States, and a Transatlantic
Faith-Healing Movement*. Cambridge: Harvard University Press.

Campbell, Catherine. 2003. *"Letting Them Die": Why HIV/AIDS Prevention Programmes Fail*.
Oxford: James Currey Press.

Canguilhem, Georges. (1952) 2001. "The Living and Its Milieu." Translated by John Savage.
Grey Room no. 3 (Spring): 6–31.

Case, Anne, Anu Garrib, Alicia Menendez, Analia Olgiati. 2013. "Paying the Piper: The High
Cost of Funerals in South Africa." *Economic Development and Cultural Change* 62,
no. 1: 1–20.

Central Statistical Office and Macro International. 2008. *Swaziland Demographic and Health
Survey 2006–07: Key Findings*. Calverton: CSO and Macro International.

Chimbindi, Natsayi, Jacob Bor, Marie-Louise Newell, Frank Tanser, Rob Baltussen, Jan
Hontelez, Sake J. de Vlas, Mark Lurie, Deenan Pillay, and Till Bärnighausen. 2015.
"Time and Money: The True Costs of Health Care Utilization for Patients Receiving
'Free' HIV/Tuberculosis Care and Treatment in Rural KwaZulu-Natal." *JAIDS: Journal
of Acquired Immune Deficiency Syndromes* 70, no. 2 (October 1): e52–e60.

Christiansen, Catrine. 2009. "The New Wives of Christ: Paradoxes and Potentials in the
Remaking of Widow Lives in Uganda." In *AIDS and Religious Practices in Africa*,
edited by Felicitas Becker and P. Wenzel Geissler, 85–116. Leiden: Brill.

Cohen, David William, and E. S. Atieno Odhiambo. 1992. *Burying SM: The Politics of
Knowledge and the Sociology of Power in Africa*. Portsmouth: Heinemann.

Cohen, Jon. 2017. "Swaziland Makes Major Strides against Its AIDS Epidemic." *Science* July 24.

Cole, Jennifer. 2009. "Love, Money, and Economies of Intimacy in Tamatave, Madagascar."
In *Love in Africa*, edited by Jennifer Cole and Lynn M. Thomas, 109–134. Chicago:
University of Chicago Press.

Comaroff, Jean. 1985. *Body of Power, Spirit of Resistance*. Chicago: University of Chicago Press.

———. 2007. "Beyond Bare Life: AIDS, (Bio)Politics and the Neoliberal Order." *Public Culture*
19, no. 1: 197–219.

Comaroff, Jean, and John L. Comaroff. 1987. "The Madman and the Migrant: Work and Labor
in the Historical Consciousness of a South African People." *American Ethnologist* 14,
no. 2: 191–209.

———. 1991. *Of Revelation and Revolution: Christianity, Colonialism and Consciousness in
South Africa*. Chicago: University of Chicago Press.

Comaroff, John L., and Jean Comaroff. 2009. *Ethnicity, Inc.* Chicago: University of Chicago
Press.

Cook, Susan, and Rebecca Hardin. 2013. "Performing Royalty in Contemporary Africa."
Cultural Anthropology 28, no. 2: 227–251.

Cousins, Thomas. 2014. "Knowledge of Life: Health, Strength and Labour in KwaZulu-Natal,
South Africa." *Anthropology Southern Africa* 37, no. 1–2: 30–41.

Crush, Jonathan. 1987. *The Struggle for Swazi Labour, 1890–1920*. Kingston: McGill-Queen's
University Press.

———. 1996. "The Culture of Failure: Racism, Violence and White Farming in Colonial Swaziland." *Journal of Historical Geography* 22, no. 2: 177–197.

Crush, Jonathan, Ines Raimundo, Hamilton Simelane, Boaventura Cau, and David Dorey. 2010. "Migration Induced HIV and AIDS in Rural Mozambique and Swaziland." Southern African Migration Programme (SAMP) and the International Organization for Migation (IOM), Migration Policy Series paper 33. Cape Town: Idasa.

Daly, John. 2001. "AIDS in Swaziland: The Battle from Within." *African Studies Review* 44, no. 1: 21–35.

Daniel, John, and Johnson Vilane. 1986. "Swaziland: Political Crisis, Regional Dilemma." *Review of African Political Economy* 13, no. 35: 54–67.

Debly, Teresa. 2014. "Culture and Resistance in Swaziland." *Journal of Contemporary African Studies* 32, no. 3: 284–301.

Decoteau, Claire Laurier. 2013. *Ancestors and Antiretrovirals: The Biopolitics of HIV/AIDS in Post-Apartheid South Africa.* Chicago: University of Chicago Press.

de Heusch, Luc. 1985. *Sacrifice in Africa: A Structuralist Approach.* Translated by Linda O'Brien and Alice Morton. Bloomington: Indiana University Press.

Denis, Phillipe, ed. 2005. *Never Too Small to Remember: Memory Work and Resilience in Times of AIDS.* Johannesburg: Cluster.

Denis, Phillipe, and Nokhaya Makiwane. 2003. "Stories of Pain, Love and Courage: AIDS Orphans and Memory Boxes in KwaZulu-Natal, South Africa." *Oral History* 31, no. 2: 66–74.

Desmond, Christopher, John King, Jane Tomlinson, Conway Sithungo, Neena Veenstra, and Alan Whiteside. 2004. "Using Undertaker's Data to Assess Changing Patterns of Mortality and their Consequences in Swaziland." *African Journal of AIDS Research* 3, no. 1: 45–50.

DeWaal, Alex, and Alan Whiteside. 2003. "'New Variant Famine': AIDS and Food Crisis in Southern Africa." *The Lancet* 362: 1234–1237.

De Witte, Marleen. 2001. *Long Live the Dead! Changing Funeral Celebrations in Asante, Ghana.* Amsterdam: Aksant Academic.

———. 2003. "Money and Death: Funeral Business in Asante, Ghana." *Africa* 73, no. 4: 531–559.

———. 2011. "Of Corpses, Clay, and Photographs: Body Imagery and Changing Technologies of Remembrance in Asante Funeral Culture." In *Funerals in Africa: Explorations of a Social Phenomena*, edited by Michael Jindra and Joël Noret, 177–206. New York: Berghahn.

Dilger, Hansjörg. 2007. "Healing the Wounds of Modernity: Salvation, Community and Care in a Neo-Pentecostal Church in Dar Es Salaam, Tanzania." *Journal of Religion in Africa* 37, no. 1: 59–83.

Dilger, Hansjörg, and Ute Luig, eds. 2010. *Morality, Hope and Grief: Anthropologies of AIDS in Africa.* London: Berghahn.

Dlamini, Betty S. 2007. "Umhlanga Reed Dance Ceremony in Swaziland: Singing Sparrows or Parrots, People or Zombies?" Paper presented at the "Popular Cultures in Africa" conference, University of Texas-Austin, March 30.

Dlamini, Dumisa. 2006. "Those Tears, Roses and Messages at Men's Funerals." *Weekend Observer* November 18.

———. 2007. "Does a Man Love His Car More Than His First Lady?" *Weekend Observer* December 21.

———. 2015. "The Forgotten, Deserted, Infected but Loyal Bride." *Weekend Observer* January 7.

Dlamini, Gabby S. 2012. "*Bantfu bentsaba*: Authenticity, Secrecy and Balances of Power." Bachelor of Arts Honors thesis, University of the Witwatersrand.

Dlamini, Jabulisa. 2013. "RFM Hospital Reports 'Parts Scandal' to Cops." *Times of Swaziland* October 1.

Dlamini, Julia F. 2016. "'Picturing' Nutritional Inclusion: Using Photo Voice to Explore School Feeding Schemes with Two Primary Schools in Manzini, Swaziland." Master of Education thesis, University of KwaZulu-Natal.

Dlamini, Nhlanhla C. 2007. "The Legal Abolition of Racial Discrimination and Its Aftermath: The Case of Swaziland, 1945–1973." PhD diss., University of the Witwatersrand.

Dlamini, Njabulo. 2005. "Inkhosikati Not at Twin Brother's Funeral." *Times of Swaziland* December 28.

Dlamini, Nonhlanhla. 2009. "Gendered Power Relations, Subversion and Sexuality in Swazi Women's Folk Songs Performed During Traditional Marriage Rites and Social Gatherings." *Muziki* 6, no. 2: 133–144.

Dlamini, Senzo. 2010. "Over E100,000 Spent on Digging Up Graves." *Times of Swaziland* May 31.

Dlamini, Welcome. 2009. "Armed Robbers Strike at Cemetery." *Times of Swaziland* September 2.

Dumbrell, Henry J. E. 1952. "Pyre Burning in Swaziland." *African Studies* 11, no. 4: 190–191.

Ebewo, Patrick. 2011. "Swazi *Incwala*: The Performative and Radical Poetics in a Ritual Practice." *South African Theatre Journal* 25, no. 2: 89–100.

Engelke, Matthew. 2007. *A Problem of Presence: Beyond Scripture in an African Church*. Berkeley: University of California Press.

Epstein, Helen. 2007. *The Invisible Cure: Why We are Losing the Fight against AIDS in Africa*. New York: Picador.

Ericson, Richard, Aaron Doyle, and Dean Barry. 2003. *Insurance as Governance*. Toronto: University of Toronto Press.

Ezer, Tamar, Aisha Glasford, Elizabeth Hollander, Lakeisha Poole, Grant Rabenn, and Alexandria Tindall. 2007. "Divorce Reform: Rights and Protections in the New Swaziland." *Georgetown Journal of Gender and Law* 8: 883–993.

Fajans, Jane. 1997. *They Make Themselves: Work and Play among the Baining of Papua New Guinea*. Chicago: University of Chicago Press.

Farmer, Paul. (1992) 2006. *AIDS and Accusations: Haiti and the Geography of Blame*. Berkeley: University of California Press.

Fassin, Didier. 2007. *When Bodies Remember: Experiences and Politics of AIDS in South Africa*. Translated by Amy Jacobs and Gabrielle Varro. Berkeley: University of California Press.

Feldman, Douglas, ed. 2008. *AIDS, Culture, and Africa*. Gainesville: University of Florida Press.

Ferguson, James. 2015. *Give a Man a Fish*. Durham: Duke University Press.

Ferme, Mariane. 2001. *The Underneath of Things: Violence, History, and the Everyday in Sierra Leone*. Berkeley: University of California Press.

Fielding-Miller, Rebecca, ed. 2017. "What the World Can Learn from Swaziland." Theme issue, *African Journal of AIDS Research* 16, no. 4.

Fielding-Miller, Rebecca, Zandile Mnisi, Darrin Adams, Stefan Baral, and Caitlin Kennedy. 2014. "'There Is Hunger in My Community': A Qualitative Study of Food Security as a Cyclically Driving Force in Sex Work in Swaziland." *BMC Public Health* 14, no. 1: 79.

Fielding-Miller, Rebecca, Kristin L. Dunkle, Hannah L. F. Cooper, Michael Windle, and Craig Hadley. 2015. "Cultural Consensus Modeling to Measure Transactional Sex in Swaziland: Scale Building and Validation." *Social Science and Medicine* 148 (November): 25–33.

Fielding-Miller, Rebecca, Kristin L. Dunkle, Nwabisa Jama-Shai, Michael Windle, Craig Hadley, and Hannah L. F. Cooper. 2016. "The Feminine Ideal and Transactional Sex: Navigating Respectability and Risk in Swaziland." *Social Science and Medicine* 158 (April): 24–33.

Finkelstein, Julia L., Pooja Gala, Rosemary Rochford, Marshall Glesby, and Saurabh Mehta. 2015. "HIV/AIDS and Lipodystrophy: Implications for Clinical Management in Resource-Limited Settings." *Journal of the International AIDS Society* 18, no. 1: 19033.

Fischer, Edward F. 2014. *The Good Life: Aspiration, Dignity, and the Anthropology of Wellbeing*. Palo Alto: Stanford University Press.

Fogelqvist, Anders. 1987. *The Red Dressed Zionists: Symbols of Power in a Swazi Independent Church*. Uppsala: Acta Universitatis Upsaliensis.

Fontein, Joost, and John Harries. 2013. "The Vitality and Efficacy of Human Substances." *Critical African Studies* 5, no. 3: 115–126.

Forrester, Bob, and Vito Laterza. 2014. *Development in Swaziland: Myths and Realities*. Mbabane and Pretoria: Sahee Foundation.

Forster, Peter, and Bongani Nsibande, eds. 2000. *Swaziland: Contemporary Social and Economic Issues*. Aldershot: Ashgate.

Friedland, Barbara A., Louis Apicella, Katie Schenk, Meredith Sheehy, and Paul Hewett. 2013. "How Informed Are Clients Who Consent? A Mixed-Method Evaluation of Comprehension among Clients of Male Circumcision Services in Zambia and Swaziland." *AIDS Behavior* 17, no. 6: 2269–2282.

Geissler, P. Wenzel, and Ruth J. Prince. 2010. *The Land Is Dying: Creativity, Contingency and Conflict in Western Kenya*. London: Berghahn.

Gershon, Ilana. 2012. *No Family Is an Island: Cultural Expertise among Samoans in Diaspora*. Ithaca: Cornell University Press.

Geschiere, Peter. 2009. *The Perils of Belonging: Autochthony, Citizenship, and Exclusion in Africa and Europe*. Chicago: University of Chicago Press.

Gifford, Paul. 2014. "Unity and Diversity within African Pentecostalism." *Pentecostalism in Africa: Presence and Impact of Pneumatic Christianity in Postcolonial Societies*, edited by Martin Lindhardt, 115–135. Leiden: Brill.

Ginindza, Mabhuza Simeon. 2012. "KaNgwane: A Life in and Beyond." *South African Historical Journal* 64, no. 1: 144–161.

Gluckman, Max. 1965. *Custom and Conflict in Africa*. Oxford: Blackwell.

Golomski, Casey. 2010. "Body Politics: Burial Disputes in the Kingdom of Swaziland." Paper presented at the University of Swaziland History Staff Seminar Series, October 23.

———. 2013. "Right Passages: Work, Ritual and Regeneration in Swaziland's Age of HIV/AIDS." PhD diss., Brandeis University.

———. 2014. "Generational Inversions: 'Working' for Social Reproduction amid HIV in Swaziland." *African Journal of AIDS Research* 13, no. 4: 351–359.

———. 2015a. "Compassion Technology: Remaking Kinship in Life Insurance in Swaziland's Age of HIV." *American Ethnologist* 42, no. 1: 81–96.

———. 2015b. "Urban Cemeteries in Swaziland: Materialising Dignity." *Anthropology Southern Africa* 38, no. 3–4: 360–371.

———. 2015c. "Wearing Memories: Clothing and the Global Lives of Mourning in Swaziland." *Material Religion* 11, no. 3: 303–327.

———. 2016a. "Risk, Mistake and Generational Contest in Bodily Rituals of Swazi Jerikho Zionism." *Journal of Contemporary Religion* 31, no. 3: 351–364.

———. 2016b. "Outliving Love: Marital Estrangement in an African Insurance Market." *Social Dynamics* 42, no. 2: 304–320.

Golomski, Casey, and Sonene Nyawo. 2017. "Christians' Cut: Popular Religion and the Global Health Campaign for Medical Male Circumcision in Swaziland." *Culture, Health & Sexuality* 19, no. 8: 884–858.

Gort, Enid. 1989. "Changing Traditional Medicine in Rural Swaziland: The Effects of the Global System." *Social Science and Medicine* 29, no. 9: 1099–1104.

Graeber, David. 1995. "Dancing with Corpses Reconsidered: An Interpretation of *Famadihana*." *American Ethnologist* 22, no. 2: 258–278.

———. 2006. "Turning Modes of Production Inside Out." *Critique of Anthropology* 26, no. 1: 61–85.

Green, Edward C. 1994. *AIDS and STDs in Africa: Bridging the Gap between Traditional Healing and Modern Medicine*. Boulder: Westview Press.

Green, Edward C., and Allison Herling Ruark. 2011. *AIDS, Behavior, and Culture: Understanding Evidence-Based Prevention*. Walnut Creek: Left Coast Press.

Guyer, Jane. 2007. "Prophecy and the Near Future: Thoughts on Macroeconomic, Evangelical, and Punctuated Time." *American Ethnologist* 34, no. 3: 409–421.

Gwebu, Titus. 2013. "Divorce Is 'Un-Swazi,' MPs Told." *IOL News* November 29.

Hall, James. 2002. *Inyandzaleyo!: Life Stories: Testimonies of Hope from People with HIV-AIDS*. Johannesburg: UNICEF.

———. 2010. "The Truth Behind Life Expectancy." *Swazi Observer* July 10.

Hardin, Jessica A. 2015. "'From Despair to Hope': Antiretroviral Therapy, Redemption, and Christianity in Africa." *Marginalia: A Los Angeles Review of Books Channel* August 18.

———. 2016. "'Healing Is a Done Deal': Temporality and Metabolic Healing among Evangelical Christians in Samoa." *Medical Anthropology* 35, no. 2: 105–118.

———. 2018. *Faith and the Pursuit of Health: Cardiometabolic Disorders in Samoa*. New Brunswick: Rutgers University Press.

Hardon, Anita, and Eileen Moyer, eds. 2014. "The Normalization of HIV in the Age of Antiretroviral Treatment: Perspectives from Everyday Practice." Theme issue. *Medical Anthropology* 33, no. 4.

Hardon, Anita, and Deborah Posel, eds. 2012. "Secrecy as Embodied Practice: Beyond the Confessional Imperative." Theme issue. *Culture, Health & Sexuality* 14, supplement no. 1.

Hardon, Anita, D. Akurut, C. Comoro, C. Ezekie, Henry F. Irunde, T. Gerrits, J. Kglatwane, John Kinsman, R. Kwasa, Janneth Maridadi, T. M. Moroka, S. Moyo, Alice Nakiyemba, Stephen E. D. Nsimba, R. Ogenyi, T. Oyabba, Florence Temu, and R. Laing. 2007. "Hunger, Waiting Time and Transport Costs: Time to Confront Challenges to ART Adherence in Africa." *AIDS Care* 19, no. 5: 658–665.

Harrison, David. 1995. "Development of Tourism in Swaziland." *Annals of Tourism Research* 22, no. 1: 136–156.

Henderson, Patricia. 2011. *AIDS, Intimacy and Care in Rural KwaZulu-Natal: A Kinship of Bones*. Amsterdam: Amsterdam University Press.

Hickel, Jason. 2012. "Neoliberal Plague: The Political Economy of HIV Transmission in Swaziland." *Journal of Southern African Studies* 38, no. 3: 513–529.

———. 2014. *Democracy as Death: The Moral Order of Anti-Liberal Politics in South Africa*. Berkeley: University of California Press.

Hlatshwayo, Sthembile. 2012. "SASO Celebrates 20 Years of Positive Living." *Times of Swaziland* May 22.

Hollan, Douglas, and Jane Wellenkamp. 1996. *The Thread of Life: Toraja Reflections on the Life Cycle*. Honolulu: University of Hawai'i Press.

Holloway, Tom. 2002. "Funeral Feasts off the Swazi Menu." *BBC News Africa* July 2.

Holmes, Thalia. 2017. "Stokvels Move with the Times." *Mail and Guardian* January 6.

Hunleth, Jean. 2017. *Children as Caregivers: The Global Fight Against Tuberculosis and HIV in Zambia*. New Brunswick: Rutgers University Press.

Hunter, Mark. 2010. *Love in a Time of AIDS: Inequality, Gender, and Rights in South Africa*. Bloomington: Indiana University Press.

ICAP (International Center for AIDS Care and Treatment Programs). 2017. "Summary Sheet: Preliminary Findings: Swaziland HIV Incidence Measurement Survey 2: A Population-Based HIV Impact Assessment: SHIMS 2016–2017." (July) New York: Columbia University's Mailman School of Public Health ICAP PHIA (Population HIV Impact Assessment) Program.

Illife, John. 2006. *The African AIDS Epidemic: A History*. Oxford: James Currey Press.

IRIN (Integrated Regional Information Networks). 2002. "School Feeding Scheme Provides Hope for Children." *IRIN* November 29.

———. 2003a. "Swaziland: Mourning Women Ordered to King's Party." *IRIN* September 1.

———. 2003b. "Swaziland: Dying Tradition as Funeral Customs Abandoned." *IRIN* July 30.

———. 2007. "Swaziland: Obesity in Times of Hunger." *IRIN* January 4.

———. 2009a. "HIV/AIDS Blamed for 25 Percent Job Absenteeism." *IRIN* February 16.

———. 2009b. "Swaziland: A Culture that Encourages HIV/AIDS." *IRIN* April 15.

———. 2011. "HIV Prevalence among Factory Workers '50 Percent.'" *IRIN* August 11.

Jackson, Michael D. 1989. *Paths Toward a Clearing*. Bloomington: Indiana University Press.

———. 2005. *Existential Anthropology: Events, Exigencies, and Effects*. London: Berghahn.

———. 2011. *Life Within Limits: Well-being in a World of Want*. Durham: Duke University Press.

James, Deborah. 2007. *Gaining Ground? "Rights" and "Property" in South African Land Reform*. New York: Routledge.

———. 2015. *Money from Nothing: Indebtedness and Aspiration in South Africa*. Palo Alto: Stanford University Press.

Jewkes, Rachel, Yandisa Sikweyiya, Robert Morrell, and Kristin L. Dunkle. 2011. "Gender Inequitable Masculinity and Sexual Entitlement in Rape Perpetration in South Africa." *PLoS One* 6, no. 12: e29590.

Jewkes, Rachel, Robert Morrell, Jeff Hearn, Emma Lundqvist, David Blackbeard, Graham Lindegger, Michael Quayle, Yandisa Sikweyiya, and Lucas Gottzén. 2015. "Hegemonic Masculinity: Combining Theory and Practice in Gender Interventions." *Culture, Health & Sexuality* 17, supplement no. 2: 96–111.

Jindra, Michael. 2005. "Christianity and the Proliferation of Ancestors: Changes in Hierarchy and Mortuary Ritual in the Cameroon Grassfields." *Africa* 75, no. 3: 356–377.

Jindra, Michael, and Joël Noret. 2011. "Funerals in Africa: An Introduction." In *Funerals in Africa: Explorations of a Social Phenomena*, edited by Michael Jindra and Joël Noret, 1–15. New York: Berghahn.

Jua, Nantang. 2005. "The Mortuary Sphere, Privilege and the Politics of Belonging in Contemporary Cameroon." *Africa* 75, no. 3: 325–355.

Junod, Henri-Alexandre. (1912) 1966. *The Life of a South African Tribe*, vol. 2. New York: University Books.

Justman, Jessica, Jason B. Reed, George Bicego, Deborah Donnell, Keala Li, Naomi Bock, Alison Koler, Neena M. Philip, Charmaine K. Mhlambo, Bharat S. Parekh, Yen T. Duong, Dennis L. Ellenberger, Wafaa M. El-Sadr, and Rejoice Nkambule. 2016. "Swaziland HIV Incidence Measurement Survey (SHIMS): A Prospective National Cohort Study." *The Lancet HIV*, published online November 15. doi: 10.1016/ S2352-3018(16)30190-4.

Kalipeni, Ezekiel, Susan Craddock, Joseph R. Oppong, and Jayati Ghosh, editors. 2003. *HIV and AIDS in Africa: Beyond Epidemiology*. Malden: Blackwell Publishing.

Kalofonos, Ippolytos. 2010. "'All I Eat Is ARVS': The Paradox of AIDS Treatment in Central Mozambique." *Medical Anthropology Quarterly* 24, no. 3: 363–380.

Kalusa, Walima T., and Megan Vaughan. 2013. *Death, Belief, and Politics in Central African History*. Lusaka: Lembani Trust.

Kamera, W. D. 2001. *Singeniso selucwaningo—Swazi Oral Literature: An Introductory Survey*. Manzini: Ruswanda Publishing.

Kappers, Sophieke. 1988. "Sitanini—Let's Help Each Other: Women and Informal Saving, Credit, and Funeral Organisations in Swaziland." In *Scenes of Change: Visions on Developments in Swaziland*, edited by Henk J. Tieleman, 163–186. Leiden: African Studies Center.

Kasenene, Peter. 1993. *Swazi Traditional Religion and Society*. Mbabane: Webster's.

Kenworthy, Nora. 2017. *Mistreated: The Political Consequences of the Fight against AIDS in Lesotho*. Nashville: Vanderbilt University Press.

Kenworthy, Nora, Matthew Thomann, and Richard Parker. 2017. "From a Global Crisis to an 'End of Aids': New Epidemics of Signification." *Global Public Health* advanced online publication (August 22).

Kiernan, J. P. 1990. "The Canticles of Zion: Song as Word and Action in Zulu Zionist Discourse." *Journal of Religion in Africa* 20, no. 2: 188–204.

King, Barbara. 2013. *How Animals Grieve*. Chicago: University of Chicago Press.

Klaits, Frederick. 2010. *Death in a Church of Life: Moral Passion in Botswana's Time of AIDS*. Berkeley: University of California Press.

Krieger, Nancy. 2013. *Epidemiology and the People's Health*. Oxford: Oxford University Press.

Kumalo, R. Simangaliso, ed. 2013. *Religion and Politics in Swaziland: The Contributions of Dr. J. B. Mzizi*. Bloemfontein: SUN Press.

Kuper, Adam. 1980. "Symbolic Dimensions of the Southern Bantu Homestead." *Africa* 50, no. 1: 8–23.

Kuper, Hilda. n.d. "Hilda Kuper Papers: Box 35, Folder 10 'Religion—traditional.'" Special Collections, Charles E. Young Research Library, University of California Los Angeles.

———. 1944. "A Ritual of Kingship among the Swazi." *Africa* 14, no. 5: 230–255.

———. 1945. "The Marriage of a Swazi Princess." *Africa* 15, no. 3: 145–155.

———. 1950. "Kinship among the Swazi." In *African Systems of Kinship and Marriage*, edited by A. R. Radcliffe-Brown and Darryl Forde, 86–100. Oxford: Oxford University Press.

———. 1965. *Bite of Hunger*. New York: Harcourt, Brace and World.

———. (1947) 1969. *The Uniform of Colour: A Study of Black-White Relationships in Swaziland*. New York: Negroes University Press.

———. 1970. *A Witch in My Heart: A Play about the Swazi People*. London: Oxford University Press.

———. 1972a. "A Royal Ritual in a Changing Political Context." *Cahiers d'etudes Africanes* 12, no. 48: 593–614.

———. 1972b. "The Language of Sites in the Politics of Space." *American Anthropologist* 74, no. 3: 411–424.

———. 1973a. "Costume and Identity." *Comparative Studies in Society and History* 15, no. 3: 348–367.

———. 1973b. "Costume and Cosmology: The Animal Symbolism of the *Ncwala*." *Man* 8, no. 4: 613–630.

———. 1978. *Sobhuza II: Ngwenyama and King of Swaziland*. New York: Africana Publishing.

———. (1947) 1980. *An African Aristocracy: Rank among the Swazi*. New York: Africana Publishing.

———. 1984. "Function, History, Biography: Reflections on Fifty Years in the British Anthropological Tradition." In *Functionalism Historicized: Essays on British Social Anthropology*, edited by George W. Stocking, Jr., 192–213. Madison: University of Wisconsin Press.

Kuper, Hilda, and Selma Kaplan. 1944. "Voluntary Associations in an Urban Township." *African Studies* 3, no. 4: 178–186.

Lambek, Michael, ed. 2010. *Ordinary Ethics*. New York: Fordham University Press.

———. 2013. "The Value of (Performative) Acts." *HAU: Journal of Ethnographic Theory* 3, no. 2: 141–160.

LaNgwenya, Maxine. 2012. "Historic Step towards Equality for Swazi Women: An Analysis of Mary-Joyce Doo Aphane v. the Registrar of Deeds." *Open Debate* 6. Parktown: Open Society Initiative of Southern Africa (OSISA).

Laterza, Vito. 2012. "Breathing Life: Labour Relations, Epistemology and the Body among Swazi Timber Workers." PhD diss., Cambridge University.

Laterza, Vito, Bob Forrester, and Patience Mususa. 2013. "'Bringing Wood to Life': Lines, Flows and Materials in Swazi Mill." In *Biosocial Becomings: Integrating Social and Biological Anthropology*, edited by Tim Ingold and Gísli Pálsson, 162–190. Cambridge: Cambridge University Press.

Leclerc-Madlala, Suzanne. 2001. "Virginity Testing: Managing Sexuality in a Maturing HIV/AIDS Epidemic." *Medical Anthropology Quarterly* 15, no. 4: 533–552.

———. 2008. "Age-Disparate and Intergenerational Sex in Southern Africa." *AIDS* 22, supplement no. 4: S17–S25.

Lee, Rebekah. 2011. "Death 'On the Move': Funerals, Entrepreneurs and the Rural-Urban Nexus in South Africa." *Africa* 81, no. 2: 226–247.

Lee, Rebekah, and Megan Vaughan. 2008. "Death and Dying in the History of Africa since 1800." *Journal of African History* 49, no. 3: 341–359.

Levin, Richard. 1997. *When Sleeping Grass Awakens: Land and Power in Swaziland*. Johannesburg: Witwatersrand University Press.

Lincoln, Bruce. 1987. "Ritual, Rebellion, Resistance: Once More the Swazi *Ncwala*." *Man* 22, no. 1: 132–156.

Livingston, Julie. 2012. *Improvising Medicine: An African Oncology Ward in an Emerging Cancer Epidemic*. Durham: Duke University Press.

Lobamba, Nxolo Nkabinde. 2015. "Imbali's Send Off for Friday's Victims." *Swazi Observer* September 1.

Luhrmann, Tanya. 2012. *When God Talks Back: Understanding the American Evangelical Relationship with God.* New York: Alfred Knopf.

Lukhele, Francis. 2016. "Tears of the Rainbow: Mourning in South African Culture." *Critical Arts* 30, no. 1: 31–44.

Mabusela, Zothile. 2007. "Dups Holdings (Pty) Ltd New Premises Opening Supplement." *Times of Swaziland* August 1.

Mabuza, Fanyana. 2005. "No More Funerals at Mangwaneni!" *Weekend Observer* December 10.

———. 2008. "No More Scramble for Bodies." *Swazi Observer* March 2.

Macmillan Boleswa. 2010. *Silulu sesiSwati: English – siSwati, siSwati – English Dictionary.* Manzini: Macmillan Boleswa Publishers.

MacMillan, Hugh. 1985. "Swaziland: Decolonisation and the Triumph of 'Tradition.'" *Journal of Modern African Studies* 23, no. 4: 643–666.

Magongo, Ellen Mary. 2009. "Kingship and Transition in Swaziland, 1973–1988." Master of Arts Thesis, University of South Africa.

Makhubu, Lydia. 1978. *The Traditional Healer.* Mbabane: Sebenta National Institute for the University of Botswana and Swaziland.

Makhulu, Anne-Maria, Beth A. Buggenhagen, and Stephen Jackson. 2010. "Introduction." In *Hard Work, Hard Times: Global Volatility and African Subjectivities*, edited by Anne-Maria Makhulu, Beth A. Buggenhagen, and Stephen Jackson, 1–27. Durham: Duke University Press.

Malinga, Lindelwa. 2014. "Pigg's Peak Morgue Collapsing." *Swazi Observer* February 17.

Manderson, Lenore, and Carolyn Smith-Morris, eds. 2010. *Chronic Conditions, Fluid States: Chronicity and the Anthropology of Illness.* New Brunswick: Rutgers University Press.

Manzini City Council. 2014. "Manzini Council Cremates 30 Paupers." *Swazi Observer* August 27.

Maphalala, Innocent. 2009. "Her Own Funeral." *Times of Swaziland* September 26.

Marsland, Rebecca, and Ruth J. Prince. 2012. "What is Life Worth? Exploring Biomedical Interventions, Survival, and the Politics of Life. *Medical Anthropology Quarterly* 26, no. 4: 453–469.

Marwick, Brian. (1940) 1966. *The Swazi.* London: Frank Cass.

Masango, Lomagugu Precious. 2009. "Reading the Swazi Reed Dance (*Umhlanga*) as a Literary Traditional Performance Art." PhD diss., University of the Witwatersrand.

Masanjala, Winford. 2007. "The Poverty-HIV/AIDS Nexus in Africa: A Livelihood Approach." *Social Science and Medicine* 64, no. 5 (March): 1032–1041.

Maseko, Zweli. 2006. "Cops Stop Funeral." *Times of Swaziland* February 4.

Masimula, Sabelo. 2008. "Another Ritual Murder March Stopped: Is Someone Prominent Behind the Killing?" *Times of Swaziland* August 15.

Mathunjwa, Nhlanhla. 2010. "Cops Stop Funeral as Defiant Family Refuses to Use Public Cemetery." *Times of Swaziland* September 26.

Matsebula, Colleen. 2014. "Forced Eviction: Losing More Than Just a Home." *Times of Swaziland* October 1.

Matsebula, James S. M. 1983. *A Tribute to the Late His Majesty King Sobhuza II.* Mbabane: Webster's.

———. (1972) 1988. *A History of Swaziland.* Cape Town: Longman.

Mattes, Dominik. 2012. "'I Am Also a Human Being!': Antiretroviral Treatment in Local Moral Worlds." *Anthropology and Medicine* 19, no. 1: 75–84.

———. 2014. "Caught in Transition: The Struggle to Live a 'Normal' Life with HIV in Tanzania." *Medical Anthropology* 33, no. 4: 270–287.

Mavuso, Winile. 2011. "SADC Insurance Industry Laws to be Harmonised." *Swazi Observer* July 28.

Maziya, Sizwe. 2010a. "Crocodile Heads, Lion Skins Found at Bus Rank." *Swazi Times* May 17.

———. 2010b. "Family of Killed Albino Girl Wants Answers." *Times of Swaziland* August 26.

———. 2011. "Bodies in Hospital Wards and Corridors." *Times of Swaziland* July 14.

Mbali, Mandisa. 2013. *South African AIDS Activism and Global Health Politics*. London: Palgrave-Macmillan.

Mbembe, Achille. 2003. "Necropolitics." Translated by Libby Meintjies. *Public Culture* 15, no. 1: 11–40.

———. (2001) 2015. *On the Postcolony*. Johannesburg: Wits University Press.

McGovern, Mike. 2012. "Turning the Clock Back of Breaking with the Past? Charismatic Temporality and Elite Politics in Côte d'Ivoire and the United States." *Cultural Anthropology* 27, no. 2: 239–260.

McNeill, Fraser. 2011. *AIDS, Politics and Music in South Africa*. Cambridge: Cambridge University Press.

Meiu, George Paul. 2016. "Belonging in Ethno-erotic Economies." *American Ethnologist* 43, no. 2: 215–229.

Meyer, Birgit. 2004. "Christianity in Africa: From African Independent to Pentecostal-Charismatic Churches." *Annual Review of Anthropology* 33: 447–474.

———. 2010. "Aesthetics of Persuasion." *South Atlantic Quarterly* 109, no. 4: 741–763.

Mfanasibili (Prince Mfanasibili). 2007. "The Story of Chief Salewebona and Mzikayise at Mkhwakhweni." *Times of Swaziland Sunday* August 5.

Mgabhi, Thoko. 1998. *Itawuphuma ehlatsini* ("Cat Out of the Bag"). Manzini: Macmillan Publishing.

Miller, Daniel. 2010. *Stuff*. Malden: Polity Press.

Ministry of Health. 2015. "Swaziland Integrated HIV Management Guidelines." Mbabane: Ministry of Health, PEPFAR, and WHO.

Ministry of Labour and Social Security. 2010. "The Swaziland Integrated Labour Force Survey 2010." Mbabane: Central Statistical Office.

Mittermaier, Amira. 2011. *Dreams That Matter: Egyptian Landscapes of the Imagination*. Berkeley: University of California Press.

Mkhwanazi, Nolwazi. 2014. "'An African Way of Doing Things': Reproducing Gender and Generation." *Anthropology Southern Africa* 37, no. 1–2: 107–118.

———. 2016. "Medical Anthropology in Africa: The Trouble with a Single Story." *Medical Anthropology* 35, no. 2: 193–202.

Mngomezulu, Mxolisi. 2010. "Reverend Grace Masilela Says ... Are Mourning Gowns for Christians." *Swazi Gospel Sun* December 2–17.

Mojola, Sanyu. 2014. *Love, Money, and HIV: Becoming a Modern African Woman in the Age of AIDS*. Berkeley: University of California Press.

Mol, Annemarie. 2010. "Moderation or Satisfaction? Food Ethics and Food Facts." In *Whose Weight Is It Anyway? Essays on Ethics and Eating*, edited by S. Vandamme, S. van de Vathorst, and I. de Beaufort, 121–132. Leuven: Acco Academic.

Monareng, Motsebi wa. 2015. "Death Toll in Swazi Accident Rises to 65." *SABC* August 30.

Morris, Rosalind. 2008. "Rush/Panic/Rush: Speculations on the Value of Life and Death in South Africa's Age of AIDS." *Public Culture* 20, no. 2: 199–231.

Motau, Phephile. 2013. "Mortuaries Act on Body Parts Scandal." *Times of Swaziland* October 2.

Motsa, Zodwa. 2001. "The Missing Link in siSwati Modern Drama." In *Precolonial and Post-Colonial Drama and Theatre in Africa*, edited by Lokangaka Losambe and Devi Sarinjeive, 32–47. Claremont: New Africa Books.

Moyer, Eileen. 2015. "The Anthropology of Life after AIDS: Epistemological Continuities in the Age of Antiretroviral Treatment." *Annual Review of Anthropology* 44: 259–275.

Mthethwa, Thulani. 2007a. "Swazi Widows Seek to End Mourning." *BBC Network Africa* October 4.

———. 2007b. "Swazi Burial after Five-Year Wait." *BBC News* December 10.

Mupotsa, Danai. 2015. "The Promise of Happiness: Desire, Attachment and Freedom in Post/Apartheid South Africa." *Critical Arts* 29, no. 2: 183–198.

Muwanga, Fred Tusuubira. 2004. "A Systematic Review of the Economic Impact of HIV/AIDS on Swaziland." Master of Public Health thesis, University of the Witwatersrand.

Mzileni, Sihle. 2007. "Bodies Pile Up at Hlathikhulu Hospital." *Swazi Times* October 22.

Mzizi, Joshua Bheki. 2005. "Is Somhlolo's Dream a Scandal for Swazi Hegemony? The Christian Clause Debate Re-Examined in the Context of Prospects for Religious Accommodation." *Missionalia* 33, no. 3: 441–458.

Nattrass, Nicoli. 2004. *The Moral Economy of AIDS in South Africa*. New York: Cambridge University Press.

Naysmith, Scott, Alex DeWaal, and Alan Whiteside. 2009. "Revisiting New Variant Famine: The Case of Swaziland." *Food Security* 1, no. 3: 251–260.

Ndzimandze, Mbongiseni. 2010. "Farmers Feed Chickens ARVS – Hlobi." *Times of Swaziland* November 9.

———. 2011. "You Feed Chickens Your ARVs, Say Nurses." *Times of Swaziland* November 4.

Ndlovu, Hebron L. 2007. "The Swazi Dual Monarchy: Its Religio-Cultural Genius." *BOLESWA Journal of Theology, Religion and Philosophy* 1, no. 3: 116–134.

Nene, Khulekani. 2013. "Siteki Mortuaries Beef Up Security." *Times of Swaziland* October 3.

Neupane, Subas, K. C. Prakash, and David Teye Doku. 2016. "Overweight and Obesity among Women: Analysis of Demographic and Health Survey Data from 32 Sub-Saharan African Countries." *BMC Public Health* 16 (January): 30.

News24. 2007. "Man to Be Buried after 5 Years." *News24* November 30.

Ngubane, Harriet S. 1977. *Body and Mind in Zulu Medicine*. New York: Academic Press.

Ngubane, Sibusiso. 2009. "Tiffany Has Been Cremated." *Times of Swaziland* August 23.

Nguyen, Vinh-Kim. 2010. *The Republic of Therapy: Triage and Sovereignty in West Africa's Time of AIDS*. Durham: Duke University Press.

Nhlapo, Ronald Thandabantu. 1992. *Marriage and Divorce in Swazi Law and Custom*. Mbabane: Webster's.

Nichter, Mark. 2008. *Global Health: Why Cultural Perceptions, Social Representations, and Biopolitics Matter*. Tempe: University of Arizona Press.

Niehaus, Isak. 2005. "Witches and Zombies of the South African Lowveld: Discourse, Accusations and Subjective Reality." *Journal of the Royal Anthropological Institute* 11, no. 2: 191–210.

———. 2007. "Death before Dying: Understanding AIDS Stigma in the South African Lowveld." *Journal of Southern African Studies* 33, no. 4: 845–860.

———. 2013. *Witchcraft and a Life in the New South Africa*. Cambridge: Cambridge University Press.

Nkambule, Mfanukhona. 2011. "Sikhutsali's Cremation Wish Granted." *Times of Swaziland* April 17.

Nkambule, Sandile. 2014a. "Grave Concern at Ngwane Park Cemetery." *Swazi Observer* March 13.

———. 2014b. "Evicted Nokwane Were Defiant." *Swazi Observer* December 13.

Ntsimane, Radikobo. 2005. "Memory Boxes and Zulu Culture." *Never Too Small to Remember: Memory Work and Resilience in Times of AIDS*, edited by Phillipe Denis, 35–40. Johannesburg: Cluster.

Núñez, Lorena, and Brittany Wheeler. 2012. "Chronicles of Death Out of Place: Management of Migrant Death in Johannesburg." *African Studies* 71, no. 2: 212–233.

Nxumalo, Mamane. 1999. "Women's Health, Sociocultural Practices, and HIV/AIDS in Swaziland." *AIDS and Development in Africa*, edited by Kempe Ronald Hope, Sr., 59–68. Binghamton: Haworth Press.

Nxumalo, Sishayi Simon. 1976. *Our Swazi Way of Life*. Mbabane: Swaziland Printing and Publishing.

Nyawo, Sonene, Patricia Mhlobo, and Zodwa Mpapane. 2009. *Religious Education in Context*. Manzini: Macmillan BOLESWA.

Nyeko, Balam. 2005. "Swaziland and South Africa since 1994: Reflections on Aspects of Post-Liberation Swazi Historiography." In *From National Liberation to Democratic Renaissance in Southern Africa*, edited by Cheryl Hendricks and Lwazi Lushaba, 23–37. Dakar: CODESRIA.

Obbo, Christine. 2006. "But We Know It All! African Perspectives on Anthropological Knowledge." In *African Anthropologies: History, Critique, Practice*, edited by Mwenda Ntarangwi, David Mills, and Mustafa Babiker, 154–169. Dakar and New York: CODESRIA and Zed Books.

Okigbo, Austin C. 2016. *Music, Culture, and the Politics of Health: Ethnography of a South African AIDS Choir*. Lanham: Lexington Books.

Olukoshi, Adebayo, and Francis Nyamnjoh. 2011. "The Postcolonial Turn: An Introduction." In *The Postcolonial Turn: Re-Imagining Anthropology and Africa*, edited by René Devisch and Francis Nyamnjoh, 1–27. Bamenda and Leiden: Langaa and African Studies Centre.

Ortner, Sherry B. 2006. *Anthropology and Social Theory: Culture, Power, and the Acting Subject*. Durham: Duke University Press.

Oxlund, Bjarke. 2014. "'A Blessing in Disguise': The Art of Surviving HIV/AIDS as a Member of the Zionist Christian Church in South Africa." *Religion and AIDS Treatment in Africa: Saving Souls, Prolonging Lives*, edited by Rijk van Dijk, Hansjörg Dilger, Marian Burchardt, and Thera Rasing, e73–e94. ProQuest Ebook Central. Farnham: Taylor and Francis.

Page, Ben. 2007. "Slow Going: The Mortuary, Modernity and the Hometown Association in Bali-Nyonga, Cameroon." *Africa* 77, no. 3: 419–441.

PANAPRESS. 2003. "Swaziland's School Programme Feeds AIDS Orphans." *PANAPRESS* (Pan African News Agency) September 11

Parikh, Shanti. 2016. *Regulating Romance: Youth Love Letters, Moral Anxiety, and Intervention in Uganda's Time of AIDS*. Nashville: Vanderbilt University Press.

Parker, Lucy A., Kiran Jobanputra, Velephi Okello, Mpumelelo Ndlangamandla, Sikhathele Mazibuko, Tatiana Kourline, Bernhard Kerschberger, Elias Pavlopoulos, and Roger Teck. 2015. "Barriers and Facilitators to Combined ART Initiation in Pregnant Women with HIV: Lessons Learnt From a PMTCT B+ Pilot Program in Swaziland." *JAIDS: Journal of Acquired Immune Deficiency Syndromes* 69, no. 1 (May 1): e24–e30.

Parsons, Michelle. 2014. *Dying Unneeded: The Cultural Context of the Russian Mortality Crisis.* Nashville: Vanderbilt University Press.

Parsons, Neil, and Robin Palmer. 1977. "The Roots of Rural Poverty: Historical Background." In *The Roots of Rural Poverty in Central and Southern Africa*, edited by Robin Palmer and Neil Parsons, 1–32. London: Heinemann.

Physicians for Human Rights. 2007. "Epidemic of Inequality: Women's Rights and HIV/AIDS in Botswana and Swaziland: An Evidence-Based Report on the Effects of Gender Inequity, Stigma and Discrimination." Cambridge: Physicians for Human Rights.

Poku, Nana K. 2005. *AIDS in Africa: How the Poor are Dying.* Cambridge: Polity Press.

Posel, Deborah, and Pamila Gupta. 2009. "The Life of the Corpse: Framing Reflections and Questions." *African Studies* 68, no. 3: 299–309.

Prince, Ruth J., Philippe Denis, and Rijk van Dijk. 2009. "Introduction to Special Issue: Engaging Christianities: Negotiating HIV/AIDS, Health, and Social Relations in East and Southern Africa." *Africa Today* 56, no. 1: v–xviii.

Ramphele, Mamphela. 1997. "Political Widowhood in South Africa: The Embodiment of Ambiguity." In *Social Suffering*, edited by Arthur Kleinman, Veena Das, and Margaret Lock, 99–118. Berkeley: University of California Press.

Ranger, Terence. 2004. "Dignifying Death: The Politics of Burial in Bulawayo." *Journal of Religion in Africa* 34, no. 1–2: 110–144.

Rasmussen, Louise Mubanda. 2014. "Negotiating Holistic Care with the 'Rules' of ARV Treatment in a Catholic Community-Based Organization in Kampala." In *Religion and AIDS Treatment in Africa: Saving Souls, Prolonging Lives*, edited by Rijk van Dijk, Hansjörg Dilger, Marian Burchardt, and Thera Rasing, e216–e235. ProQuest Ebook Central. Farnham: Taylor and Francis.

Raviv, Shaun. 2015. "The Killers of Swaziland." *The Big Roundtable* March 4.

Reis, Ria. 1996. *Sporen van Ziekte: Medische Pluraliteit en Epilepsie in Swaziland.* Hague: Het Spinhuis.

———. 2002. "Medical Pluralism and the Bounding of Traditional Healing in Swaziland." In *Plural Medicine, Tradition and Modernity, 1800–2000*, edited by Waltraud Ernst, 95–112. New York: Routledge.

———. 2008. "Inventing a Generation: The Revitalisation of 'Umcwasho' in Swaziland in Response to the HIV/AIDS Crisis." In *Generations in Africa: Connections and Conflicts*, edited by Erdmute Alber, Sjaak van der Geest, and Susan Reynolds Whyte, 169–182. Berlin: Lit Verlag.

Rhine, Kathryn. 2016. *The Unseen Things: Women, Secrecy, and HIV in Northern Nigeria.* Bloomington: Indiana University Press.

Robbins, Joel. 2007. "Between Reproduction and Freedom: Morality, Value, and Radical Cultural Change." *Ethnos* 72, no. 3: 293–314.

Rödlach, Alexander. 2006. *Witches, Westerners, and HIV: AIDS and Cultures of Blame in Africa.* Walnut Creek: Left Coast Press.

Root, Robin. 2009. "Religious Participation and HIV-Disclosure Rationales among People Living with HIV/AIDS in Rural Swaziland." *African Journal of AIDS Research* 8, no. 3: 295–309.

———. 2010. "Situating Experiences of HIV-Related Stigma in Swaziland." *Global Public Health* 5, no. 5: 523–538.

———. 2011. "'That's When Life Changed': Client Experiences of Church Run Home-Based HIV/AIDS Care in Swaziland." Durban: HEARD.

———. 2014. "Being HIV Positive: A Phenomenology of HIV Disclosure in Swaziland." In *Disclosure in Health and Illness*, edited by Mark Davis and Lenore Manderson, 36–55. New York: Routledge.

Root, Robin, and Arnau van Wyngaard. 2011. "Free Love: A Case Study of Church-Run Home-Based Caregivers in a High Vulnerability Setting. *Global Public Health* 6, supplement no. 2 (October): S174–S191.

Root, Robin, and Alan Whiteside. 2013. "A Qualitative Study of Community Home-Based Care and Antiretroviral Adherence in Swaziland." *Journal of the International AIDS Society* 16 (October 8): 17978.

Root, Robin, Arnau van Wyngaard, and Alan Whiteside. 2015. "Reckoning HIV/AIDS Care: A Longitudinal Study of Community Home-Based Caregivers and Clients in Swaziland." *African Journal of AIDS Research* 14, no. 3: 265–274.

———. 2017. "'We Smoke the Same Pipe': Religion and Community Home-Based Care for PLWH in Rural Swaziland." *Medical Anthropology* 36, no. 3: 231–245.

Rose, Laurel. 1992. *The Politics of Harmony: Land Dispute Strategies in Swaziland*. New York: Cambridge University Press.

Russell, Margo. 1984. "Beyond Remittances: The Redistribution of Cash in Swazi Society." *Modern African Studies* 22, no. 4: 595–615.

Rutherford, Danilyn. 2012. "Kinky Empiricism." *Cultural Anthropology* 27, no. 3: 465–479.

Rycroft, David K. 1981. *Concise siSwati Dictionary*. Pretoria: J. L. van Schaik.

Saethre, Eirik, and Jonathan Stadler. 2017. *Negotiating Pharmaceutical Uncertainty: Women's Agency in a South African HIV Prevention Trial*. Nashville: Vanderbilt University Press.

Sangaramoorthy, Thurka. 2014. *Treating AIDS: Politics of Difference, Paradox of Prevention*. New Brunswick: Rutgers University Press.

Shaw, Cassandra. 2011. "Govt Cuts E200 Million on Sikhuphe/Mbadlane Road." *Times of Swaziland* June 6.

Shipton, Parker. 2009. *Mortgaging the Ancestors: Ideologies of Attachment in Africa*. New Haven: Yale University Press.

Shongwe, Nosipho. 2014. "Exam Room Entry Points Smeared with Olive Oil." *Times of Swaziland* October 7.

Sibbald, Barbara. 2012. "Making Sense of the World's Highest HIV Rate." *CMAJ* 184, no. 17: E882–E884.

———. 2013. "Cultural and Societal Obstacles in Responding to Swaziland's HIV Epidemic." *CMAJ* 185, no. 4: E181–E182.

Siedner, Mark J., Data Santorino, Alexander Lankowski, Michael Kanyesigye, Mwebesa B. Bwana, Jessica Haberer, and David Bangsberg. 2015. "A Combination SMS and Transportation Reimbursement Intervention to Improve HIV Care Following Abnormal CD4 Test Results in Rural Uganda." *BMC Medicine* 13 (July 6): 160.

Sihlongonyane, Mfaniseni. 2003. "The Invisible Hand of the Royal Family in the Political Dynamics of Swaziland." *African and Asian Studies* 2, no. 2: 155–187.

Simelane, Gugu. 2017. "Schools Have Enough Food—Govt." *Swazi Observer* February 1.

Simelane, Hamilton Sipho. 1991. "Landlessness and Imperial Response in Swaziland, 1938–1950." *Journal of Southern African Studies* 17, no. 4: 717–741.

———. 2011. "'Sharing My Bed with the Enemy': Wives and Violent Husbands in Post-Colonial Swaziland." *Journal of Contemporary African Studies* 29, no. 4: 493–512.

Simelane, Hamilton Sipho and Jonathan Crush. 2004. "Swaziland Moves: Patterns and Perceptions of Migration in Swaziland." Southern African Migration Programme (SAMP) and the International Organization on Migration (IOM), Migration Policy Series paper 32. Cape Town: Idasa.

Simelane, Lethumusa. 2014. "Malagwane Accident, the Cultural History." *Sunday Observer* May 11.

Simelane, Nomcebo Olivia. 1987. "Household Morbidity Patterns and Choice of Health Care Service Utilized in Manzini District, Swaziland." PhD diss., Clark University.

Simpson, Anthony. 2014. "'God Has Again Remembered Us!' Christian Identity and Men's Attitudes to Antiretroviral Therapy in Zambia." In *Religion and AIDS Treatment in Africa: Saving Souls, Prolonging Lives*, edited by Rijk van Dijk, Hansjörg Dilger, Marian Burchardt, and Thera Rasing, e92–e108. ProQuest Ebook Central. Farnham: Taylor and Francis.

Smith, Daniel Jordan. 2014. *AIDS Doesn't Show Its Face: Inequality, Morality, and Social Change in Nigeria.* Chicago: University of Chicago Press.

Stoebenau, Kirsten, Lori Heise, Joyce Wamoyi, and Natalia Bobrova. 2016. "Revisiting the Understanding of 'Transactional Sex' in Sub-Saharan Africa: A Review and Synthesis of the Literature." *Social Science and Medicine* 168 (November): 186–197.

Sukati, Sibongile. 2009. "No More Funerals!" *Times of Swaziland* June 21.

———. 2010. "MPs Angry Over ARV Chickens Statement." *Times of Swaziland* November 30.

Sukati, Zwelihle. 2009. "Pastors Slammed on Funeral Traditions." *Times of Swaziland* July 15.

Susser, Ida. 2009. *AIDS, Sex, and Culture: Global Politics and Survival in Southern Africa.* Malden: Wiley-Blackwell.

Tevera, Daniel, Nomcebo Simelane, Graciana Peter, and Abul Salam. 2012. "The State of Food Insecurity in Manzini, Swaziland." Urban Food Security Series, no. 15. Cape Town and Kingston, Ontario: African Food Security Urban Network, and Southern African Research Center, Queen's University.

Thomas, Kylie. 2014. *Impossible Mourning: HIV and Visuality after Apartheid.* Lewisburg: Bucknell University Press.

Thornton, Robert. 2008. *Unimagined Community: Sex, Networks, and AIDS in Uganda and South Africa.* Berkeley: University of California Press.

Thwala, Phumelele. 1999. "Sexual Abuse, HIV/AIDS, and the Legal Rights of Women in Swaziland." *AIDS and Development in Africa*, edited by Kempe Ronald Hope, Sr., 69–82. Binghamton: Haworth Press.

Thwala, Thabani. 2013. "The Politics of Placing Princes in Historical and Contemporary Swaziland." Master of Arts thesis, Faculty of Humanities, University of the Witwatersrand.

Timberg, Chris. 2004. "A Brutal Sexual Assault Galvanizes Swazi Women." *Washington Post* October 4.

Times of Swaziland. 1945. "From South Swaziland: Swazi Customs." *Times of Swaziland* February 22.

———. 1986. "End of Mourning." *Times of Swaziland* November 3.

———. 2007. "Manzini Cemetery: Where Angels Fear to Tread." *Times of Swaziland* August 6.

———. 2010. "'Do Not Eat at Funerals': Pastor Justice Says It Gives an Opportunity for Demons to Enter." *Times of Swaziland* September 27.

———. 2011. "A Rather Strange Funeral for Chief Nguduza." *Times of Swaziland* February 20.

———. 2013. "ARVs (Not HIV) Are Killing Africans." *Times of Swaziland* June 2.

Tishkin, Joel, and Andreas Heuser. 2015. "'Africa Always Brings Us Something New': A Historiography of African Zionist and Pentecostal Christianities." *Religion* 45, no. 2: 153–173.

Tofa, Eliot. 2014. "'In Jesus' Name You Are Free': HIV, ARVs and Healing Space in Selected African Initiated Churches." *UNISWA Research Journal* 27 (March): 70–85.

Togarasei, Lovemore. 2010. "Christian Theology of Life, Death and Healing in an Era of Antiretroviral Therapy: Reflections on the Responses of Some Botswana Churches." *African Journal of AIDS Research* 9, no. 4: 429–435.

Treichler, Paula. 1999. *How to Have Theory in an Epidemic: Cultural Chronicles of AIDS.* Durham: Duke University Press.

Tsai, Alexander, David Bangsberg, and Sheri D. Weiser. 2013. "Harnessing Poverty Alleviation to Reduce the Stigma of HIV in Sub-Saharan Africa. *PLoS Medicine* 10, no. 11: e1001557.

Tsai, Alexander, Abigail M. Hatcher, Elizabeth A. Bukusi, Elly Weke, Lee Lemus Hufstedler, Shari L. Dworkin, Stephen Kodish, Craig R. Cohen, and Sheri D. Weiser. 2017. "A Livelihood Intervention to Reduce the Stigma of HIV in Rural Kenya: Longitudinal Qualitative Study." *AIDS and Behavior* 21, no. 1: 248–260.

Twala, Mashumi. 1986. "AIDS Shockwave." *Times of Swaziland* November 3.

Twala, Regina G. 1951. "Beads as Regulating the Social Life of the Zulu and Swazi." *African Studies* 10, no. 3: 113–125.

Ukah, Asonzeh F. K. 2008. *A New Paradigm of Pentecostal Power: A Study of the Redeemed Christian Church of God in Nigeria.* Trenton: Africa World Press.

UNAIDS (Joint United Nations Programme on HIV/AIDS). 2006. "Revival of Old Traditions Brings Hope to Orphans in Swaziland." UNAIDS Press Centre Feature Story, August 30.

———. 2012. "Monitoring the Political Declaration on HIV and AIDS: Swaziland Country Progress Report. Mbabane: NERCHA and UNAIDS.

———. 2014. "Swaziland Global AIDS Response Progress Reporting 2014." Mbabane: Government of the Kingdom of Swaziland and NERCHA.

———. 2016. "On the Fast-Track to an AIDS-Free Generation: The Incredible Journey of the Global Plan towards the Elimination of New HIV Infections among Children by 2015 and Keeping Their Mothers Alive." Geneva: UNAIDS.

UNDP (United Nations Development Programme) and CANGO (Coordinating Assembly of NGOs). 2007. "Swaziland Human Development Report: HIV and AIDS and Culture." Mbabane: United Nations Development Programme in Swaziland.

United States Department of State. 2011. "International Religious Freedom (IRF) Report: Swaziland." Washington, DC: Bureau of Democracy, Human Rights and Labor.

———. 2013. "Swaziland 2013 Human Rights Report." Country Reports on Human Rights Practices for 2013. Washington, DC: Bureau of Democracy, Human Rights and Labor.

van der Geest, Sjaak. 2006. "Between Death and the Funeral: Mortuaries and the Exploitation of Liminality in Kwahu, Ghana." *Africa* 76, no. 4: 485–501.

van Dijk, Rijk, Hansjörg Dilger, Marian Burchardt, and Thera Rasing, eds. 2014. *Religion and AIDS Treatment in Africa: Saving Souls, Prolonging Lives.* ProQuest Ebook Central. Farnham: Taylor and Francis.

van Schalkwyk, Cari, Sibongile Mndzebele, Thabo Hlophe, Jesus Maria Garcia Calleja, Eline Korenromp, Rand Stoneburner, and Cyril Pervilhac. 2013. "Outcomes and Impact of HIV Prevention, ART and TB Programs in Swaziland—Early Evidence from Public Health Triangulation." *PLoS One* 8 (July 26): e69437.

van Wyk, Ilana. 2014. *The Universal Church of the Kingdom of God in South Africa: A Church of Strangers*. Cambridge: Cambridge University Press.

van Wyngaard, Arnau, Robin Root, and Alan Whiteside. 2017. "Food Insecurity and ART Adherence in Swaziland: The Case for Coordinated Faith-Based and Multi-Sectoral Action." *Development in Practice* 27, no. 5: Advanced online publication.

Verdery, Katherine. 1999. *The Political Lives of Dead Bodies: Reburial and Postsocialist Change*. New York: Columbia University Press.

Vernooij, Eva, Mandhla Mehlo, Anita Hardon, and Ria Reis. 2016. "Access for All: Contextualising HIV Treatment in Swaziland." *AIDS Care* 28, supplement no. 3: 7–13.

Vilakati, Faith. 2010. "Funeral Drama: Prince's Widow Goes Bananas, Bolts Out of Mourning House." *Swazi Observer* December 20.

Von Schnitzler, Antina. 2014. "Performing Dignity: Human Rights, Citizenship and the Techno-Politics of Law in South Africa." *American Ethnologist* 41, no. 2: 336–350.

Wastell, Sari. 2007. "Being Swazi, Being Human: Constitutionalism, Custom and Human Rights in Swaziland." In *The Practice of Human Rights: Tracking Law between the Global and the Local*, edited by Mark Goodale and Sally Engle Merry, 320–342. Cambridge: Cambridge University Press.

Weeks, Kathi. 2011. *The Problem with Work: Feminism, Marxism, Antiwork Politics, and Postwork Imaginaries*. Durham: Duke University Press.

Weiser, Sheri D., Abigail Hatcher, Lee Hufstedler, Elly Weke, Shari Dworkin, Elizabeth Bukusi, Rachel Burger, Stephen Kodish, Nils Grede, Lisa Butler, and Craig Cohen. 2017. "Changes in Health and Antiretroviral Adherence among HIV-Infected Adults in Kenya: Qualitative Longitudinal Findings from a Livelihood Intervention." *AIDS and Behavior* 21, no. 2: 415–427.

Werbner, Richard. 2011. *Holy Hustlers, Schism and Prophecy: Apostolic Reformation in Botswana*. Berkeley: University of California Press.

———. 2015. *Divination's Grasp: African Encounters with the Almost Said*. Bloomington: Indiana University Press.

White, Hylton. 2004. "Ritual Haunts: The Timing of Estrangement in a Post-Apartheid Countryside." In *Reproducing African Futures: Ritual and Reproduction in a Neo-Liberal Age*, edited by Brad Weiss, 141–166. Leiden: Brill.

———. 2010. "Outside the Dwelling of Culture: Estrangement and Difference in Postcolonial Zululand." *Anthropological Quarterly* 83, no. 3: 497–518.

———. 2011. "Beastly Whiteness: Animal Kinds and the Social Imagination in South Africa." *Anthropology Southern Africa* 34, no. 3–4: 104–113.

———. 2012. "A Post-Fordist Ethnicity: Insecurity, Authority, and Identity in South Africa." *Anthropological Quarterly* 85, no. 2: 397–427.

———. 2013. "Spirit and Society: In Defence of a Critical Anthropology of Religious Life." *Anthropology Southern Africa* 36, no. 3–4: 139–145.

Whiteside, Alan, and Fiona Henry. 2011. "The Impact of HIV and AIDS Research: A Case Study from Swaziland." *Health Research Policy and Systems* 9, supplement no. 1: S9.

Whiteside, Alan, and Amy Whalley. 2007. "Reviewing 'Emergencies' for Swaziland: Shifting the Paradigm in a New Era," edited by Scott Naysmith. Mbabane and Durban: NERCHA and HEARD.

Whiteside, Alan, Chris Desmond, John King, Jane Tomlinson, and Conway Sithungo. 2002. "Evidence of AIDS Mortality from an Alternative Source: A Swaziland Case Study." *African Journal of AIDS Research* 1, no. 1: 35–38.

Whiteside, Alan, Catarina Andrade, Lisa Arrehag, Solomon Dlamini, Themba Ginindza, and Anokhi Parikh. 2006. "The Socio-Economic Impact of HIV/AIDS in Swaziland." Mbabane and Durban: NERCHA and HEARD.

Whyte, Susan Reynolds. 2005. "Going Home? Belonging and Burial in the Era of AIDS." *Africa* 75, no. 2: 154–172.

———. ed. 2014. *Second Chances: Surviving AIDS in Uganda*. Durham: Duke University Press.

Wilson, Anika. 2013. *Folklore, Gender and AIDS in Malawi: No Secret under the Sun*. New York: Palgrave-MacMillan.

WLSA (Women and Law in Southern Africa). 1998. *Family in Transition: The Experience of Swaziland*. Manzini: Ruswanda Publishing.

Woubshet, Dagmawi. 2015. *The Calendar of Loss: Race, Sexuality and Mourning in the Early Era of AIDS*. Baltimore: Johns Hopkins University Press.

Wyrod, Robert. 2016. *AIDS and Masculinity in the African City: Privilege, Inequality, and Modern Manhood*. Berkeley: University of California Press.

Yamashita, Shinji. 1994. "Manipulating Ethnic Tradition: The Funeral Ceremony, Tourism, and Television among the Toraja of Sulawesi." *Indonesia* 58 (October): 69–82.

Zigon, Jarrett. 2010. *"HIV Is God's Blessing": Rehabilitating Morality in Neoliberal Russia*. Berkeley: University of California Press.

Zulu, Joseph. 2009a. "Body Parts Go Missing at Morgue." *Times of Swaziland* September 28.

———. 2009b. "Town Planners Grill Town Council About Morgue in Residential Area." *Times of Swaziland* December 3.

———. 2015. "SD Rated 2nd Highest Obese Nation in Africa." *Times of Swaziland* July 10.

Zwane, Ackel. 2006. "Drama at Gavu's Funeral." *Times of Swaziland* April 26.

Index

CASEY GOLOMSKI is Assistant Professor of Anthropology at the University of New Hampshire.

Lightning Source UK Ltd.
Milton Keynes UK
UKHW01f1817270918
329653UK00010B/658/P